Uncivil Religion

University of Denver
Center for Judaic Studies

Stanley M. Wagner, Director

UNCIVIL RELIGION

———— ✦ ————

Interreligious Hostility in America

Edited by Robert N. Bellah
and Frederick E. Greenspahn

CROSSROAD • NEW YORK

1987

The Crossroad Publishing Company
370 Lexington Avenue, New York, N.Y. 10017

Printed in the United States of America

Library of Congress Cataloging in Publication Data

Uncivil religion.

1. United States—Religion. 2. Religions—Relations.
I. Bellah, Robert Neely, 1927–   . II. Greenspahn,
Frederick E., 1946–   .
BL2525.U53   1987   291.9′0973   86-24163
ISBN 0-8245-0976-9

Contents

Introduction

FREDERICK E. GREENSPAHN

G eorge Washington described America as a country where "it is now no more that toleration is spoken of, as if it was by the indulgence of one class of people, that another enjoyed the exercise of their inherent natural rights. For happily the government of the United States . . . gives to bigotry no sanction, to persecution no assistance."[1]

The facts of American life have not always been as benign as the United States' official policy of tolerant religious pluralism. In the last century, Mormons were subjected to the kind of persecution more commonly associated with the Middle Ages, and American Protestants have long rejected Roman Catholics as an alien presence. A poll taken during World War II disclosed that more than twice as many people considered Jews to be a "menace to America" than were concerned about Japanese or Germans.[2]

This country has harbored many kinds of interreligious antagonisms. Some are deeply rooted in Western culture and were merely imported to this "New World." Others are indigenous, reflecting tensions unique to the American experience.

Because America originated as a predominantly Protestant culture, Protestant-Catholic hostility has been largely a matter of anti-Catholicism, with Catholic hostility most often an immigrant minority's defensive response. Jewish-Christian tensions have also, for the most part, been a one-sided affair, nourished by a long tradition of Christian anti-Judaism[3] as well as the relatively late arrival of the vast majority of the

Jewish population. That Catholics and Jews have more recently come to care less about maintaining a low profile and been willing to engage in the conflict of American political life on behalf of their own priorities probably speaks much about their growing sense of comfort.

In any event, such "traditional" tensions by no means exhaust the varieties of interreligious hostility to be found in this country. Time and again, accepted and successful religious communities have united in opposition to newer groups, whether American-born or "imported." There is some irony in this. After all, one would expect the newer and smaller groups to feel threatened, as indeed their symbolism and rhetoric suggest they have, rather than those that are well established.

In recent years the term "cult" has come to designate those new religions whose treatment belies our vaunted religious tolerance.[4] The ways in which that term is used are remarkably revealing. A recent book on "cults" published by a conservative Protestant press deals with the Mormons, Jehovah's Witnesses, Christian Scientists, Unitarian-Universalists, Black Muslims, and Worldwide Church of God,[5] while an official resolution of the Reform Jewish rabbinate applies the same term to the "Unification Church, Hebrew-Christian Missionaries, the Divine Light Mission, the Hari [*sic*] Krishna, the Church of God movement, [and] Jews for Jesus."[6] The term clearly means different things to different people. Common to all is the view that cults, perceived as dangerous caricatures of religion, do not merit the tolerance accorded more acceptable communities.

Such feelings reflect a kind of generational conflict between religious communities. Both Judaism and Christianity enjoyed charismatic leadership early in their own histories. But religion, like all human endeavors, must become institutionalized to survive beyond the enthusiasm of early generations. And the bureaucracies that institutions require are bound to be uncomfortable with the charismatic leadership typical of newly emergent communities.[7] This distrust is exacerbated by the universal and exclusive language typical in claims of religious truth. Ironically, as the groups that elicit such fear become themselves established, they are prone to feel threatened by still newer sects.

Not all religious hostility is interdenominational. Internal tensions and even schisms were a prominent characteristic of American religious life at the time of the Civil War, over a century ago. In recent years polarization between liberals and conservatives has become increasingly evident within almost all religious groups, corresponding in part to the growing divergence between liberals and conservatives throughout American life. As a result, many people now feel more comfortable with those similarly inclined in other religious communities than with some members of their own denomination.

All these diverse forms of religious hostility share certain characteristics. Although expressed in theological language, they reflect a sense of fear, fear that the other groups are not just wrong, but dangerous. The sheer emotion with which American evangelicals inveigh against Jehovah's Witnesses, or their more liberal counterparts against fundamentalists, or Jews against the Jews for Jesus demonstrates that such groups are seen not merely as rivals, but as a profound threat. Hostility is a sign of underlying insecurity, a sense not only of personal danger, but of religious uncertainty, with deep-seated social and psychological concerns masked by theological language.

Despite the passion that often accompanies interreligious relations, it is probably fair to say that religious persecution has caused fewer deaths in America than in most Western countries over a comparable period. We must, therefore, not only note the reality of religious hostility, but also explain its *relatively* small proportions.

One probable factor is the growing secularization of recent American life, in which other priorities have come to play a far greater role than religion in defining our sense of self. Bluntly put, many Americans do not regard religion as important enough to fight for. On the other hand, if religion refers to one's truest and deepest commitment, then many Americans' "true religion" may not be Roman Catholicism, Presbyterianism, or Conservative Judaism, but rather what has been called "civil religion."[8] Here it is clear that our tolerance has not always been great. Indeed, underlying many of the tensions charted in these pages is a perceived threat to the "American way of life," however that is understood.

The American situation is thus more complex than one might first expect. Intergroup hostility has been as real a fact of American life as the rhetoric of tolerance. If there has not always been the tension that this book's title and structure seem to suggest, that may be testimony to the power of the ethos Americans have sought to create. And where hostility does exist, it reminds us of the distance we must go if that ethos is to be realized fully.

Notes

1. Morris U. Schappes, *Documentary History of the Jews in the United States 1654–1875*, rev. ed. (New York: Citadel Press, 1952) 80.

2. Charles Herbert Stember, *Jews in the Mind of America* (New York: Basic Books, 1966) 128.

3. See Rosemary Ruether, *Faith and Fratricide: The Theological Roots of Anti-Semitism* (New York: Seabury Press, 1974).

4. Although it does not appear in the *Oxford English Dictionary*, the term's pejorative connotation has a long history in American usage; see, for example, Fred S. Miller, *Fighting Modern Evils That Destroy Our Homes; A Startling Exposition of the Snares and Pitfalls of the Social World Vividly Depicting How Homes Are Wrecked and Souls Destroyed Through the Wiles and Trickery of Mystic Cults* (Chicago: Homewood Press, 1913), especially pp. 219–20 where the term is applied to Hinduism and Buddhism; similarly Jan Karel van Baalen, *The Gist of the Cults: Christianity Versus False Religions* (Grand Rapids: Wm. B. Eerdmans, 1944).

5. M. Thomas Starkes, *Confronting Popular Cults* (Nashville: Broadman Press, 1972).

6. *CCAR Yearbook* 86 (1976) 63.

7. Max Weber, *On Charisma and Institution Building*, ed. S.N. Eisenstadt (Chicago: University of Chicago Press, 1968), especially pp. 48, 51, 54–61.

8. Cf. Robert Bellah, "Civil Religion in America," *Daedalus* 96:1 (Winter 1967) 1–21.

Uncivil Religion

I

JEWISH-CHRISTIAN TENSIONS

Tension between Jews and Christians began when these communities diverged two thousand years ago. The New Testament already ascribes the rejection of Christianity to the Jews,[1] and the early church fathers responded to this felt abuse in kind. "Indeed, a whole day would not suffice to tell all [about Jews . . . the] most miserable of all men," wrote John Chrysostom in the fourth century.[2]

Since the middle of this century, there has emerged a tripartite understanding of American religion, in which Protestantism, Catholicism, and Judaism are treated as equally legitimate.[3] Jews have, therefore, encountered an unexpectedly tolerant America. On a theological level, Franz Rosenzweig's view of Christianity as the "Judaism of the Gentiles"[4] has achieved widespread acceptance.

Yet old feelings die slowly. As recently as 1954, the World Council of Churches proclaimed that "In view of the grievous guilt of Christian people towards the Jews throughout the history of the Church, we are certain that the Church cannot rest until the title of Christ to the Kingdom is recognized by His own people according to the flesh."[5]

While their minority status has effectively limited Jewish assertiveness, creating a situation in which official tolerance is in the Jewish community's best interest, their attitude has hardly been benign. Several observers have described an attitude of superiority, to which some attribute theological roots, albeit in a radically secularized form.[6]

Whether the ambivalence of this two-thousand-year-old relationship can reasonably be expected to disappear in any environment other than one of complete indifference is difficult to ascertain. That several cycles of anger and toleration have passed in just recent years reminds us how active and important an element of modern American life religion continues to be, secularism and apathy notwithstanding.

Notes

1. See Douglas R.A. Hare, *The Theme of Jewish Persecution of Christians in the Gospel According to St. Matthew* (Cambridge: Cambridge University Press, 1967), especially pp. 19–79.
2. *Adversus Judaeos* 1.7, PG 48.853.
3. Will Herberg, *Protestant–Catholic–Jew: An Essay in American Religious Sociology* (Garden City, NY: Anchor Books, 1960). Tolerance of Judaism may not be entirely as new as Herberg's thesis would suggest; see Robert Handy, *A Christian America: Protestant Hopes and Historical Realities* (New York: Oxford University Press, 1971) 59.
4. So Seymour Siegel in "The State of Jewish Belief: A Symposium," *Commentary* 42:2 (August 1966) 143; for a Christian version of this position, see A. Roy Eckardt, *Elder and Younger Brothers: The Encounter of Jews and Christians* (New York: Schocken Books, 1973), especially pp. 160–61.
5. *The Evanston Report: The Second Assembly of the World Council of Churches, 1954* (New York: Harper & Brothers, 1955) 327.
6. E.g., Hannah Arendt, *Antisemitism* (New York: Harcourt, Brace & World, 1968) ix; see also Arnold Eisen, *The Chosen People in America: A Study in Jewish Religious Ideology* (Bloomington, IN: University of Indiana Press, 1983) 143–48.

1

Jewish-Christian Hostility in the United States: Perceptions from a Jewish Point of View

JONATHAN D. SARNA

My medieval ancestors would have had no difficulty with my subject here. "Jewish-Christian hostility?" they would have exclaimed, somewhat incredulously. "Why that is due to the fact that Christians hate Jews. That is all there is to it." This censorious attitude did not merely reflect age-old prejudice. It also seemed to comport with reality as experienced on a day-to-day basis: the abuses, the vilifications, the persecutions. With a few notable exceptions, medieval Jews quite generally viewed interreligious hatred as something inevitable, and they found rabbinic exegesis that supported their claims. Rabbinic midrash taught that "all the nations of the world hate Israel"; Rabbi Simeon bar Yokhai considered the fact that "Esau [interpreted as Christianity] hates Jacob" to be an "axiom."[1]

With the coming of the Enlightenment and the gradual theological shift toward an emphasis on love, these attitudes began to change. Jews and Christians became far better acquainted with one another; they discovered how much they held in common, and gradually a few brave souls replaced the old rhetoric of enmity with a new rhetoric of tolerance and amity. Moses Mendelssohn, the great German-Jewish philosopher of the Enlightenment, boasted that he had "the good fortune of having for a friend many an excellent man who is not of my faith. We sincerely love

I am grateful to Professor Michael Cook for his invaluable comments on an earlier draft of this paper, and to the American Council of Learned Societies and the Memorial Foundation for Jewish Culture for supporting some of the research upon which this essay is based.

each other, though we suspect that in matters of religion we hold totally different opinions." Mendelssohn's Christian friends, at least in their letters to him, agreed.[2] Similar expressions of toleration and even philo-Semitism echoed through Holland, France, and England. Throughout Western Europe and in America too, enlightened Jews and Christians saw a new age aborning.[3]

A second look, however, revealed that many Christians coupled their love for Jews and support for Jewish rights with the hope that Jews would ultimately be incorporated into the Christian fold. In dispensing love, in other words, Christians concealed a hidden agenda: to persuade Jews to convert to the majority faith. Seen from a Jewish perspective, this was a cynical stratagem, a new tactic designed to further the same old purpose. Christians still hoped to make Jews see the light, only now, rather than coercing them into apostasy, they tried to love them into it instead. The verb changed, but the trouble remained the same. Where once Christians hated Jews, now they loved them too well and sought to embrace them too closely.[4]

To trace this theme fully with all of its many implications for Jewish-Christian relations in modern times would require a full volume in itself. My effort here is more modest. First of all, I want to offer several American examples of love used as a conversionist tool in order to prove that this has not just been a European Jewish problem. Second, I shall argue that conversionist philo-Semitism inevitably carries with it the insistence that Jews, beloved as they may be, remain in various ways inadequate or deficient, justifying the effort to Christianize them. Finally, to restore some semblance of balance, I shall suggest a series of factors that have mitigated interreligious hostilities between Jews and Christians in America, conversionism notwithstanding. If my first two sections seem unremittingly negative, I promise at least to conclude on a positive note.

I

The idea that Jews should be treated with love rather than tortured by persecutions has its Protestant roots in the early writings of Martin Luther, those that precede the virulently anti-Semitic phase of his life. In his *That Jesus Christ Was Born a Jew*, Luther deplored Catholic behavior toward the Jewish people, and insisted that "if we really want to help them, we must be guided by Christian love, not by popish legalism." Luther made no attempt to hide the conversionist aims that underlay his strategy. By receiving Jews cordially and allowing them to trade and work amidst Christians, he thought that "some may be won over." "So long as we treat them like dogs," he continued, "how can we expect to work any good among them?"[5]

An early echo of this idea in the United States may be found in the writings of Dr. Abiel Holmes, grandfather of Justice Oliver Wendell Holmes, Jr. In the biography of his father-in-law, Ezra Stiles (1798), which was subsequently quoted by Hannah Adams in her *History of the Jews* (1812), Holmes lamented that "instead of being treated with that humanity and tenderness which Christianity should inspire, they [Jews] are often persecuted and condemned as unworthy of notice or regard. Such treatment tends to prejudice them against our holy religion, and to establish them in their infidelity." Holmes naturally held Stiles up as a counterexample for his "civility and catholicism towards the Jews." He then proceeded to associate this benevolence with missionizing, deploring the fact that other Americans were not doing "what ought to be done towards the conversion of this devoted people."[6]

Christian missions to American Jews, when they began in 1816, took up Holmes's challenge and accepted the relationship between loving and converting Jews as a self-evident proposition. The numerous publications of the American Society for Meliorating the Condition of the Jews, for example, regularly condemned Jewish persecutions and described the state of the Jews in heartrending terms that indicated genuine feelings of contrition. *Israel's Advocate*, the missionary society's first newspaper, lived up to its name—given Protestant assumptions. Jews, of course, viewed the title—and indeed the titles of many subsequent missionary publications—as pure deception. They looked with similar disdain upon most other missionary activities, for what Christians saw as charity and benevolence, manifestations of their own boundless love for God's people, Jews scorned. "You mock us," a Jewish opponent of missionaries sneered, "by offering to bribe us like children with toys."[7]

A remarkable illustration of these two contradictory perceptions—the missionary view that one loved Jews by converting them, and the Jewish view that interpreted this exchange of love for Jewish souls as pure bribery—may be seen in the following citation from the twentieth report of the American Society for Meliorating the Condition of the Jews' Board of Directors:

> And here the Board would pause a moment, while they would endeavor to impress on the minds of their Christian friends and brethren, what they believe to constitute the true secret of successful effort upon the Jewish mind. It must be approached through the heart. We must make them feel that we love them, and desire to do them good. For how many years, nay centuries, has a different course been pursued by the Christian world? Ever since the days of the persecutions, when the Jews

were hunted outlaws, what have we done to make them love us? What have we done to make them think otherwise than that we were still, as of old, the enemies of their religion and their race? We have complained of the bitterness of their prejudices, the hardness of their hearts, and their unconquerable aversion to Christianity; nay some have gone so far as to express an utter want of faith in the possibility of their conversion through any human means. But, during all this time, we have done nothing for them; we have not gone among them, nor invited them among us. We have been willing at heart that they should remain as they have been, a separate people; nay, some of us have often shrunk from the idea of daily and intimate fellowship with a Jew. Let us honestly confess it—the prejudice and bigotry have been ours scarcely less than theirs, and why should we wonder at the result? But approach a Jew (as we have recently been led to do) in the spirit of kindness and Christian love, visit him in his distress, speak comfortably to him, let him see that we desire to relieve his wants, and we find that he has the heart of a man, and that it will respond to our own. . . .

Our missionary has already made himself extensively respected, and even beloved, among the Jewish population of this city. His visits, instead of being repelled with rudeness, are looked for and welcomed; the Bibles he carries with him, instead of being rejected, are gratefully received, read and treasured; the children cluster round him when he enters their humble apartment, and often welcome him with a kiss; nay, he has been saluted in this affectionate manner by aged men! What a revolution is here begun in the Jewish heart![8]

According to this missionary perspective, the frustrating failure of earlier efforts to convert Jews stemmed from the inadequate amounts of love devoted to the enterprise. Jews had to *feel* loved before they would convert. When they did feel love, in tangible form, the results according to this report seemed most promising. Jews, needless to say, read this same account quite differently. To them it stands as startling confirmation of what Isaac Mayer Wise called missionaries' "rascality."[9]

The link between loving Jews and converting them has by no means been confined to missionaries.[10] Zebulon B. Vance, North Carolina's prominent governor and then senator, was without doubt friendly toward Jews, and his frequently delivered address entitled "The Scattered Nation"—a so-called "classic of American eloquence"—was one of the more outspoken pleas on their behalf in all of late nineteenth-century America. Vance termed the Jew "the most remarkable man of this world —past or present" and viewed Jewish history as "the history of our civilization and progress in this world and our faith and hope in that which is to come." He pointed out the Jewish roots of Christianity ("Strike out all of Judaism from the Christian church and there remains nothing but an unmeaning superstition"), enumerated various "debts" Christians owed to Jews, described Jewish "characteristics and peculiarities," and held up to shame the persecutions and sufferings meted out against Jews "by Christian people and in the name of Him, the meek and lowly, who was called the Prince of Peace and the harbinger of good will to men."

Yet for all the love that Vance genuinely felt toward Jews, he nevertheless believed that "the Christian is simply the successor of the Jew," and that the Jews would ultimately abandon "their exclusion and preservation." He looked to the day when Jews would become "as other men," learning "that one sentence in our Lord's prayer which is said not to be found in the Talmud and is the key-note of the differences between Jew and Gentile, 'Forgive us our trespasses *as we* forgive them who trespass against us.' " Vance did not come right out and call upon Jews to convert, but Christians in his audience surely understood the conversionist premillennial tenor of his words:

> So may the morning come, not to them alone but to all the children of men who, through much tribulation and with heroic manhood, have waited for its dawning, with a faith whose constant cry through all the dreary watches of the night has been, "though He slay me, yet will I trust in Him!"[11]

By the twentieth century, the "love" approach to the so-called Jewish problem had become broadly accepted, in line with the general movement from fear to love in American Protestant theology. At the two world conferences on Jewish evangelization, chaired by America's great Protestant lay leader, John R. Mott, and held in Budapest and Warsaw in 1927, everyone professed to love Jews. The volume that emerged from these conferences, entitled *The Christian Approach to the Jew*, carried a forthright philo-Semitic declaration:

> We desire to put on record our goodwill and friendly feeling toward the Jewish people; we deplore the long record of injustice and ill-usage of Jews on the part of professedly Christian people; we declare such conduct to be a violation of the teaching and spirit of Christ, and we call upon Churches and Christians everywhere to oppose injustice and ill-usage of Jews. . . .

That done, conference members settled down to discuss at length "the urgent and growing need for special evangelisation among the Jews of the world." From the point of view of those assembled, the interrelationship of love and conversion was simply assumed.[12] The assumption continues, at least in many evangelical circles, down to the present day.[13]

II

For all that Jews may have condemned those who equate love with
conversion, they have surely preferred them to enemies of old who relied
on persecution to effect the same end. Christian missions to American
Jews never resulted in Jewish martyrdom, and even those who converted
to Christianity of their own free will were free to convert back if they so
chose. In their battles for equal rights and against prejudice, and later in
their Zionist efforts, Jews knew that they had allies in the evangelical
camp. The 1891 Blackstone Memorial, the influential resolution entitled
"Palestine for the Jews," signed by leading Americans and presented to
President Benjamin Harrison, is only the best known of many such Christian endeavors on Jews' behalf.[14] For their part, Jews could hardly af-
ford to be too troubled by support from those who sought ultimately to
convert them. As a beleaguered minority group, they quite understanda-
bly accepted help from anyone kind enough to extend it.

Still, despite these pro-Jewish efforts, those who sought to convert
Jews could not escape casting aspersions on the religion they wanted
Jews to leave. No matter how often they sang Jews' praises, they still had
to insist that Jews were deficient, lacking in those advantages that ac-
crued to all who recognized Jesus as the Messiah. By definition, a conversionist had to believe that Jews were beset by faults that only conversion
could cure. This being the case, one can understand why Jews have so often classed those who profess to love them in the same category as those
who openly hate them, for both alike have criticized Jews in ways that
Jews find offensive.

Typical love-inspired criticisms of Jews may be found in the address
delivered by the Rev. Philip Milledoler, later president of Rutgers, at the
1816 organizational meeting of the American Society for Evangelizing
the Jews (the name was changed to Meliorating the Condition of the Jews
in 1820, when a state charter was obtained). Milledoler, describing the
state of the Jews, referred to the "strong plea of humanity" that inspired
the missionary effort being undertaken. "Is not their situation," he cried,
"calculated to excite our sympathy and call forth our exertions? And
shall we slumber in apathy over their tremendous misery?" The misery
he had in mind consisted of such things as that "with the New Testament, which is founded upon and indissolubly connected with the Old,
the great body of that people are almost wholly unacquainted." That
"though arraigned and condemned before the bar of God, and their own
consciences, as sinners, yet by the deeds of the law they still hope to be
justified before God." That "their religious exercises are scarcely con-

ducted with the form, much less with the spirit, of devotion." And that they suffer from "laxness of morals . . . the female character among them holds a station far inferior to that which it was intended to occupy by the God of nature of providence." In short, from Milledoler's perspective, Jews closed their eyes to the obvious truth of Christianity, misread the Bible, were both religiously and morally decadent, and remained in need of salvation.[15]

Although Christian criticisms of Judaism have changed since 1816, in many cases the charges still sound obnoxiously familiar, at least to Jewish ears. *The Christian Approach to the Jew*, referred to above, reported that "the majority of educated Jews have turned to agnosticism or atheism. Religious apathy or indifference grows apace, morals have suffered . . . decadence is apparent almost everywhere." It then proceeded to reaffirm that "the religion of the New Testament is the necessary completion of the Old Testament religion," that "misunderstanding of the Old Testament" hindered "the acceptance of the Christian message by the Jew," and that Christianity possessed a "higher moral standard" that acted "as a deterrent to many Jews."[16] More recently, Gregory Baum, the liberal Catholic theologian who has often criticized fellow Catholics for their negative attitudes toward Jews, pointed out the painful dilemma that makes such criticisms almost inevitable: "It is not easy to proclaim Jesus Christ without at the same time implying a negation of the Jews. As the Church, we see ourselves as the chosen people replacing the Jewish people which by its infidelity is considered to have set itself outside the divine covenant. That is what Matthew's Gospel already clearly states."[17]

Four themes emerge from this love-inspired Christian critique of Judaism that deserve special attention. When Jews talk about Jewish-Christian hostility, these are what they usually have in mind. First, there is the manifold problem of Christian triumphalism. All religions have some degree of triumphalism attached to them, just as all countries do; triumphalism is to some extent a function of self-respect. Jews, however, have always had considerable difficulty with the frequently encountered Christian view that salvation lies *only* in the church. Perhaps because Jews have been taught that the righteous of all nations have a share in the world to come, they have taken offense at the notion that so long as they refuse to believe in Jesus of Nazareth their eternal prospects are, as one nineteenth-century missionary termed them, "dark and dismal even when compared with Pagan nations."[18] To Jews the idea that "if we don't repent and convert we will nosedive directly into the waiting jaws of hell" is anathema.[19]

Continuing with this same theme, Jews have also taken offense at the triumphalistic view that Christianity is simply Judaism fulfilled. This idea

has been traced to the Book of Revelations (2:9, 3:9) and featured prominently in medieval disputations.[20] In America, Ralph Waldo Emerson
believed that "Jews have at last flowered perfectly into Jesus," and the
Catholic World explained in 1878 that "Judaism . . . is related to Christianity not as the seed to the plant, but as the well-prepared soil to the
harvest, as the figure to the reality, as the prophecy to its accomplishment, as the harbinger to the King whose coming he announces to the
populations who are to receive him."[21] Jews have always disagreed and
find Christian doctrines of *praeparatio* and *Verus Israel* freighted with
anti-Judaism.

Finally, with regard to this first theme, Jews have had trouble with
triumphalistic Christian millennial views that foresee ultimate Jewish
conversion. Jews certainly prefer those who call for their *ultimate* conversion to those who work for their *immediate* conversion. Still, the link
drawn in so many Christian minds between the much heralded end of
days and the simultaneous end of the Jewish people is profoundly dis-
turbing. Some assume that "the Jews in God's own time will become
Catholic Christians." Others of a more Adventist bent believe, as
William Cummins Davis described in his poem "The Millennium," that
"We'll find the world without a Jew. The Pope, and Devil, known no
more . . . / And Jew and Gentile now the same/ Rejoice to wear the Christian name." On this one point Catholics and anti-Catholics both agree:
Jews will ultimately disappear.[22]

A second prominent Christian theme that has long been a source of
trouble to Jews is the idea that the Bible is really a Christian book, con-
taining a so-called Old Testament that predicts Jesus' coming and a New
Testament superseding the Old and bringing forth gospel truth to mankind. This view, of course, has long been a pervasive one. In America,
William Holmes McGuffey's *Eclectic Third Reader* (1836–7) taught a
full generation that "the Scriptures are especially designed to make us
wise unto salvation through Faith in Christ Jesus." The "Old Testament," according to the reader, was the Jews' "own sacred volume," and
contained "the most extraordinary predictions concerning the infidelity
of their nation, and the rise, progress, and extensive prevalence of Christianity."[23] *The New York Observer*, in 1865, found it "strange" that
Jews "cannot see that the Old Testament as well as the New is full of Jesus Christ." The *Church Review* charged that "the literature of the prophetic books was misapprehended and perverted, as everything else was,
by the carnally-minded Jews."[24] Such quotations could easily be multiplied.

Buttressing all these claims was the fact that many Bibles published in

America, particularly in the nineteenth century, contained headings over every page and before every chapter that read Christian interpretations into the text: "The Prediction of Christ" over Psalm 110; "A Description of Christ" over Song of Songs 5; "Christ's Birth and Kingdom" over Isaiah 9. Translations, from the American Bible Society's edition of the King James Bible down to the recent Good News Bible, have also contained thoroughly Christological understandings of the original Hebrew. Such words as "saviour" and "spirit" abound, and prophecies from "Shiloh" in Genesis to the "Son of Man" in Daniel have been rendered into English with an eye toward Christian exegesis and New Testament parallels.[25]

These theologically charged translations do not, from a Jewish perspective, capture the literal meaning of the biblical idiom. Instead, they distort the text, reduce the sanctity and significance of the Hebrew Bible, and engender interreligious hostility. To this day, the arsenals of groups such as "Jews for Jesus" are heavily stocked with arguments based on biblical prooftexts, and their missionaries, like Moishe Rosen, confidently report that "examining the clear continuities between the Old and New Testaments can be a fascinating experience for Jews," for "these prophecies clearly show that Jesus is our long-awaited Messiah."[26]

A third area of hostility between Jews and Christians emerges from the word "decadence" which, as we have seen, both nineteenth- and twentieth-century critics employed in characterizing the Jewish situation. Many Christians—not all—have always assumed that there is a straight-line relationship between Christianity, morality, and modernity, and as a consequence, they have looked upon Jews as being both amoral (if not immoral) and primitive. The very word "Christian," in popular usage, carries with it overtones of morality and civilization, as in the phrase "a Christian thing to do." In writing to Thomas Jefferson, the Jewish leader Mordecai Noah thus once used the phrase "in the civilized, or if you please in the Christian world." Quite a few American Jews, Noah among them, similarly took the phrase "you are truly a good Christian" to be a high compliment.[27]

Referring to a few Jews as "good Christians," however, does not solve the overall problem of whether Jews *can* be moral and modern. Missionaries have usually insisted that Jews cannot be—a view that provoked one early critic of missions to charge the whole enterprise with aiming "to place the Jew below the level of the Christian. It presupposes the former to be in a degraded and uncultivated state, and the latter completely civilized. It recognizes the impolitic principle . . . that Christianity ought to be the predominant religion; that those who do not profess it must necessarily be immoral persons, undeserving of the rights of citizens, and whose condition is incapable of amendment or amelioration, under the profession of any other faith."[28]

Various nineteenth-century descriptions of Judaism agreed with missionaries about Judaism's primitive character. A popular volume entitled *The Jew At Home and Abroad*, revised from a British edition by the American Sunday School Union (1845), reported on "the absurd and superstitious practices which are so numerous and diversified in the private and public exercises of the Jews."[29] A later work professed to detail Jews' "religious prejudices, superstitions, and fables, their sacred reverences for trifling traditions and useless ceremonies and customs." Other works, particularly the autobiographies of converts, continued to characterize Judaism in this fashion down through the twentieth century.[30]

Given this view of Judaism—and as readers of Lyman Beecher's *A Plea for the West* (1835) know, Catholics were not treated in any more friendly a light—it followed that America for its own good had to be Protestant. Daniel Webster spoke for many when he insisted that "the Christian religion"—to him synonymous with the Protestant religion—"must ever be regarded among us as the foundation of civil society." If that meant that a Jewish school for the poor "would not be regarded as a charity" since it taught "doctrines . . . contrary to the Christian religion," so be it. Similar pronouncements, as Robert Handy has shown, echoed down through the nineteenth century and beyond.[31] To be full Americans according to this view, to be seen, in other words, as moral, modern, and thoroughly civilized, Jews had to convert. Needless to say, Jews have vigorously demurred.

The last in this sad litany of Christian hostility as seen from a Jewish point of view is the problem of the "mythical Jew" and the "Jew next door," the clash between received wisdom about ancient Jews and perceived wisdom about modern ones. Many Christians have always experienced difficulty distinguishing Jews they read about in the Bible from those they meet on the street, and they ascribe to the latter characteristics, if not indeed guilt, attributed to the former. The editor of the *Richmond Whig* in 1829 may have been somewhat carried away when he wrote that:

> When we see one of this people, and remember that we have been told
> by good authority, that he is an exact copy of the Jew who worshiped in
> the Second Temple two thousand years ago—that his physiognomy and
> religious opinions—that the usages and customes of his tribe are still
> the same, we feel that profound respect which antiquity inspires.[32]

Still the sentiments he expressed have found many echoes.

Had "profound respect" been the universal response to this anachronistic view of Jews, it seems safe to assume that Jews would happily have overlooked the problem. Unfortunately, however, that was not to be. Instead, many Jews have found themselves pilloried not only for their own sins, but for the reputed sins of their ancestors. Thus the abolitionist leader William Lloyd Garrison once attacked Mordecai Noah as "that lineal descendant of the monsters who nailed Jesus to the cross between two thieves," and concluded that "Shylock will have his 'pound of flesh' at whatever cost."[33] Oliver Wendell Holmes admitted that he grew up with the view that Jews formed "a race lying under a curse for their obstinacy in refusing the gospel." Others remember being chased with cries of "Christ-killer" and "sinner."[34]

Problems connected with Christian efforts to reconcile the increasingly apparent differences between the "mythical Jew" and the "Jew next door" cannot be considered here.[35] Suffice it to say that Jews have found it particularly galling to discover that even when they have gone to great lengths to "modernize" themselves by conforming to Western norms they continue to be viewed as if nothing had changed for them since Pharisaic days. Missionaries, indeed, have quite generally viewed all deviations from strict Orthodox Judaism to be anathema;[36] to their mind, as we have seen, modernization cannot take place without Christianization. According to this way of thinking, Jewish history ceased to develop independently soon after the year 1, for "with the appearance of Christ, the account of the Jewish branch of the church properly ends." Jews from then on could only be acted upon; they could not act themselves. Jews alive today are consequently fossils. Modern Jews are a contradiction in terms.[37]

III

I have so far portrayed Jewish-Christian relations in the United States in rather dismal tones. I have argued that many Christians love Jews by trying to convert them, and that they express their love of Judaism by insisting on the superiority and ultimate triumph of Christianity. In making these claims, I have wandered with seeming abandon across the full spectrum of American Christianity, ignoring critical theological differences, and I have leaped back and forth across two centuries in time, ignoring obvious historical changes. I have done this deliberately to suggest the existence of an ongoing Christian tradition, deeply troubling to Jews, cen-

tered neither in any one Christian denomination nor in any single historical period, and available for use as part of the cultural baggage that
American Christianity carries on its back.

It would, however, be a gross distortion to imply that this tradition
forms the sum and substance of Jewish-Christian relations in the United
States, for precisely the opposite is true. Jewish-Christian hostility in the
United States has always been balanced by genuine manifestations of amity. Jews who interact socially with Christians know that not every Christian seeks to convert Jews, nor does every Christian wish that Judaism
would disappear. To underscore this point—forgotten with surprising
frequency by those who write on this subject—I shall now switch directions and briefly outline five factors that promote Jewish-Christian harmony in the United States, mitigating problems that do exist. I do not
claim that these are the only factors involved, nor that they have invariably succeeded in thwarting the kinds of love-inspired anti-Jewish sallies
that I have enumerated. I do maintain, however, that any discussion of
Jewish-Christian hostility would be incomplete without devoting at least
some attention to these countervailing tendencies.

1. *Freedom of Religion.* The first amendment's guarantee—"Congress
shall make no law respecting an establishment of religion or prohibiting
the exercise thereof"—reiterated by American presidents, duplicated in
state constitutions, and enshrined in American tradition, generally taints
as "un-American" anything that smacks of religious intolerance. Conversionism, anti-Catholicism, anti-Mormonism, and other expressions of religious zealotry and narrow-mindedness have, to be sure, sometimes elicited support from leading Americans; religious liberty in this country has
always meant different things at different times to different people. But
constitutional guarantees have at least put those who seem illiberal on
the defensive. Those, by contrast, who speak out on behalf of boundless
religious tolerance generally win far more widespread approval.

2. *Religious Pluralism.* Even before the Revolution, American social
and religious diversity mandated the reality of pluralism among some
Protestants. A denominationalist conception of the church arose which,
within limits, accepted each Protestant communion as acceptably Christian, differences notwithstanding. Full religious pluralism followed logi-
cally, many coming to accept the view that *all* who love and fear God
may claim legitimacy. This widely embracing idea—preserved in such
phrases as "one nation under God"—permitted Jews an equal place in
the panoply of American religion. As early as 1789, when Philadelphians
celebrated their state's ratification of the Constitution, onlookers witnessed a parade of "the clergy of the different Christian denominations,

with the rabbi of the Jews, walking arm in arm."[38] In 1860, a Jew was for the first time invited to deliver the prayer opening a session of Congress.[39] Later, Jews and various Christian denominations formed temporary informal coalitions based on shared common interests. While, as we have seen, pluralism continued to have its opponents, and religious triumphalism never did die, the fact that America's religious tradition made a place for Jews has again meant that those who deny Jews independent religious legitimacy must answer to the bar of public opinion. Most Americans seem to prefer one or another pluralistic model of religion, assuming as they do that real religion, whatever the brand, must be all right.

3. *Voluntaryism.* All religious groups in America depend for survival on voluntary support from a committed laity. This results in competition among different faiths and would at first glance seem to exacerbate rather than inhibit hostility such as that between Jews and Christians. In fact, however, competition has in the long run acted as a moderating force in American religion. Most religious groups have learned that unfair or dishonorable competitive practices are responded to in kind, to the ultimate detriment of religion generally. Faiths have gained far more by promoting their own virtues than by badmouthing opponents, for competitors in America are still expected to display respect for one another. America's competitive religious situation does, of course, continue to promote discord; competition always does. But at least in the case of Jews, interfaith rivalry has also had a beneficial effect. Challenges, even if they weakened Judaism at first, have ultimately led to changes that made for a stronger and more viable Judaism than existed before.[40]

4. *Coalitionism.* As American religious groups began to worry about their declining influence, issues that divided them tended to loom less large than the need to display unity in the face of formidable adversaries. Secularism, the advent of new religions, and menacing political developments all posed challenges that cut across denominational lines. Religious coalitions took shape in response. The new stress on common areas of agreement did not close off areas of disagreement. Still, the knowledge that Jews could serve as valuable allies has resulted in new sensitivity toward Jewish concerns, and in some cases—Reinhold Niebuhr's for example—important theological reevaluations.

5. *Interfaith and Community-Relations Organizations.* Organizations designed to further "better understanding" between Jews and Christians, all of them products of the twentieth century, have played an increasingly important role in building a spirit of amity between Jews and Christians.[41] Their financial resources, prestige, political savvy, and high-level connections have enabled them both to mold opinions, particularly those

reflected in the media and in textbooks, and on occasion to shape policy. While it is easy to exaggerate the contribution of these groups—often their contributions have been more show than substance—they have by their existence and message served to counter the idea that Christians seek merely to convert Jews, if not one way then another. The National Conference of Christians and Jews, for example, goes out of its way to emphasize to Christians that "dialogue is *not* a soft-sell approach to conversion." It quotes "an evangelical layman" who considers it "illegitimate" to utilize dialogue to make converts, and stresses that "the purpose of dialogue is not to convert but to create mutual understanding and respect."[42]

Of course, five factors[43] do not harmonious relations make. There is instead an ongoing tension among various Christian approaches to the Jew, some reflecting hostility, some amity. The tangled web of conflicting Jewish, Christian, and American traditions, the simultaneous attraction of contending religious and political ideologies, and the contradictory demands of competing authority figures of different persuasions together ensure a level of complexity in Jewish-Christian relations that defies attempts at glib generalization. Feelings of love and hate, tolerance and intolerance, triumphalism and pluralism all coexist uneasily not only within different religious groups, but often within individuals themselves. At any given moment in American history there has been reason for despair and reason for hope. American Jews have experienced trouble from Christians, but they have enjoyed manifold blessings from them too.

Notes

1. Genesis Rabbah 63:7 and Sifre 69; cf. Rashi on Genesis 33:4. Jacob Katz, *Exclusiveness and Tolerance* (New York: Schocken Books, 1962); Shmuel Almog, ed., *Antisemitism through the Ages* (Hebrew, Jerusalem: Zalman Shazar Center, 1980); and Gerson Cohen, "Esau as Symbol in Early Medieval Thought," in *Jewish Medieval and Renaissance Studies*, ed. A. Altmann (Cambridge: Harvard University Press, 1967) 19–48, especially p. 26, explore aspects of this medieval view.

2. Alexander Altmann, *Moses Mendelssohn* (University, AL: University of Alabama Press, 1973) 220; cf. pp. 50, 592.

3. David S. Katz, *Philo-Semitism and the Readmission of the Jews to England* (New York: Oxford University Press, 1982); Alan Edelstein, *An Unacknowledged Harmony: Philo-Semitism and the Survival of European Jewry* (Westport,

CT: Greenwood Press, 1982); Arthur Hertzberg, *The French Enlightenment and the Jews* (New York: Columbia University Press, 1968) 248–313.

4. In addition to works cited in note 3, see Abraham Gilam, *The Emancipation of the Jews in England* (New York: Garland Publishing, 1982) 26–32; and Paul R. Mendes-Flohr and Jehuda Reinharz, *The Jew in the Modern World* (New York: Oxford University Press, 1980) 7–46.

5. Gordon Rupp, "Martin Luther in the Context of His Life and Times," *Face to Face: An Interreligious Bulletin* 10 (Spring 1983) 6; Armas K. E. Holmio, *The Lutheran Reformation and the Jews* (Hancock, MI: Finnish Lutheran Book Concern, 1949).

6. Joseph L. Blau and Salo W. Baron, *The Jews of the United States 1790– 1840: A Documentary History* (New York: Columbia University Press, 1963) I:91.

7. Ibid., III:769.

8. *The Twentieth Report of the Board of Directors of the American Society for Meliorating the Condition of the Jews* (New York, 1843) 12–13.

9. Jonathan D. Sarna, "The American Jewish Response to Nineteenth-Century Christian Missions," *The Journal of American History* 68 (June 1981) 45.

10. John Adams concluded a pro-Jewish letter with the hope that "once restored to an independent government and no longer persecuted they would . . . possibly in time become liberal Unitarian Christians": Adams to Mordecai M. Noah, 15 March 1819, reprinted in M. Davis, *With Eyes toward Zion* (New York: Ayer, 1977) 19.

11. Zebulon B. Vance, *The Scattered Nation* (New York: J. J. Little & Co., 1904), especially pp. 10, 14, 25, 40, 42; see also Selig Adler, "Zebulon B. Vance and the Scattered Nation," *The Journal of Southern History* 7 (August 1941) 357–77; and for Vance's views on "the elevating and refining influence of the Christian religion," Clement Dowd, *Life of Zebulon B. Vance* (Charlotte, NC: Observer Printing and Publishing House, 1897) 121–22; cf. p. 287.

12. *The Christian Approach to the Jew* (London: Edinburgh House Press, 1927), quotes from pp. 36, 18; see also pp. 178, 189. For other views on Mott and the Jews, see C. Howard Hopkins, *John R. Mott, 1865–1955: A Biography* (Grand Rapids: Wm. B. Eerdmans, 1979); and C. Howard Hopkins and John W. Long, "American Jews and the Root Mission to Russia in 1917: Some New Evidence," *American Jewish History* 69 (March 1980) 342–54.

13. Arnold Seth Stiebel, "The Marketing of Jesus: An Analysis of Propaganda Techniques Utilized by Christian Missionaries in Their Attempt to Proselytize the American Jew" (Ord. thesis, Hebrew Union College-Jewish Institute of Religion, 1982).

14. William E. Blackstone, "Palestine for the Jews" (1891), reprinted in *Christian Protagonists for Jewish Restoration* (New York: Arno Press, 1977). On Blackstone, see I. S. Meyer, ed., *Early History of Zionism in America* (New York, 1958) 164–70; Yona Malachy, *American Fundamentalism and Israel* (Jerusalem: Magnes Press, 1978) 136–42; and Carl Ehle, "Prolegomena to Christian Zionism in America: The Views of Increase Mather and William E. Black-

stone Concerning the Doctrine of the Restoration of Israel" (Ann Arbor: University Microfilms International, 1978). For other examples, see Jonathan D. Sarna, "From Necessity to Virtue: The Hebrew-Christianity of Gideon R. Leder," *Iliff Review* 37 (Winter 1980) 31; B. Eugene Griessman, "Philo-Semitism and Protestant Fundamentalism: The Unlikely Zionists," *Phylon* 37 (Fall 1976) 197–211; and David Rausch, *Zionism within Early American Fundamentalism* (New York: Edwin Mellen Press, 1979).

15. *Religious Intelligencer* 1 (1817) 555–57; for later echoes of these charges, see Bernhard E. Olson, *Faith and Prejudice* (New Haven: Yale University Press, 1963); and Charles Y. Glock and Rodney Stark, *Christian Beliefs and Anti-Semitism* (New York: Harper & Row, 1966), especially pp. 60–80.

16. *The Christian Approach to the Jew*, pp. 95, 98–99; cf. Frank E. Talmage, "Christianity and the Jewish People," in Talmage, ed., *Disputation and Dialogue* (New York: Ktav Publishing, 1975) 240–53; and B. Z. Sobel, *Hebrew Christianity: The Thirteenth Tribe* (New York: Wiley, 1974) 76–92.

17. Gregory Baum, "Foreword," in Charlotte Klein, *Anti-Judaism in Christian Theology* (Philadelphia: Fortress Press, 1975) xi.

18. Elnathan Gridley, "The Character of the Jews," *Memoirs of American Missionaries Formerly Connected with . . . Andover Theological Seminary* (Boston: Peirce and Parker, 1833) 295.

19. Eli N. Evans, *The Provincials* (New York: Atheneum, 1973) 126.

20. Marcel Simon, *Verus Israel* (Paris: E. de Boccard, 1948); David Berger, *The Jewish-Christian Debate in the High Middle Ages* (Philadelphia: Jewish Publication Society of America, 1979) 287–89.

21. Alfred R. Ferguson and Ralph H. Orth, eds., *The Journals and Miscellaneous Notebooks of Ralph Waldo Emerson* (Cambridge: Harvard University Press, 1977) 13:120; F. Doncat, "Relations of Judaism to Christianity," *Catholic World* 27 (June 1878) 352.

22. P. Girard, "The Present State of Judaism in America," *Catholic World* 25 (June 1877) 375; William C. Davis, "The Millennium" (1811), quoted in Le Roy Edwin Froom, *The Prophetic Faith of our Fathers* (Washington, DC: Review and Herald, 1954) 4:222. For the medieval background, see Berger, *The Jewish-Christian Debate*, p. 268.

23. John H. Westerhoff, *McGuffey and His Readers* (Nashville: Abingdon Press, 1978) 138–39.

24. *New York Observer*, 24 August 1865, p. 268; *Church Review* 24 (April 1872) 271.

25. Nahum M. Sarna and Jonathan D. Sarna, "Jewish Bible Scholarship and Translations in the United States," in Ernest S. Frerichs, ed., *The Bible and Bibles in America* (forthcoming).

26. Moishe Rosen with William Proctor, *Jews for Jesus* (Old Tappan, NJ: Fleming H. Revell, 1974) 47–48.

27. Jonathan D. Sarna, *Jacksonian Jew* (New York: Holmes & Meier, 1981) 133; idem, "The 'Mythical Jew' and the 'Jew Next Door' in Nineteenth Century America," in David Gerber, ed., *Anti-Semitism in American History* (Urbana: University of Illinois Press, 1986) 65, 76.

28. *Israel Vindicated* (New York: Abraham Collins, 1820) vi; on this work see Jonathan D. Sarna, "The Freethinker, the Jews, and the Missionaries: George Houston and the Mystery of *Israel Vindicated*," *AJS Review* 5 (1980) 101–14.

29. *The Jew at Home and Abroad* (Philadelphia: American Sunday-School Union, 1845) 111.

30. Charles Freshman, *The Autobiography of the Reverend Charles Freshman* (Toronto: S. Rose, 1868) vii; cf. Stuart A. Federow, "Convert Autobiographies As a Genre of Literature" (Ord. thesis, Hebrew Union College-Jewish Institute of Religion, 1982), especially pp. 66–68, 98. See also George Sweazy, *Effective Evangelism* (New York: Harper, 1953) 58: "It is normal to be a Christian; it is abnormal to be away from Christ."

31. Daniel Webster, "The Christian Ministry and the Religious Instruction of the Young," in *The Works of Daniel Webster* (Boston: C. C. Little and J. Brown, 1851) 6:166–67; Robert T. Handy, *A Christian America* (New York: Oxford University Press, 1971). See also Ferene M. Szasz, "Protestantism and the Search for Stability: Liberal and Conservative Quests for Christian America, 1875–1925," in Jerry Israel, ed., *Building the Organizational Society* (New York: Free Press, 1972) 88–102; and for the European background, Jacob Katz, *From Prejudice to Destruction* (Cambridge: Harvard University Press, 1980) 195–202.

32. *The Richmond Constitutional Whig*, 9 January 1829, in Herbert T. Ezekiel and Gaston Lichtenstein, *The History of the Jews of Richmond*, (Richmond, VA: H. T. Ezekiel, 1917) 56.

33. Louis Ruchames, "The Abolitionists and the Jews," in Bertram W. Korn, ed., *A Bicentennial Festschrift for Jacob Rader Marcus* (Waltham: American Jewish Historical Society, 1976) 508.

34. Oliver Wendell Holmes, *Over the Teacups* (Boston: Houghton, Mifflin and Co., 1891) 194; cf. Louis Harap, *The Image of the Jew in American Literature from Early Republic to Mass Immigration* (Philadelphia: Jewish Publication Society of America, 1974) 87–90.

35. See my article cited in note 27 above.

36. *The Jew at Home and Abroad*, pp. 152–53, thus condemns Moses Mendelssohn; for an analysis of this theme in more recent missionary writings see Norman S. Lipson, "An Enquiry into Hebrew Christianity" (Ord. thesis, Hebrew Union College-Jewish Institute of Religion, 1972) 45–49.

37. W. H. Ryder, "Church of the Jews," *Universalist Quarterly Review* 15 (July 1858) 319. For Jewish responses to the fossil theme in general and particularly to Arnold Toynbee who gave the theme currency, see Maurice Samuel, *The Professor and the Fossil* (New York: Alfred A. Knopf, 1956); and Oscar Rabinowicz, *Arnold Toynbee on Judaism and Zionism: A Critique* (London: W. H. Allen, 1974).

38. Edwin Wolf II and Maxwell Whiteman, *The History of the Jews of Philadelphia from Colonial Times to the Age of Jackson* (Philadelphia: Jewish Publication Society of America, 1956) 150.

39. Bertram W. Korn, "The First Jewish Prayer in Congress," *Eventful Years and Experiences* (Cincinnati: American Jewish Archives, 1954) 98–124.

40. On this theme, see Jonathan D. Sarna, "The Impact of Nineteenth Century

Christian Missions on American Jews," *Journal of Ecumenical Studies* (forthcoming).

41. See Lance J. Sussman, "'Toward Better Understanding': The Rise of the Interfaith Movement in America and the Role of Rabbi Isaac Landman," *American Jewish Archives* 34 (April 1982) 35–51. David Berger, "Jewish-Christian Relations: A Jewish Perspective," *Journal of Ecumenical Studies* 20 (Winter 1983) 5–32, came to hand after this essay was substantially complete. Berger offers important insights into the impact of dialogue, as well as on the problem of triumphalism dealt with above.

42. Dean M. Kelly and Bernhard E. Olson, *The Meaning and Conduct of Dialogue* (New York: National Conference of Christians and Jews, 1970) 11–12.

43. For related discussions, see Winthrop Hudson, *The Great Tradition of the American Churches* (New York: Harper, 1953); Sidney E. Mead, *The Lively Experiment* (New York: Harper & Row, 1963); and Jonathan D. Sarna, "Anti-Semitism and American History," *Commentary* 71:3 (March 1981) 42–47.

2

The Elephant and the Angels; or, The Incivil Irritatingness of Jewish Theodicy

JOHN MURRAY CUDDIHY

According to an old joking story, of which every group has its version, a professor assigned term papers on the topic of "The Elephant" to a small seminar of independent-study students. The German student wrote on "The Taxonomy of Elephants"; the French student wrote on "The Elephant and Romantic Love"; the Jewish student wrote on "The Elephant and the Problem of Anti-Semitism."

There is a long tradition of connecting Jews with matters that, on the surface at least, have little or nothing to do with them. A recent issue of the *Jewish Week*, for example, notes that " 'The Jewish Contribution to the Olympic Games' will be broadcast as a multi-part series from now through the 1984 Summer Games, on 'Page One,' the syndicated news-magazine program produced by the Simon Wiesenthal Center. Richard Trank, program director, will interview sports buff Richard Macales, who will provide *little-known facts* concerning Jewish Olympians."[1]

Such an egregious tradition, which sees the salience of Jews and anti-Semitism for such an extraordinarily broad range of subjects, events, and topics "makes it all the more notable, then," Professor Berel Lang writes,

> that anti-Semitism, which has been such a coercive factor in Jewish history, should be viewed as not part of the "Jewish Question" at all, but as an issue which, since it could only have been defined by non-Jews, remains quite fully *their* question: to answer, as well as to answer for. The reasonable, indeed urgent, concern to understand anti-Semitism—its origins and causes, its forms of expression—has, *for once*, nothing to

do with the Jews. This view, furthermore . . . has served as a premise in the most serious historical attempts to analyze the phenomenon of anti-Semitism—in standard works, for example, by Poliakov and Parkes and, hardly less noticeably, in the general Jewish histories by such figures as Graetz, Dubnow, and Baron. . . . This resistance to the possibility of a connection between anti-Semitism and Jewish history is understandable, but it has also been pernicious. Consideration of that possibility is, in fact, crucial to a grasp of the phenomenon of anti-Semitism; its avoidance has, in fact, persistently distorted the analysis of anti-Semitism as a general occurrence and has skewed the accounts of even such specific, ponderable expressions of anti-Semitism as the Holocaust itself.[2]

"The Jewish Contribution to the Olympic Games"—such contributions are common, but the "Jewish Contribution to the Jewish Question"? To this problem the Jewish contribution is claimed to be nonexistent.

Recently the position that anti-Semitism has nothing to do with Jews and everything to do with gentiles was formulated in its pure form: "The notion that anti-Semitism can be, in the slightest degree, the fault of Jews," writes Cynthia Ozick, "is in itself—even when it crops up, as it frequently does, among Jews—a species of anti-Semitism. In three indelible sentences of irrefutable clarity," she continues, "Barbara Tuchman blows away this foolishness: 'Anti-Semitism,' she says, 'is independent of its object. What Jews do or fail to do is not the determinant. The impetus comes out of the needs of the persecutors.'"[3] Not only does anything Jews do or refrain from doing have nothing to do with anti-Semitism, but any *attempt* to explain anti-Semitism by referring to the Jewish contribution to anti-Semitism is itself an instance of anti-Semitism!

This *reductio ad absurdum* has stunning implications. It means that Jews have not been causal agents in their own history. Nothing about them has "contributed" to the emergence of anti-Semitism. They did not act and interact causally and historically with other groups in history. Morally blameless, the Jews in this self-conception escaped the rough give-and-take of history. They were outside history, aspiring to what Lionel Trilling calls in another connection, "unconditioned spirit." Following Maritain, let us call this "angelism."[4]

Theodicy, as we know, is a traditional branch of classical moral theology. It endeavors to understand evil, to reconcile God's goodness and omnipotence, on the one hand, with the fact of evil—sin, pain, death, cruelty—on the other. How does one reconcile a benevolent and omnipotent God with the existence of evil? Milton wrote the epic of an evil fall, a *Paradise Lost*, in order, he writes, "to justify the ways of God to man." A book on theodicy written by a rabbi led the nonfiction bestseller list for much of 1983. It was called *When Bad Things Happen to Good People*.⁵

Jewish theodicy is the way Jews—ordinary Jews, secular or religious—handle the problem of evil in everyday life and in their writings and literature and art. For Jews, the problem of evil takes paramount shape as the problem of anti-Semitism, and the problem of anti-Semitism is climaxed in the Holocaust. In the course of performing their theodicy, the discourse of Jews is frequently irritating. Not necessarily wrong, or inaccurate, or immoral or illegal, but just simply annoying.

Why? Because, I would hold, of its presumption of total innocence on the part of Jews in relation to the historical phenomenon of anti-Semitism. In this theodicy, the Jewish people become as blameless and benevolent as God himself is supposed to be in the dilemma of classical theodicy. The problem becomes, "How do bad things [read: anti-Semitism] happen to this good people?"

If this people in practice really considers itself blameless, as sinned against by other groups, itself not sinning against them, it is driven by its own logic to a kind of Manichean view of the world in which a small, weak, good group (the Jews) is dispersed among a large, strong, bad group (the nations, the *goyim*). This small, good group is self-defined as a victim of the large, strong, bad, Christian group that victimizes it.

It was not ever thus with Jewish theodicy. The classical theodicy blamed the Jews themselves for the woes of exile. The earlier lamentations were intrapunitive. I define Jewish secularization and emancipation as precisely a shift in the direction of blame: from a deserved punishment from God for violating the covenant to blaming the instruments of his wrath, the nations. The vector of blame shifts from intrapunitive to exteropunitive, leaving the Jews themselves relatively blameless.

Jewish theodicy so conceived finds nothing morally problematic about its claimed status as victim. Jews blame the victimizer, the anti-Semite. They see the anti-Semite as blaming the victim, the Jew. This they take to be very problematic and irrational. Yet, when Jews' own historical actions, in the Middle East for example, create a stateless people who, in turn, blame the Jews and the Israelis, what does Jewish theodicy do? It blames the victims, the Palestinians, and sees nothing irrational in this. This presumption of blamelessness is irritating because it violates reciprocity.

Let me try to supply some concrete, often random, contemporary examples of this kind of self-regarding moral complacency. I believe that, in the main, they are typical, rather than exceptional.

Stuart E. Eisenstat, former assistant to President Carter for domestic affairs (1977–81), speaks of American support for Israel as based on many things, including "the enlightened ethics of Israel."[6] The shape of the phrase itself is odd. Would anyone say, for example, that Margaret Thatcher's England supports American policy because of "the enlightened ethics of the United States"? Or our support of England—would we say that it was based on "the enlightened ethics of England"? Simply as a locution, it is odd, even apart from the problem of whether or not it is true.

Another example: As David Denby writes, Woody Allen's "*Broadway Danny Rose*, conceals a good deal of Jewish self-regard—indeed, the Jews-are-more-moral-than-other-people sentiments get a little sticky here, especially as all the Italians apart from Tina [played by Mia Farrow] are pictured as outright slobs."[7] In *Danny Rose*, Denby continues, Woody Allen plays "a small-time Jewish entertainment figure so insistently moral that he lingers in a restaurant to lay down a tip even as Mafia hit men are coming in the door to bump him off."[8]

This moral smugness and self-regard can take the form of imputing envy to "the world," to the gentile, to the *goyim*. Hence Elie Wiesel's remarks at the Western Wall shortly after its "liberation" in the 1967 war: "Let's not fool ourselves. The world already envies our victory. Already we can hear the strident voices. . . . Even our 'friends' are not likely to forgive that we were victorious—that it was such an impolitely swift victory, so complete, so magnificent, it is understandable. We have suddenly stripped them of the chance to pity us."[9] Notice Wiesel's curious certitude that the *goyim* "envy" Jews their victory; but, he adds, given that the victory was so "impolitely swift . . . so complete, so magnificent," such envy is "understandable." This public *kvelling* and sanctimonious moralizing are all rolled into the familiar Wieselian bolus. It is irritating. And yet the New York pundit and critic John Leonard announces, "If we stop reading [Wiesel]—if we stop listening—we will lose our souls."[10]

This matter of Christians envying Jews is revived by Jewish intellectuals and their allies in every era. The question is always *what* is being envied and *why*? Thirty years ago, the Jewish social thinker Karl Polanyi addressed this problem in the course of his review of the late Benjamin Nelson's *The Idea of Usury, From Tribal Brotherhood to Universal Otherhood*.[11] The Deuteronomic ban on tribal usury—the taking of interest on a loan to one's brother Jew—was waived in the case of the gentiles. Medieval Catholicism universalized this prohibition: no usury from anyone. What Polanyi describes as a "monstrous situation" arose, a situation in which Jews were envied by Christians for "having evaded the cross of the supererogatory ethic." The Jew must have been aware, Polanyi writes, that he enjoyed a "*privilegium odiosum* conferred on him by the restriction of the Deuteronomic injunction to his own kind."

Hence, he concludes, the idea of usury in the West has dramatic implications and "bears the imprint of the Jewish-Christian calvary."[12]

The vicissitudes of interreligious envy, unlike those of interreligious hostility, remain a curiously underresearched topic. To return to Elie Wiesel: Was "the world" he deemed envious of the Six-Day War—"so impolitely swift . . . so complete, so magnificent"—envying its magnificence or was it envying, when and if it did, perhaps, a *privilegium odiosum*, an *immunity* from criticism in the Christian West? America would have been swift to condemn, had a Third World country won a similarly "magnificent" war.

What is it that enables Jews and Jewish spokesmen so often to occupy the moral high ground with such confidence? To answer this, we need more case material.

Several years ago the following appeared in the *Jewish Week:*

Brooklyn's ex-D.A., now Jerusalemite, Finds Israel Rewarding

A reporter ran across a familiar face and familiar Brooklyn accent in the Jewish Quarter of the Old City of Jerusalem and asked Eugene Gold, new immigrant, how he liked it in Israel, how Israel compared with America.

That was an unfair question, the former District Attorney of Kings County (Brooklyn) said. "It's unfair to compare Israel with America. *Materially*, there's no land like the States, but that's not what we came here for anyway," he said over a glass of wine with a reporter for "Israel Scene," the slick magazine of the World Zionist Organization.

Gold practically stepped out of his office in Brooklyn when his term in office ended six months ago and onto an aircraft, with his wife, to take them to Israel to live.

"Why they went on aliyah?" "Sure," he said. "In New York we had a much higher standard of living. But we wanted to be part of a state that reflects the uniqueness of being Jewish—the morals, the justice." He looked at his wife, Ronnie. "Well, didn't we?" he asked her. She beamed assent.[13]

What is so irritating, to me anyway, about Gold's contrast between America and Israel is the facile identification of America with "materialism" and a "higher standard of living" versus Israel, with its "uniqueness of being Jewish—the morals, the justice," its idealism and higher standard of morality and justice. Anybody can understand and sympathize with the feeling of the American immigrant, toward the end of his life, returning to the old country—or the new country, or the *Altneuland*—to live out his days on Social Security. You don't have to be a cultural anthropologist to empathize with the good feeling of being "at home" among "your own," with familiar sounds, and laughs, and tears. But Gold's ordinary human contentment is inseparable from the Zionist ideology of the Jewish state as morally superior to other states. The Golds made *aliyah* for high-minded motives, for moralistic reasons. The Diaspora they leave behind is damned with faint praise: "Materially, there's no land like the States, but that's not what we came here for . . . ." In fact, they made a sacrifice in going; they traded in a higher standard of living for a higher standard of morality. The ideology buried (and not so buried) in this interview is irritating and incivil and, I think, tied ultimately to Jewish theodicy and "why bad things happen to good people." The "impulse to moral aggrandizement," to use Lionel Trilling's phrase, to group moral aggrandizement, appears here with appalling frankness.

The self-image of the Jew as morally superior to the *goyim* is embedded in the situation of Jewish emancipation. Being marginal and relatively powerless, in other words, being *luftmenschy*, enabled Jews, especially Jewish intellectuals, to become very moralistic, very critical of the Diaspora. Ideologies like Marxism, Freudianism, Hebraism, and Reform Judaism embody this high-minded thrust. The luxury of powerlessness ended with the founding of Israel. In becoming Israelis, Jews dirtied their hands. But, despite *les mains sales*, the old-time theodicy of victimage continued, especially in the Diaspora. There is a strain, a conflict, between two rhetorics—between the Diaspora Reform rhetoric of the Jew as ethical, moralistic, and pacifistic and the Israeli rhetoric of Sabra victory and pride, between, if you will, *New York Times* editorial talk and the talk of Menachem Begin and General Ariel Sharon.

There are, of course, attempts to keep the Diaspora rhetoric alive. We turn again to Elie Wiesel, who writes: "How do Jews respond to violence?" With retaliation? No. "When the enemy is mad, he destroys; when the killer is mad, he kills. When we are mad, we sing."[14] But the Israelis also have guns. The *Times* knows this. In its 1977 Christmas editorial on Bethlehem we read, "Atop [*sic*] the Church of the Nativity, Jewish lads tug idly at their slung firearms and scan ocher hills that command our [*sic*] history. What is sovereign there in Bethlehem? And who?"[15] This is transition rhetoric, bridging powerlessness and power; a vista of Diaspora Jewish lads protecting Christian pilgrims, tugging idly at slung firearms, scanning ocher hills. It is Wordsworth cum Uzi, a pastoral "occupation."

Earlier, Rabbi Jacob Neusner had noted the way Israel seeks "to make war without fanaticism, to wage peace with selflessness . . . above all its hatred of what it must do to survive."[16] Prime Minister Golda Meir's statement that she might be able to forgive the Arabs their killing of Israelis but that she could never forgive their having turned Israelis into killers of Arabs has become famous. Reviewing an Israeli book on the Six-Day War, American Jewish writer Hugh Nissenson observes that the soldiers' "victory agonizes them. They refuse to discard the immemorial Jewish sense of identity with the victim . . . they are horrified to become conquerors."[17] Accompanying the review is a photo of an Israeli soldier who looks like a *tzaddik*.

There is an almost conscious search on the part of Jewish writers to find a rhetoric, and metaphors, and analogies that will hold on to both images at once: the Jew as agonized, good, and victim together with the Jew as victorious soldier. The Hebrew Bible seems to offer the ideal synthesis—the image of David and Goliath, with Israel as David, of course, and the Arab world as Goliath. When Random House brought out Yigal Allon's story of Israel's armed forces in 1970, it was called *The Shield of David*. In February of the following year, again Random House published Shimon Peres's account of Israel's military and industrial strength; it was titled *David's Sling*.

How *does* one cling to the old image and yet acknowledge the new? Novelist Herbert Gold turns the rhetorical trick by using a metaphor taken from born-again Christianity: "I grieved with the twice-born steely ones of the Israeli army."[18]

The figure of the Diaspora Jew as schlemiel is retained by Diaspora Jews and incongrously combined with the confident, even brash, Sabra. In European Jewish writing, Ruth R. Wisse notes, "The fool appears in many guises: on the battlefield he cries: 'Stop shooting! Someone might, God forbid, lose an eye!' "[19]

Somehow, the Diaspora rhetoric of the Jew as schlemiel, as a fumbling, bumbling, inept loser—as a Christ-figure, even—continues even as contradictory reports pour in. The 1982 invasion of Lebanon and siege of Beirut was a severe test for Diaspora Jewry's traditional theodicy. Who were the bad people? What were the "bad things" that were happening to "good people"? Who were the good people?

On August 5, New Yorkers read a dispatch in the *Times* by James F. Clarity, datelined Jerusalem and headlined, "Begin Says 'Nobody Should Preach to Us'": "The Prime Minister [addressing 200 American members of the U.J.A.] evoked loud applause discussing the Israeli army. 'It is the most valiant army in the world,' he said. 'It is the most humane army in the world. Our boys get killed in order not to hurt civilians. Nobody is going to preach to us humanitarianism. . . . Nobody, nobody,' he nearly shouted, 'is going to bring Israel to its knees. The Jews do not kneel but to God.' "[20]

On that same day, Washingtonians read a front-page dispatch in their

Post by William Branigan, datelined Beirut, and headlined, "Nowhere to Run As Shells Rain On Downtown Beirut": "For many there seemed nowhere to run on this day of terror as Israeli shells and bombs launched from land, sea and air fell nonstop from midnight until just after dark. . . . The pattern of nearly 20 hours of shelling appeared to be *indiscriminate* to reporters and other observers . . . ."[21]

Was this "the most humane army in the world," with Israelis getting killed in order *not* to hurt Arabs, as the prime minister told his American U.J.A. visitors? Or was this an "indiscriminate" bombing of civilians in a nonstop siege, as William Branigan told the *Washington Post?* The two images of Israeli Jewry were clashing in August 1982.

It so happened that a *Times* correspondent had also described the bombing as "indiscriminate": "On August 6 . . . Thomas L. Friedman, the *New York Times'* bureau chief in Beirut, cabled his Manhattan editors in outrage when he awoke to discover that they had summarily cut the word 'indiscriminate' from his lead on the previous day's Israeli bombing of Beirut. The bombing had 'the apparent aim of terrorizing its [Beirut's] civilian population,' said Friedman's Telex. His editors had been [he wrote] 'afraid to tell our readers,' and the correspondent thought it 'thoroughly unprofessional.' "[22]

Why were the editors of the *New York Times* "afraid" to tell their readers that the Israeli bombing had, for twenty hours, been "indiscriminate"? What were they "afraid" of? As we have seen, Branigan's dispatch to the *Washington Post* on the same day had also described the bombing as "indiscriminate," and his editors had not seen fit to censor the word.

No published comments on the siege and the siege coverage, Roger Morris writes in the *Columbia Journalism Review*, are more telling than the heretofore unpublished text of Thomas Friedman's "impassioned Telex" to his *Times* editors when the paper deleted the adjective "indiscriminate" from his August 5 lead on the Israeli bombing. "He had always been careful, Friedman said (and his dispatches would document the claim), 'to note in previous stories that the Israelis were hitting Palestinian positions and if they *were* hitting residential areas to at least raise the possibility that the Palestinians had a gun there at one time or another.' He [Friedman] had used 'a strong word' such as 'indiscriminate' only after he had taken a hazardous tour of the city with Branigan of the *Post* and had concluded that 'what happened yesterday was something fundamentally different from what has happened on the previous 63 days [of the siege]. The 'newspaper of record should have told its readers and future historians' about the Israeli terror bombing, Friedman went on. It was [he Telexed] the 'very essence of what was new yesterday. . . . What can I say?' he concluded. 'I am filled with profound sadness by what I have learned in the past afternoon about my newspaper.'

"Sent over the Reuters open wire and widely read in the profession, Friedman's cable provided a remarkable inside look at the conscientiousness of reporters in Beirut and their awareness of the sensitivity at home of what they were reporting. In a sense," Morris concludes, "it would be a more eloquent rebuttal to critics of the war coverage than any dispatch from the front."[23]

What is this "sensitivity at home" that made the *Times* resort to the censorship of one of its own bureau chiefs? What was the *Times* afraid of? Readers? Yes. Jewish readers? Yes. Jewish organizations? Yes. All would probably have come down on them heavily. But I think a deeper fear was the fear of losing an illusion, a theodicy, a carefully constructed and maintained "social construction of reality." For a millennium, if any Diaspora Jew were to hear news about "bad things happening to good people" there would be very little doubt in his mind about who the "good people" were and who were the perpetrators of the "bad things." This presumption of Jewish victimhood, of Jewish blamenessness, had never been publicly rebuttable. But it *was* rebutted that week in Beirut. And all the efforts of the Anti-Defamation League to include the Beirut press coverage in their annual audit of defamation have failed.

In fact, the surfeit with what I call Jewish angelism did not have to wait till 1982. There already had been murmurings in the wake of the 1967 war. When, for example, psychoanalyst Erik Erikson defended the Israeli occupation in a passage in his book on Gandhi, writing that "the triumph of Israeli soldiery is markedly subdued, balanced by a certain sadness over the necessity to reenter historical actuality by way of military methods not invented by the Jews and yet superbly used by them,"[24] Princeton anthropologist Clifford Geertz was slightly nauseated by what he calls the "moral double-talk" of this passage. He goes on to say that he prefers "the bleak candor of *Realpolitik* to images of a saddened soldiery fighting to advance the cause of pacifism . . ."[25] But, even after Beirut, what Geertz calls the "moral double-talk" goes on. Author Herman Wouk, for example, on his way to visit his two sons in Israel, one in the navy the other in the army, wrote that the Israeli army is "the strangest" army in the world. Why? Because the army hates war "as much as the anti-nuclear marchers do."[26] If only Wouk, a professional writer, had said, "*almost* as much as the anti-nuclear marchers do," but no, he must go all the way, for it is Israel and his own sons he is writing about, and Beirut must become another Aldermaston.

After the siege of Beirut came the September massacre at the Sabra and

Shatila camps, committed by the Christian Phalange while their Israeli ally looked the other way.[27] There was an outcry against Israel. Prime Minister Begin resisted calls for a commission of inquiry. After having visited Begin, Reform Jewish leader Rabbi Alexander M. Schindler asked, "What has given us, historically, the strength to withstand the attacks of the world?" And he answered his own question as follows: "Our sense of rightness. The only thing that has enabled us to withstand the torments of the centuries, the martyrdom, was our sense of moral superiority."[28]

Underlying all the ideologies of Diaspora Jewish intellectuals—secular ideologies like Marxism and Freudianism, religious ideologies like Reform Judaism and Hebraism, national ideologies like Bundism and Zionism—there is a generic ideology that I call the ideology of Jewish moralism. Like all ideology in the modern sense this one both reveals and conceals—conceals by generalizing—an interest. "*Cui bono?*" we ask of this posture of moral high-mindedness. "The Jews," Susan Sontag notes, "pinned their hopes for integrating into modern society on promoting the moral sense . . . for every sensibility is self-serving to the group that promotes it."[29]

The premise of this generic ideology was superiority to the surrounding environment, the nations, the *goyim*, superiority to what Jews like Begin and Wiesel call grandly "the world." The ideology remains group-enhancing. It performs this function even if it is not, in fact, true. Plausibility is enough.

Since the establishment of the state of Israel in 1948, this ideology is no longer very useful and is being cast aside. The Jewish ideology passes; the Jewish interest abides. That interest no longer centers in a politics of redistribution. In fact, few Diaspora Jewish intellectuals use the old moralistic vocabulary in discussing foreign policy. The word "justice" has fallen into disuse. Jacobo Timerman is old-fashioned. Expelled from Argentina, he used on Israel the same moralism that Diaspora intellectuals had been using on the claims and pretensions of the Diaspora nations for generations.[30] His stay in Israel was a short one.

So, the old free-floating Jewish intellectuals of Karl Mannheim vintage, these classical intellectual skywriters, these *luftmenschen* have ever since 1948 done a long, slow free-fall down, out of the circumambient air. They hit the ground running, running away from the old "interstices" and into the arms of the new conservatives.

The origin of this Jewish ideology of moralism—Mathew Arnold and S. D. Luzzatto called it "Hebraism"[31]—is in the secularization of the doctrine of Jewish election, Jewish chosenness. This affirmation of chosenness secularized itself into a value attitude of moral superiority. What the late Harold Nicolson wrote about the early Christians applies *a fortiori* to the Jews: "The prejudice against the Galileans was not due to their doctrine or their form of worship so much as to their bad manners. It was their attitude towards the non-elect that irritated people; not their faith."[32]

Brandeis University sociologist of religion Marshall Sklare notes that Jews "still possess a feeling of superiority, although more in the moral and intellectual realms now than in the area of spiritual affairs. While the [Jewish] feeling of superiority is a factor which has received comparatively little attention from the students of the problem [of explaining Jewish survival], it is of crucial importance because it operates to retard assimilation. Leaving the group . . . is viewed not as advancement, but as cutting oneself off from a claim to superiority."[33]

In more recent times, chosenness was inherited as a sense of one's betterness, one's betterness to the *goyim*. What a Jewish child in mid-century America inherited, writer Philip Roth told an Israeli audience, was "no body of law, no body of learning and no language, and finally, no Lord—which seems to me a significant thing to be missing." But what one did receive, Roth went on, "was a psychology, not a culture and not a culture in its totality. What one received whole, however, what one feels whole, is a kind of psychology; and the psychology can be translated into three words—'Jews are better.' This is what I knew from the beginning: somehow Jews were better. I'm saying this as a point of psychology; I'm not saying it as a fact."[34]

In a recent book, Dennis Prager and Joseph Telushkin maintain that, in fact, "Jews generally have led higher quality lives than their Gentile neighbors" owing to the higher values instilled in them by their Judaism, and that gentiles, perceiving Jews as "better than" themselves, resent and envy them precisely for this.[35] This, they claim, is the cause of anti-Semitism. This is, clearly, the obverse side of Barbara Tuchman and Cynthia Ozick's statement that the very effort to explain anti-Semitism as a response to anything Jews do or don't do is itself anti-Semitism: *les extrèmes se touchent*. Here anti-Semitism is related *intrinsically* to Jewish values and Jewish behavior, to Judaism itself: it is the compliment vice pays to virtue. Jews *are* better morally and superior culturally and are perceived as such by others. And this, not scapegoating or projection, Praeger and Telushkin claim, is the reason for anti-Semitism.

But, Joseph Sobran objects, "most people in the West have tended to look on Jews as backward, not superior. The popular sociology that made 'jew' and 'gyp' slang terms for sharp dealing may have been crude and cruel, but it hardly expressed a sense that Jewish and Gypsy life were worthy of envy. Prager and Telushkin overlook the sheer *ethnocentrism* of other cultures, because they are possessed by an ethnocentrism of their own. . . . [The book] *Why the Jews?* assumes that Jewish self-absorption is matched by a Gentile absorption with Jews."[36]

A final point: After a particularly atrocious terrorist attack on women and children in Israel on Saturday, March 11, 1978, Prime Minister Menachem Begin wrote in the *Jewish Press* that these women and children were slain by murderers "*only* because they were Jews, *only* because they were citizens of Israel. They fell at the hands of murderers who pointed their arrows at the Jewish heart."[37] These words contain the whole of this paper.

The scapegoat theory "is popular," Robert Segal writers, "because in refusing to explain anti-Semitism historically it precludes any possible apology for anti-Semitism."[38] But if the scapegoat theory thus makes anti-Semitism capricious and irrational, Begin's Zionist ideology, where no historical explanation is needed because Jews were slain "*only* because they were Jews," makes anti-Semitism an eternal, Manichean problem. This type of explanation is, Segal writes, "likewise antihistorical: *a priori* anti-Semitism rather than any *a posteriori*, historical anti-Semitism stems from the same fear as that underlying the scapegoat theory: the fear that a historical explanation will make the Jews responsible for anti-Semitism, and will thereby excuse it."[39] "To say that [Jews] are singled out simply for being Jewish is to speak not only tautologically but also nonhistorically," Segal concludes.[40]

To make this point clearer, let me use a fanciful example. Suppose that the Irish, deeming themselves the "lost tribe of Israel," had, in a fit of irredentism, returned in force and occupied Palestine in 1948, thus inheriting all the Arab world's hatred that Jews have, in fact, inherited. Suppose, further, that Arab terrorists had blown up a bus full of Irish women and children on March 11, 1978, and that the Irish prime minister cried out, "These women and children were slain by murderers *only* because they were Irish." Would it not be clear to almost everyone that they had *not* been killed for their Irishness, but rather for their behavior, for what the Arabs believed they had *done*, for their actions, their occupation?

In Begin's account of Israelis being killed for their Jewishness *as such*, the Jews are at least not marginalized as they would be in a historical or general social-science analysis of the atrocity. They were not killed, he is telling us, as scapegoats, as projections or displacements for some other hostility, territorial or otherwise. They were murdered because they were Jews and, as he writes, "*only* because they were Jews." This makes Jewishness the center of everything.

In the illusion of that centrality there reappears what Hannah Arendt calls the Zionist ideology of eternal ahistorical anti-Semitism.[41] In the conviction that the Israelis were murdered for their *being* (for *being* Jews) and not for their *doing*, we find the heart of the secular Jewish theodicy. And in this theodicy, which is a tautology, we find at work what theodicies always do—consolation.

Jews come honorably by their paranoia. Nevertheless, when it comes to their own behavior, they go on a moral holiday, legitimated by their secular, post-emancipation ideology. And if consoling to Jews, it is irritating to many non-Jews.

Notes

1. *Jewish Week*, 20 April 1984, p. 28.
2. Berel Lang, "Anti-Semitism—A Jewish Question," *Judaism* 26:1 (Winter 1977) 68–69.
3. Cynthia Ozick, "Debate: Ozick vs. Schulweis," *Moment* 1:10 (May–June 1976) 78.
4. Jacques Maritain writes about that *beata nox* of November 1619, when the fertile idea of the reform of reason—"sparkling with angelic lustre"—was conceived by Descartes in a little heated room in Germany (*The Dream of Descartes Together with Some Other Essays* [New York: Philosophical Library, 1944] 21).
5. Harold Kushner, *When Bad Things Happen to Good People* (New York: Schocken Books, 1981).
6. Address at the Ben-Gurion Memorial Ceremony, Sde Boker, Israel, 13 November 1983.
7. David Denby, "Movies: Guy and Doll," *New York Magazine* 17:6 (6 February 1984) 66.
8. Ibid., p. 64.
9. Elie Wiesel, "Holy Place," from *Hadassah* magazine, reprinted as part of *Israel*, a special advertising supplement in the *New York Times Magazine*, 11 September 1983, p. 15) sponsored by the Israel-American Friendship Committee, in association with Zaham Publications, Ltd.
10. John Leonard, advertisement for Summit Books, distributed by Simon & Schuster, *New York Times*, 29 April 1981, p. C28.
11. Princeton: Princeton University Press, 1949 (2d ed. published by the University of Chicago Press in 1969).
12. Karl Polanyi, "The Brother and the Other," *Commentary* 10:2 (August 1950) 193 and 194.
13. *Jewish Week*, 6 August 1982, p. 6 (my italics).
14. *A Jew Today* (New York: Random House, 1978) 180.
15. "The Command of Bethlehem," *New York Times*, 25 December 1977, p. 10E.
16. Jacob Neusner, "Judaism and the Zionist Problem," *Judaism* 10:3 (Summer 1970) 32.

17. Hugh Nissenson, reviewing *The Seventh Day: Soldiers' Talk about the Six-Day War*, ed. Avraham Shapira (New York: Charles Scribner's Sons, 1971), in *New York Times Book Review*, 2 May 1971, p. 41.

18. "On Being a Jew," *Commentary* 53:3 (March 1972) 63.

19. Ruth R. Wisse, *The Schlemiel As Modern Jewish Hero* (Chicago: University of Chicago Press, 1971) 23.

20. *New York Times*, 5 August 1982, p. A2, col. 4.

21. *Washington Post*, 5 August 1982, p. A1 (my italics).

22. Roger Morris, "Beirut—and the Press—Under Siege," *Columbia Journalism Review* 21:4 (November/December 1982) 24.

23. Ibid., p. 30 (my italics).

24. Erik H. Erikson, *Gandhi's Truth: On the Origins of Militant Nonviolence* (New York: W. W. Norton, 1969) 376.

25. Clifford Geertz, "Gandhi: Non-Violence as Therapy," *New York Review of Books* 13:9 (20 November 1969) 4.

26. Herman Wouk, "Must Wars Occur?" *Parade* (supplement in the *Washington Post*, 6 February 1983) p. 7.

27. Despite Israeli Foreign Ministry denials, David K. Shipler's dispatch to the *New York Times*, 19 September 1982, pp. 1 and 14, reads: "Nevertheless, as early as the second week of the war last June, Israeli officials were speaking privately of a plan, being considered by Defense Minister Ariel Sharon, to allow the Phalangists to go into West Beirut and the camps against the Palestinian Liberation Organization. The calculation was that the Phalangists, with old scores to settle and detailed information on the Palestinian fighters, would be more ruthless than the Israelis and probably more effective."

28. David K. Shipler, "In Israel, Anguish over Moral Questions on Beirut," *New York Times*, 24 September 1982, p. A10. The massacre was September 17–19.

29. Susan Sontag, "Notes on 'Camp,'" in *Against Interpretation and Other Essays* (New York: Farrar, Straus & Giroux, 1966) 290.

30. Cf. Jacobo Timerman, *The Longest War: Israel in Lebanon* (New York: Alfred A. Knopf, 1982).

31. Cf. John M. Cuddihy, *The Ordeal of Civility: Freud, Marx, Lévi-Strauss, and the Jewish Struggle with Modernity* (New York: Basic Books, 1974) 183–84.

32. Harold Nicolson, *Good Behaviour: Being a Study of Certain Types of Civility* (London: Constable, 1955) 89.

33. Marshal Sklare, *Conservative Judaism: An American Religious Movement* (Glencoe, IL: Free Press, 1955) 34.

34. Philip Roth, "Second Dialogue in Israel," panel on The Jewish Intellectual and Jewish Identity, *Congress Bi-Weekly* 30:12 (16 September 1963) 21.

35. *Why the Jews? The Reason for Anti-Semitism* (New York: Simon and Schuster, 1983) 34.

36. Joseph Sobran, "Anti-Semites All," *National Review* 35:15 (5 August 1983) 948.

37. "Prime Minister of Israel Menachem Begin Speaks," *Jewish Press*, 24 March 1978, p. 3 (italics mine).

38. Robert A. Segal, "The Historical Inexplicability of Anti-Semitism," *Contemporary Jewry* 5:2 (Fall/Winter 1980) 66.

39. Ibid., p. 67.

40. Ibid., p. 68.

41. *The Jew as Pariah* (New York: Grove Press, 1978) 141. Elsewhere she writes of Diaspora Jews' conviction "that the eternal and ubiquitous nature of anti-Semitism [has] been the most potent *ideological* factor in the Zionist movement since the Dreyfus Affair" (*Eichmann in Jerusalem: A Report on the Banality of Evil* [New York: Viking Press, 1965] 10 [italics added]).

II

PROTESTANT-CATHOLIC TENSIONS

The inevitability of conflict is inherent in the very names of American Christianity's two major branches: The Roman Church's designation as Catholic, with its meaning "universal," is an assertion against which the very existence of Protestantism protests.

This centuries-old theological rivalry was brought to America by the earliest settlers, providing the language with which the existing population could express its fear of social dislocation. As increasing numbers of Catholic immigrants arrived, nativism and nationalism took on a distinct anti-Catholic guise. The papacy's role, embodied in the First Vatican Council's decree of infallibility, was used to cast doubt on Catholic loyalty; indeed, the legitimacy of the Roman church was itself challenged because of both its anti-democratic structure and suspicions about its sometimes private practices.

The long history of resentment and the variety of problems that American anti-Catholicism has masked make this tension's recent dissipation especially striking, occasional resurgences notwithstanding. Should we find this reassuring, demonstrating how much can change in a very short period of time? Or should it evoke a nervous skepticism, making us suspicious that present tolerance owes less to a truly ecumenical spirit than to the current mood of religious indifference? It is perhaps telling that as Roman Catholicism has become acceptable, many of the charges once directed against it are now levelled at various "cults." The fears that make such accusations credible seem to outlast the vulnerability of their target.

3

From Maria Monk to Paul Blanshard: A Century of Protestant Anti-Catholicism

BARBARA WELTER

Americans historians are willing to spare few of our cherished illusions. George Washington's cherry tree and Thomas Jefferson's family life have vanished with our lost passenger pigeons. It is, therefore, not surprising that our boast to be a nation dedicated to religious freedom has also been refuted.

When the Statue of Liberty, symbol of a safe harbor for tempest-tossed souls, was completed in 1886, its symbolic lamp was dimmed by the prior publication of Josiah Strong's *Our Country*, a best seller extolling undiluted Anglo-Saxon racial and religious purity.[1] The Haymarket Riot, which John Higham termed "the most important single incident in late nineteenth-century nativism,"[2] occurred in the same year. It was, however, only one incident in a very long line of nativist hostilities, of which those involving Roman Catholics and Protestants were perhaps closest to the original concept of what well-ordered religious hostility should be about in this new Jerusalem.

The origins of this conflict and its linear growth on this continent have been well traced in several monographs, and I do not intend to repeat the chronology of these tensions from colonial times to the present.[3] I should like only to recapitulate some of the enduring themes in this most Christian crusade, especially those most appropriate to the New World, and then focus on two texts written more than a century apart in order to illustrate some of the peculiarly institutional arguments.

Maria Monk's *Awful Disclosures of the Hotel Dieu Nunnery of Mon-

treal was a best seller in 1836, and Paul Blanshard's *American Freedom and Catholic Power* achieved the same status in 1949. I suggest that the themes and even the language—metaphor, invective, connotative adjectives—are remarkably similar. Best sellers rarely demonstrate great literary imagination or intellectual rigor, but they do show what a large segment of the Republic wants to be told at a given time. When books are reprinted over and over, as has been the case with Monk's work, they reveal at the very least attitudes and ideas that appeal to many generations.

Historians of nativism—Ray Allen Billington, John Kane, John Higham, David Brion Davis, Richard Hofstadter, and Sydney Ahlstrom among them—uniformly denounce and categorically deny the objective reality of this anti-Catholic prose. The writers of these inflammatory tracts are dismissed as "hatemongers," "fanatics," and, most damning of all to the healthy historical mind, "paranoids."[4] I should like to suggest, if only as a kind of devil's advocate for popular culture, that these popular writings be reexamined, not as embarrassing blots on the national copybook of rights or as the ravings of a lunatic fringe of un-American Americans. I suggest that these two documents (and others in the same vein) be taken seriously as the expression of serious concern on the part of perfectly rational Americans.

Consensus is a way of dealing with controversies, not of denying them. The inflamed rhetoric of the anti-Catholic tracts, like the actual conflagration of anti-Catholic mobs, sprang from deep concern for values and for a way of life based on that most fragile value of all, personal liberty. Paranoids may be persecuted or, more often, may remember a time when they were persecuted. When anguish translates into hate literature and mob violence, it may reflect a passionate although inarticulate commitment to a genuinely endangered specific. Popular delusions and the madness of crowds are not hallucinatory in origin, however illusory in accomplishment. When there is widespread fear, as Mrs. Willy Loman might have defended her class, "Attention must be paid."

The litany of Protestant grievances against Catholics is a long and bitter one, as long and bitter as its reverse would be. Any list of grievances in any national catalogue of collected injustices tends to run to many pages, incorporating many varieties of experience, religious and political. To recite them, or even to list them all, sounds perilously like "How do I not love you? . . . Let me count the ways." In this particular litany it might include: "We dislike your men (priests), your women (nuns) and your children (Boy Scouts), and a few institutions; we dislike the arrogance and elitism of claiming to be the 'one, holy, catholic and apostolic church'; we dislike the reliance on authority, rather than on individual judgment;

we dislike the substitution of a parochial for a public school system; we find celibacy unwholesome and perverse for the clergy (indeed, for practically anyone); we oppose inflexible social rules masquerading as immutable natural laws; we oppose censorship in books; we prefer to read the Bible for ourselves and scorn official interpretation; we deplore the level of taste in architecture, statuary, and hymns; we shudder at the superstition surrounding the Virgin and the saints; and we deplore intransigence in the face of progressive reform, especially in temperance and women's rights." Now, although the most casual perusal of Puritan doctrine and law would find equal or greater violations of all the above without leaving the boundaries of Massachusetts, that does not deny the fact that Protestants believed themselves to be the upholders of these yeoman, self-evident truths, which they believed Catholics opposed.

Catholics have historically responded to these accusations with such helpful arguments as: "You do not understand, and because you are not a member of the One True Church there is not a prayer that you ever could understand," or, "Only certain benighted ethnic or social groups believe that," or, "Have you stopped burning your witches lately?" Historians and liberal Protestants have been equally quick to deny any lingering validity on their side of the controversy. They metaphorically stuff Maria Monk and Paul Blanshard into the closet, saying soothingly to liberal Catholics, "We know that you, like us, have nothing to do with the clods who read bad books and burn convents. That's un-American and frightfully low, but neither side can be responsible for its 'crazies.'" This argument is both anti-historical and evasive.

When historians actually address themselves to the question of why the unenlightened Protestant has gotten these ideas so firmly fixed, they respond with a litany of their own:

> the English anti-Catholic tradition dates back at least to the Armada;

> it was intensified by an anti-Irish bias dating at least to Cromwell and extending, with all its ugly stereotypical ramifications, across the ocean;

> American Protestantism has been quick to refer to its honorable scars from Reformation Wars, even though the Reformation predated the founding of this country;

> the anti-Catholic rhetoric of the Puritans was intensified by popular books and sermons (John Foxe's *Book of Martyrs* was, after all, one of the few books a Protestant child could read on Sunday);

the Quebec Act of 1774 had galvanized Americans into revolutionary action as they saw the spread of American Protestantism
checked;

France and Spain, which represented continual threats to American
independence, were identified with moral decadence and woeful dis-
regard of the work ethic;

the large influx of Catholics to American cities represented what one
historian refers to as a "disruption of America's agrarian dream,"[5]
and those same immigrants posed an economic threat to American
labor and an overburdening of very modest social-welfare agencies;

a "Protestant frontier thesis" saw winning the West as a religious
rather than a territorial race, with "Presbyterians and Jesuits" as a
more sober version of "Cowboys and Indians";

the gradual loss of status and prestige by American Protestants
called forth a "backlash" which was expressed in the historical
terms most familiar to the threatened group, namely, Reformation
rhetoric.[6]

Seeking to explain the persistence of the anti-Catholic bias, David
Brion Davis sees the nineteenth-century stereotyped Catholic as the "pre-
cise antitheses of American ideals, an inverted image of Jacksonian democracy."[7] Since the Jacksonian "ideals" were, in fact, largely composed
of mythful thinking, constantly challenged by internal and external
events, they were all the more in need of a countervailing demonic force.
John William Ward argues that the need for a hero was so strong that if
the age had not in fact produced Andrew Jackson, it would have invented
him.[8] A similar need for an anti-hero produces the inverse of that thesis:
If the age had not produced Catholics, it would have invented them as the
necessary negative image of the proposed national virtue. This early Republic nationalism culminated in the most widely publicized burst of
anti-Catholic violence, the burning of the Ursuline convent in Charlestown, Massachusetts, and the publication of that remarkable nativist
tract, *The Awful Disclosures* of Maria Monk.[9]

The period before the American Civil War saw the "Beast of Rome"
invading even this new Eden, as a series of highly visible conversions
brought Americans from well-known American families (Sophia Dana
Ripley, for example) and the "Seeker for Truth," Orestes Brownson, into
the Catholic church. The Paulist Fathers were founded by another such
convert, Isaac Hecker, for the avowed purpose of bringing the United
States into the "True Church."[10] Hecker's visionary prose added to the

bombastic transcendentalism of Brownson suggested to many Americans that Protestantism was being attacked for being too permissive, too secular, and too democratic. Since Protestants themselves were split over recent liberal changes in theology and society, this was a very palpable hit. Lyman Beecher went full tilt against the pernicious influence of convents in general and the Ursuline convent in particular, starting in 1830 when the convent had already been successfully educating young women for a dozen years.[11]

Besides the traditional Protestantism at war with the more relaxed tenets of Unitarians, the "New Light" versus the "Old Light," and other quasi-theological controversies, there was the persistent class structure, denied by both church and state and equally pervasive in both institutions. To the lower-class bricklayers in Charlestown, the Ursuline convent represented luxury and mystery. The vagaries of heterodox and orthodox were mere puffs of smoke compared to the concrete fury generated by the flight of a young woman, Elizabeth Harrison, from the convent in 1834. Here was something a man could protest with all his strength and be proud in the blow he was striking for free American womanhood. The young Ursuline nun subsequently repented of her decision and asked Bishop Fenwick to allow her to return to her convent, but by this time all of Boston was involved. The selectmen were invited to tour the convent in order to put the more lascivious rumors to rest, but they were embroiled in a separate controversy with the bishop over a Catholic cemetery and dragged their feet. By the time they had their tour and published their report guaranteeing Miss Harrison's freedom and safety, a mob had burned the building, to the cheers of a large crowd.[12]

The persistent focus on convents as the most feared element in Catholic life involved more than just maintaining the female as scapegoat or even than substituting sexual for political issues in order to make the latter seem more threatening. This was a period in which American women, consistently described by themselves and foreign observers as the "free female in a free country" and "uniquely blessed among women in Christian lands," were beginning to exert themselves. Most Americans hoped to combine the traditional roles for women with a belief that these roles were carried out in the New World in such a way as to make them part of democratic life, liberty, and happiness. The existence of groups of women in convents was both a persistent threat and a frightening alternative to the cult of domesticity.

The prospectus of the school run by the Ursulines differed almost not at all from those of similar "female seminaries" of the period, and there is no evidence of overt religious proselytizing. In fact, it would appear that at this school, as well as in similar schools staffed by Roman Catholic

Sisters, the curriculum was highly traditional and ornamental. In many parts of the country these convent schools were eagerly prized because they taught the rather raw young women at least some of the graces associated with civility, gentility, and the dubious values of young ladyism. Since it was widely believed that it took three generations to turn a young man into a gentleman but only one to make the woman into a lady, this crash course in social mobility was all the more prized.[13]

Americans' fascination for convents—illustrated in the twentieth century by the popularity of *The Nun's Story*[14]—was explained by one nineteenth-century British visitor, Frederick Marryat, as a national feeling that nothing must be kept veiled, an inherent commitment to freedom of information and open covenants openly arrived at. "Americans," he wrote in 1839, "cannot bear anything like a secret—that's *unconstitutional*."[15] In the absence of knowledge, they constructed their own fantasies, aided by a small but lurid literature of "ex-priest" and "ex-nun" aubobiographies.[16] What went on after the Portress closed the heavy doors to those mysterious buildings surrounded by high walls? What mysterious sounds, smells, ceremonies took place in an atmosphere that, for many Protestants, literally reeked with incense and with sin? Simplicity in church liturgy and architecture, along with services in the vernacular, were identified with the vigor and strength of the country. Would not these virtues be eroded, smothered in the images, obscured by the Latin, shrouded by the very mysteries and authorities from which Protestants had presumably fled in escaping to America?

The most popular tale of all was that constructed by Maria Monk and presented to the public in 1836. (Monk's work is a sort of revenant of anti-Catholicism, most recently wafted through the country in the wake of John F. Kennedy's presidential campaign.) Although refutations appeared almost immediately, challenging both her authorship and her sanity (in a published interview with her mother it was revealed that a slate pencil had entered Maria's head as a child and she was never the same since), nature in this case proved no match for art.[17] And in this particular art the public most definitely knew what they wanted. Interestingly enough, however, although there certainly was the requisite discussion of hanky-panky in the confessional and elsewhere, the majority of the pages were devoted to a diatribe against Catholics because of their resistance to democracy, rather than their immorality.[18] The focus of attack was the complete authority that the priests had over the nuns and that the Mother Superior exercised over her charges. No matter how repugnant the act required might be, blind obedience replaced reason or independent judgment. Unspeakable humiliation was sanctioned in the name of obedience to authority. It is of interest that "breaking the will," a staple mandate in child-rearing manuals, was under attack in this period, and the parental authority formerly invested in the rod was being replaced by a "dominion of love and reason."[19]

The traditional mainspring of Protestant conviction, the independent reading of the Bible, was a long-standing matter of controversy between the two religions. Monk solemnly averred that she was not allowed to read the Bible and indeed never had, although a few chapters of scripture had been read aloud in her presence. When she asked her superiors why Catholics did not read the New Testament, she was told, "Because the mind of man is too limited and weak to understand what God has written."[20] The young women systematically became automatons, until they could say to their priests (not their God), "Not my will, but thine be done." Instead of encouraging a nation of sturdy yeoman, pulling their forelocks to no man, the network of Catholic clergy demanded a subservience based not on Jefferson's "elite of virtue and intellect," but on the hierarchy of religion. Superstition was rampant, and the Blessed Virgin was a terrible role model for the American girl. At a time when what William James dubbed "the religion of positive thinking" was replacing the negativism of earlier years, such acts of penance as putting a pin through one's cheek or disciplining the flesh with a whip brought new revulsion.[21] The grim enthusiasms of Cotton Mather and Jonathan Edwards might have produced equal consternation if offered to this new generation, but the "mortification of the flesh" once so much a part of Puritan life was identified with the negative aspects of Catholicism.

One of the things most noticeable about Monk's book is the specificity of her charges. The reader is given detailed descriptions of the layout of the convent, the room for *accouchement* so conveniently placed next to the room where the priests strangled the babies after first baptizing them to secure "their everlasting happiness."[22] If these details were so accurately drawn, the overall theme of obedience and authoritarianism replacing independent thought and democratic process seemed equally true. These were the same Americans who, according to amazed travelers' accounts, let their hired girls sit at the dinner table and declined to respect titles or degrees. Samuel F. B. Morse, painter and inventor, allegedly became an ardent anti-Catholic when a soldier in Rome knocked off his hat as a religious procession was passing.[23]

The fragility of democracy seemed real, and the tightrope between European reaction and European revolution was difficult for Americans to walk during the tumultuous years before the Civil War. The threat from Catholicism was even more serious, since it combined the outer threat of external rule—the pope and his "guards"—with the inner threat of subversion, especially of the minds and wills of young women, future mothers of democratic men. Protestantism consistently defined itself as the liberator of women. This was the primary theme used to recruit women missionaries, urging them to volunteer in order to bring their benighted heathen sisters the blessings American Protestantism had conferred on women.

As the missionary movement increased in energy and numbers during the nineteenth century, it was often defined as a "war" between Catholics and Protestants for the dominion of the earth. One of its early themes was the impending millennium, which could take place only if the world was converted. This was interpreted as meaning not only the required baptism of the "heathen," but also the reconversion of what Protestants termed "nominal Christians" or Roman Catholics. This passion resulted eventually in a plaque that adorns the walls of the Vatican to this day, announcing the coming of the American Baptists in 1870 on their mission of "conversion."

The rivalry on the mission field usually consisted in harmless attempts on the part of the Protestants to harass their boards and their congregations by demanding more money or missionaries. Roman Catholic nuns were allegedly drawing away prospective women converts in China by dint of their beautiful embroidery. A call went out for Protestant girls with similar skills — a call not well heeded, it might be said. The popularity of the Catholic priest Father Damien resulted in the demand for a "Protestant leper," which was partially met through the work of Mary Reed, although stories about her never achieved the virtual cult of Damien. The Catholic Indian saint Catherine Tegawitha was responded to with a call for a Protestant Indian saint. Duly converted and duly dead, Henrietta Brown, young and pious though she was, somehow never captured the public imagination as did the "Lily of the Mohawks." At a more virulent level, however, Protestants charged that the Whitman Massacre, which occurred in Oregon in 1847, was the result of the Jesuits inciting "their" Indians to remove the threat of a Protestant Northwest.[24]

Violence was the exception, not the rule, even during the demonstrations and confrontations of the school Bible controversy and other rock-throwing, name-calling incidents. Rather than consider these well-documented incidents, let me instead point to the permeation of cultural anti-Catholicism in virtually every area of American popular culture.

What my colleague John Cuddihy has called "Protestant taste" became the measure of American taste — other religions were, by definition, lower on the aesthetic ranking and fell short of approved literary and artistic standards.[25] A brief examination of the children's literature popular from the mid-nineteenth to the mid-twentieth century is replete with examples of almost offhand anti-Catholicism, often associated with convents. Although there is nothing as avowedly polemical as the work of the English writer "Charlotte Elizabeth," the Elsie Dinsmore series by Martha Finley and the numerous works of "Pansy" are imbued with the principles of Protestantism and of Chautauqua.[26] A "convent" is the threat with which a wicked adult attempts to control an innocent child.

There are no comparably popular books of Catholic literature preaching against Protestants, at least not until the twentieth century, but one vivid example of Catholic retaliation, even if it never reached the bestseller list, is the 1874 work purporting to be the autobiography of Lizzie St. John Eckel.[27] This earnest work was entitled *Maria Monk's Daughter* and told of the career of the former nun's illegitimate child. (There is a parallel here, perhaps a case of nature imitating art again, in which the sequel to the best seller *Charlotte Temple* is the story of her illegitimate daughter, who lives a life of Christian piety and self-denial as redemption for her mother's sin.) Maria Monk's daughter had nothing good to say for her parent, who left her to fend for herself after her birth in 1837. A passion for self-improvement ("I had always been fond of studying encyclopedias"[28]) kept her mind alive through the drudgery of menial employment. When at the age of thirty she visited a convent for the first time, she shrieked aloud a prayer for enlightenment. As she listened in wonder to the happy laughter of the nuns, "a moral light" illumined her soul and she quickly joined the Roman Catholic Church.[29] The church became her real mother, "for it was she who took me by the hand and raised me out of the abyss of spiritual misery, into which the faults of my parents had helped to plunge me."[30] Her mother's book is specifically repudiated: "In my heart of hearts I *am sure* that my mother's book is a lie."[31] But this is only the penultimate conclusion. The real meaning of her work she saves for the final page, where she addresses her book "to the hearts of those women who consider themselves strong-minded. . . . Could they only see themselves as they are in the sight of God, they would find themselves to be the weakest of their weak sex. For the truly strong-minded woman is she who strives to conquer herself, and by charity and humility to assist Christ in establishing His kingdom on earth . . . not she who seeks to take the position which God had assigned on this earth to men"; the most important truth for woman is to realize that she cannot escape "the law of suffering."[32]

In a similar vein, Orestes Brownson used the presumed model of the Blessed Virgin to speak against the woman's movement. Catholic females, "trained up in the love and imitation of her virtues . . . are trained to be wives and mothers, or holy virgins, spouses of Jesus Christ."[33] He identified the demand for the vote with "hostility to the marriage law, and the cares and drudgery of maternity and human life."[34] It is not surprising that with friends like these the Catholic Church had its enemies among the ranks of the women's movement, although even Elizabeth Cady Stanton (who claimed to dislike Catholics, Protestants, and Jews as equally inimical to woman's progress) had a grudging admiration for the communal kitchens of convent life.[35] In its feminist category, the *Dictionary of Notable American Women* (whose deaths occurred before 1950) lists only three born Catholics, two of whom lost their faith, and one Catholic convert.[36]

The anti-Catholicism of popular literature was also present in the etiquette manuals where "Bridget" was assumed to be a slothful, drunken, and immoral person, the heritage of her Irish nationality and Catholic religion. The Protestant housewife, although she was told to let her servants attend their own church, was also told to force them to attend family prayers, to give them copies of the Bible ("which they have never been allowed to read") and to equate civil order with Protestantism, in the home and on the streets.[37] Similarly, in the literature of the philanthropic organizations of the nineteenth century, the "fallen" woman was to be rehabilitated through conversion to Protestantism. The "lady visitors" of such organizations as the Magdalen Society reserved their highest praise for the reclamation of the "lamb that had strayed," in which renouncing her former religion was synonymous with renouncing her former way of life.[38] Even when such factors as class, ethnicity, and gender were specified, religion had a kind of moral override as the significant differentiating factor between virtue and vice.

In the years between Maria Monk's outcry and the publication of Paul Blanshard's more sophisticated attack there were relatively few overt hostilities. The role of women continued to change, and Catholicism continued to be identified with a more patriarchal, authoritarian structure, whether in terms of gender or politics. In 1949, while Catholics responded to the charges in *American Freedom and Catholic Power* with shock and horror, it became clear that the cultural anti-Catholicism embodied in the area of taste, popular literature, and reform had kept alive many of the same issues attacked with crude but effective force by Maria Monk. The "Awful Disclosures" of Paul Blanshard covered much of the same territory.

Catholic surprise was a measure of their own sense of acceptance.[39] There were Catholic members of Congress, even a Catholic Supreme Court Justice. There were Bing Crosby and Loretta Young. Such separatism as did exist was in itself upper-directed and relatively affluent: the Catholic universities, the separate coming-out parties for Catholic girls at the Cardinal's Ball, Catholic country clubs. The American Catholic felt that his dues were paid and that he did not any longer consider himself, if he ever had, to be in alien territory, a stranger in a strange land. Blanshard spoke to this lack of comprehension on the part of both Catholics and Protestants. With the zeal of the reformer, he wanted attention to be paid to the difference between American values and Catholic values, a difference which threatened the very existence of the American values.[40]

Blanshard's first and most often repeated charge was the same as that used a century before by Maria Monk, the overwhelming "absolute rule of the clergy." Constantly he asked rhetorically, is this what free-born Americans should do? How can any American voluntarily relinquish his (or her, because women were specifically called upon to protest) autonomy? " 'Is not such servility utterly contrary to American tradition?' 'What good American kneels to any man?' "[41] Through his denunciations passed whole generations of Americans who refused to perform the kowtow in Imperial China or to wear knee breeches at the Court of St. James. The rhetoric was the same as that used in a Know-Nothing tract of 1855 in which Senator Brooks attacked Archbishop Hughes, recently returned from the Vatican: "Fresh from the court of Rome . . . the Bishop could not all at once realize that Senator Brooks, in his plain American dress, was just as good a man as the Archbishop Hughes in all his scarlet robes and golden trappings."[42] According to Blanshard, "The central structure of the Church is completely authoritarian, and the role of laymen is completely passive."[43] Blanshard's categorical denial of the role of the laity was directly opposed to the fears expressed by Leo XIII in his 1895 encyclical *Longinque Oceani*, in which he condemned "Americanism" precisely because there was too little authority invested in the clergy and too much in the laity.[44]

Blanshard's second major argument against the Catholics was based on the system of parochial schools. Here he had two separate arguments, although he chose to treat them as one: the appropriateness of such schools at all, and their quality. Again, as in the case of the apparent contradiction in Leo XIII's encyclical, Blanshard may have pointed out the lessons ·Catholics had learned from former brushes with authority, especially in the burning of the Ursuline convent. Blanshard wanted to know, "Are the Catholic schools worthy of national support? Are they democratic? . . . Do they teach tolerance and national solidarity?"[45]

The value Americans attached to the public-school system and its relationship to the controversy with Catholics had been expressed long before Blanshard got into print. In 1890 Cardinal Gibbons wrote to Leo XIII that divisions between Roman Catholics and Protestants in the United States "are caused above all by the opposition against the system of national education which is attributed to us, and which, more than any other thing, creates and maintains in the minds of the American people the conviction that the Catholic Church is opposed by principle to the institutions of the country and that a sincere Catholic cannot be a loyal citizen of the United States."[46] Similar questions might have been raised about the private-school system in which religion played a minimal or nonexistent role, but they would not have fit in with the thrust of Blanshard's arguments. He wanted to alert the American people to the use of schools as propaganda tools and as vehicles for authoritarian decision-making. With horror he quoted from the 1929 encyclical of Pius XI, "Christian Education of Youth," which reserved the function of education primarily to the church, not to the parent or state.[47] With equal loathing he cited Bishop McIntyre, who opposed a New York bill prohibiting racial and religious discrimination in the schools. The bishop defined the bill as "what we mean by the infiltration of Communist ideas" because it gave to the states decision-making rights in education.[48] As a civil libertarian, Blanshard was opposed to any form of social coercion, even if the individuals involved voluntarily accepted their chains. In fact, nothing annoyed him more than supposedly rational Americans denying the validity of his arguments with an "it can't happen here" insouciance. To him, the pope as "a Foreign Potentate" was just as real a threat as any other dictator who claimed special privilege from his office.

Again, the rhetoric had been heard in America before. During the days of Know-Nothingism, the nominal complaint was about the use of the Protestant Bible in the school. Catholics claimed that they did indeed read the Bible; they even received "indulgences" for reading it fifteen minutes a day (an argument not calculated to placate their fiercer critics). Protestants continued to maintain that Catholics didn't read the Bible at all, because they didn't read the "authorized" or King James Version. The controversy escalated into an attack on the presumed wealth and tax exemption of the Catholic Church, also one of the weapons in Blanshard's arsenal. In the midst of the fray a New York paper came up with an "authentic" oath, taken by every Jesuit as a soldier in the pope's army: "I, Son of the Holy Father, promise and swear to sustain the altar and the Papal throne, and to exterminate the heretics, liberals, and enemies of the Church, without pity for the cries of children, or of men and women, so help me God."[49] Although the rhetoric of both the New York paper and Blanshard verges on absurdity, its hyperbole is an exaggerated form of the fear expressed by such serious students of liberty as Thomas Jefferson and Abraham Lincoln about the conflict of interest and allegiance when loyalty to the state is, or is perceived to be, in conflict with other loyalties, either to an individual or an institution.

Critics of Blanshard's extreme position denied the existence of any justifiable reservations.[50] When expressed in more abstract (and less popular) terms, this seemed reasonable and even important to consider. Catholic reviewers and spokespersons denied any possible conflict on their part and pointed to active participation in every war fought by the country. In 1884 Bishop Ireland, speaking to the last Plenary Council, promised, "There is no conflict between the Catholic Church and America . . . and when I assert, as I now solemnly do, that the principles of the Church are in thorough harmony with the interest of the Republic, I know in the depths of my soul that I speak the truth . . ."[51] But such protests fell on deaf ears. In vain did Catholics point out not only the heroism of American Catholic men, but also the splendid role played by the nursing Sisters during the Civil War. Such citations only brought forth more of Blanshard's attacks, like those of Monk most agitated when discussing the position of women within the Catholic Church. Blanshard flatly considered nuns "completely subordinate to the men . . . Catholic nuns may vote in American political elections but not in their own church."[52] The convent itself was a sinister "sorority," in which the superiors "attempt to cleanse the mind of each postulant of the desire for romantic relations and motherhood, and to sublimate the libido in passionate religious devotion."[53] The "unhygienic costumes and their medieval rules of conduct" not only "establish a barrier between themselves and the outside world" . . . but "reflect a medieval attitude of piety and feminine subordination that seems utterly alien to the typically robust and independent spirit of American womanhood."[54] Clearly Blanshard's knowledge of the convent had not included reminiscences of the "Sister Mary Ignatius" variety or even rueful memories of gentle Sister Mary Grace slamming her little parochial student into the blackboard.

Monk had combined concern for undemocratic practices with a discussion of the immorality and lewd activities practiced in the convents. Blanshard had a different set of atrocity stories; and before detailing them, he goes Ms. Monk one better in warning the gentle reader that his argument may "include some items that are physically revolting and some readers may prefer to skip this section."[55] He assures the strong-minded (and stomached) reader that his reason for quoting the "gruesome particulars" is no vulgar desire to shock, but rather to show "how the Catholic hierarchy attempts to make Catholic nurses into diligent priestesses of the faith."[56] What follows is a description of botched abortions and monster births that make the "strangled babies" of the Hotel Dieu seem lucky in comparison. In his anxiety to present Planned Parenthood as the rational alternative to such horrors, Blanshard virtually elevates Margaret Sanger to sainthood, which would have been quite a shock even to her supporters and quite possibly to the lady herself. In fact, far from being the calm, serene rationalist of Blanshard's praise, much of Sanger's effectiveness, as well as the controversy surrounding her, came because she actively sought confrontation. It was not really necessary to choose lecture halls in close proximity to Catholic churches, but Sanger enjoyed the challenge and identified the Catholic Church with her father as the exploiter and betrayer of women.[57]

The century of anti-Catholic attitudes exemplified in the Monk and Blanshard works saw major changes in the ethnic and religious population of the United States. It was not, however, necessary to be Protestant in order to be anti-Catholic. The enduring themes exemplified in these two best sellers and fortified by popular culture during the intervening years were genuine fears of a population unsure about the parameters of individual liberty in the face of necessary authority and about the role of women and the family amidst rapid social change. In both cases Catholicism was seen as opposing individual initiative and constructive autonomy, of being something other than not necessarily what Protestants had actually achieved, for then the need for an enemy would not have been so strong, but what they had hoped to achieve and had fallen short of. The controversy over the pope's domination should be seen in the midst of considerable difference of opinion over the prerogatives of the president; the charges against the lack of liberty for women against a background that promised more than it achieved; the supposed failures of the parochial-school system were at least partially an attempt to ignore the real failures of the public schools.

Vatican II brought about many of the changes inherent in Protestant criticism and in the criticism of Catholics themselves.[58] Some differences between the two groups, however, have not been blurred with indifference or surgically removed by reform. In the literature of anti-Catholicism an anecdote persistently recurs: A four-year-old Protestant girl decides to go swimming with a four-year-old Catholic boy, although they have forgotten their bathing suits. The little girl looks at her companion and remarks, "Oh, my, Catholics really *are* different from Protestants!" The changes of the past decade suggest that while that may still be true, in the case of both Protestants and Catholics—and boys and girls —the more hopeful response is, "Yes, but not as different as they used to be."

Notes

1. Josiah Strong, *Our Country: Its Possible Future and Its Present Crisis* (rev. ed., New York: American Home Missionary Society, 1891). The publisher

claimed that by the time of this edition more than 140,000 volumes had been printed. The fifth chapter (pp. 46–52) deals with the "Conflict of Romanism with the Fundamental Principle of our Government."

2. John Higham, *Strangers in the Land: Patterns of American Nativism 1860–1925* (original edition 1963; reprinted Westport, CT: Greenwood Press, 1980) p. 54.

3. John Higham identifies four major periods of "virulent" nativism: the late 1790's, the 1850's, 1886 through 1896, and the years following World War I. Basic histories of religion in the United States, especially Sydney E. Ahlstrom's *A Religious History of the American People* (New Haven: Yale University Press, 1972); Winthrop S. Hudson's *Religion in America* (2d ed., New York: Charles Scribner's, 1973); and William Warren Sweet's *The Story of Religion in America* (2nd ed., New York: Harper & Row, 1950), also discuss manifestations of anti-Catholicism as do the histories of the Roman Catholic Church in America. See, for example, Thomas T. McAvoy, C.S.C., *A History of the Catholic Church in the United States* (Notre Dame, IN: Notre Dame University Press, 1969); John Tracy Ellis, *American Catholicism* (Chicago: University of Chicago Press, 1956); Andrew M. Greeley, *The Catholic Experience* (New York: Doubleday & Co., 1967); and the treatise that was itself virtually a primary source for these tensions, John D. Gilmary Shea, *History of the Catholic Church in the United States 1843–1866* (New York: J. G. Shea, 1892), and its companion volume *Our Faith and Its Defenders* (2 vols., New York: Office of Catholic Publishing, 1894).

Eighteenth century manifestations are described by Thomas More Brown, "The Image of the Beast: Anti-Papal Rhetoric in Colonial America," in *Conspiracy: The Fear of Subversion in American History*, ed. Richard D. Curry and Thomas M. Brown (New York: Holt, Rinehart and Winston, 1972) 1–20. See also J. Higham, *Strangers in the Land*; Carlton Beals, *Brass-Knuckle Crusade: The Great Know-Nothing Conspiracy* (New York: Hastings House, 1960); Reuben Maury, *The Wars of the Godly* (New York: R. M. McBride & Co., 1928); Gustavus Myers, *History of Bigotry in the United States* (New York: Random House, 1945); Seymour Mandelbaum, *The Social Setting of Intolerance* (Chicago: Scott, Forsman, 1964); Harry Carmen, "Some Aspects of the Know-Nothing Movement Reconsidered," *South Atlantic Quarterly* 39 (1940) 213–34; Donald L. Kinzer, *An Episode in Anti-Catholicism: The American Protective Association* (Seattle: University of Washington Press, 1964); and especially Ray Allen Billington, *The Protestant Crusade 1800–1860: A Story of the Origins of American Nativism* (New York: The Macmillan Company, 1938).

Catholic responses include a series of monographs based on dissertations at the Catholic University of America and published by its press, for example, Marie Fell, *The Foundation of Nativism in American Textbooks, 1783–1860* (Washington, DC: Catholic University of America Press, 1941); Agnes McGann, *Nativism in Kentucky to 1860* (Washington, DC: Catholic University of America Press, 1944); Carroll J. Noonan, *Nativism in Connecticut 1829–1860* (Washington, DC: Catholic University of America Press, 1938); and Evangeline Thomas, *Nativism in the Old Northwest 1850–60* (Washington, DC: Catholic University of America Press, 1936). Other Catholic presentations include Dorothy Dohen,

Nativism and American Catholicism (New York: Sheed and Ward, 1967); and Robert Francis Hueston, *The Catholic Press and Nativism 1840–60* (New York: Arno Press, 1976)

4. See S. Ahlstrom, *A Religious History of the American People*; R. A. Billington, *The Protestant Crusade*; and J. Higham, *Strangers in the Land*; as well as David Brion Davis, "Some Themes of Countersubversion: An Analysis of Anti-Masonic, Anti-Catholic and Anti-Mormon Literature," *Mississippi Valley Historical Review* 47 (1960) 205–24, and his introduction and notes to *Fear of Conspiracy* (Ithaca, NY: Cornell University Press, 1971); Richard Hofstadter, *The Paranoid Style in American Politics* (New York: Knopf, 1965); and John J. Kane, *Catholic-Protestant Conflicts in America* (Chicago: Regnery, 1955). In a rare display of unanimity, these sources all treat nativism as an aberration. They disagree only as to whether its source is primarily religious or ethnic; most of the Protestant historians accept the latter interpretation, and the Catholic historians the former. In a paper delivered at the April 1978 meeting of the Organization of American Historians, Stanley Coben offered a bio-historical theory, equating "nativism" with the behavior of lizards with brain lesions.

5. S. Ahlstrom, *A Religious History of the American People*, p. 556.

6. See the Catholic historians cited in note 3 and J. Kane in *Catholic-Protestant Conflicts*, especially pp. 1–14 ("A Hundred Years of Anti-Catholicism"). Also Theodore Roemer, *The Catholic Church in the United States* (St. Louis: B. Herder, 1957), especially pp. 50–75; Anson Phelps Stokes and Leo Pfeffer, *Church and State in the United States* (rev. ed., New York: Harper & Row, 1964); Jerome G. Kerwin, *The Catholic Viewpoint on Church and State* (Garden City, NY: Hanover House, 1959); and Richard J. Regan, S.J., *American Pluralism and the Catholic Conscience* (New York: Macmillan, 1963); as well as the documents in Thomas McAvoy, *Roman Catholicism and the American Way of Life* (Notre Dame: Notre Dame University Press, 1960).

7. D. B. Davis, "Some Themes of Countersubversion," p. 208.

8. John William Ward, *Andrew Jackson: Symbol for an Age* (New York: Oxford University Press, 1955).

9. *Awful Disclosures of the Hotel Dieu Nunnery of Montreal* (New York: Howe & Bates, 1836). In his introduction to the facsimile edition published by Archon Books (Hamden, CT: 1962), Ray Allen Billington claims that "in all the long, sad saga of man's mistreatment of man, few books have played such a malicious role" (p. 1).

10. Elwyn A. Smith, *Religious Liberty in the United States* (Philadelphia: Fortress Press, 1972) 85–209. For a nineteenth-century tract on conversion, see Charles Constantine Pise, *Letters to Ada* (New York: Harper, 1834). For the conversion experience, see Peter Hardeman Burnett, *The Path Which Led a Protestant Lawyer to the Catholic Church* (New York: D. Appleton and Co., 1860); Levi Silliman Ives, *The Trials of a Mind in Its Progress to Catholicism: A Letter to Old Friends* (Boston: Patrick Donahoe, 1854). The best source for Orestes Brownson is "The Seeker" himself, in the twenty volumes of his works. The works which most reflect Isaac Thomas Hecker's spirit are *Aspirations of Nature* (New York: J. P. Kirker, 1857), *The Catholic Church in the United States: Its*

Rise, Relations with the Republic, Growth, and Future Prospects (New York: Catholic Publication Society, 1879), and *The Church and the Age* (New York: Catholic Book Exchange, 1896). In his 1879 volume, Hecker asserted, "There is scarcely an American family, distinguished either by its ancestry, or its social position, which today has not one or more representatives among the converts to the Catholic Church" (p. 7). Archbishop John Ireland said that Hecker "assumed that the American people are naturally Catholic" (Introduction to Walter Elliott's *Life of Father Hecker* [2nd ed., New York: Columbus Press, 1894] p. xi). The French translation of Elliott's biography was one cause of the "Americanism" controversy of the 1880s and 90s. Good biographies of Hecker are Vincent Holden, *The Yankee Paul: Isaac Thomas Hecker* (Milwaukee, WI: Bruce Publishing Co., 1958); and Joseph McSorley, *Father Hecker and His Friends* (St. Louis, MO: B. Herder, 1952). See also John Arina, *An American Experience of God: The Spirituality of Isaac Hecker* (New York/Ramsay, NJ: Paulist Press, 1981) and *Hecker Studies: Essays on the Thought of Isaac Hecker* (New York/Ramsay, NJ: Paulist Press, 1983). Edward J. Mannix's attempt to explain the phenomenon of conversion to the Roman Catholic Church (*The American Convert Movement* [New York: Devin-Adair Co., 1923]) lacks historical perspective.

11. Lyman Beecher, *A Plea for the West* (2nd ed., Cincinnati: Truman & Smith, 1835). Beecher believed it plain that "in the province of God" the United States was "destined" to lead the way in the moral and political emancipation of the world" and "equally plain that the religious and political destiny of our nation is to be decided in the West" (p. 11). His idea that the West was to be "won" for Protestantism is responsible for his particular resentment of Catholic educational and missionary enterprises.

12. The social and historical background of the burning of the Ursuline Convent (Mount St. Benedict) at Charlestown is described in S. Ahlstrom, *A Religious History of the American People*, pp. 560–61; and R.A. Billington, *The Protestant Crusade*, pp. 71–75. Contemporary documents include *Papers of the Vigilance Committee*, 15 December 1834–January 1835 (Boston: *Municipal Proceedings*, 1835); James T. Austin, *Argument of James T. Austin, Attorney General, before the Supreme Judicial Court in Middlesex on the Case of John R. Buzzell, charged with being concerned in destroying the Ursuline Convent in Charlestown* (Boston: Ford and Damrell, 1834); and *The Charlestown Convent* . . . (Boston: New England News Co., 1870). Its publication date notwithstanding, this latter, valuable volume is "compiled from authentic sources," as promised. Later historical treatments include Mrs. Louisa (Goddard) Whitney, *The Burning of the Convent . . . As Remembered by One of the Pupils* (Boston: J. B. Osgood, 1877), and Carmine A. Prioli, "The Ursuline Outrage," *American Heritage* 33 (February/March 1982) 101–5.

A very popular American novel based on the Charlestown fire was Justin Jones, *The Nun of St. Ursula or The Burning of the Convent, a Romance of Mt. Benedict*, written under the pseudonym of Harry Hazel (Boston: F. Gleason, 1845). His *The Convent's Doom* and *The Haunted Convent* were published together in a fifth edition in 1854 (Boston: Graves & Weston).

13. Ursuline work in the United States is discussed in P. W. Browne, "The

Oldest Institutions of Learning for Women in North America," *Catholic Education Review* 30 (1932) 87–99; and Ettie Madeline Vogel, "The Ursuline Nuns in America," *American Catholic Historical Society of Philadelphia, Proceedings* 1 (1887) 214–43. There is no single monograph for the larger role of nuns in American society; see, for example, Elizabeth Kolmer, A.S.C., "Catholic Women Religious and Women's History," in *Women in American Religion*, ed. Janet Wilson James (Philadelphia: University of Pennsylvania Press, 1980) 127–40. Mary Ewens covers more limited topics in *The Role of the Nun in Nineteenth-Century America* (New York: Arno Press, 1978), which is largely a study of fictional sources, and "The Leadership of Nuns in Immigrant Catholicism," in *Women and Religion in America*, ed. Rosemary Radford Ruether and Rosemary Skinner Keller (New York: Harper & Row, 1981) vol. I (19th Century) 101–7. See also Ellen Ryan Jolly, *Nuns of the Battlefield* (Providence: Providence Visitors Press, 1927).

For a comparison of the curriculum at the Ursuline Convent (given in the appendix to *The Charlestown Convent* [n. 12 above]) see the catalogues of such contemporary institutions as Boston's Monitorial Female Seminary (1812) and Pittsfield's Young Ladies' Institute (1842). James Frothingham Hunnewell provides a general discussion of the area itself in *A Century of Town Life: A History of Charlestown, Mass. 1775–1887* (Boston: Little, Brown and Co., 1888).

One of the main charges of the anti-convent literature was that even with the best intentions—which the writers were unlikely to concede to them—the nuns could not help but proselytize. See, for example, the very influential work of Timothy Dwight, who insists that "by every artful measure which they can adopt (and they are the most artful of all human beings), by every insinuation, every captivating ceremony which can be presented to the youthful mind and the excited imagination, they steal upon their fancies, and by sly but dangerous artifices gradually attach them to the most destructive system of faith and morals which the history of the Christian world has ever known (*Open Convents* [New York: Van Nostrand and Dwight, 1936] 128–29). Dwight also suggests that the convents were inferior in science, mathematics, and, of course, religious teaching. *The Know-Nothing Almanac* for 1856 also suggests deficiency in subject matter as well as in ideology when it denounces convent education because "even if they teach French, or some other frivolous or secondary branch better than other schools near them, they teach none of the grand and indispensable sciences thoroughly and correctly, if at all" (*The Know-Nothing Almanac or True American's Manual* [New York, 1856]). To these charges, the defenders of the convents responded that since the majority of the young women were Protestants, *a priori* the convent became a "Protestant" convent. See the testimony of Samuel K. Williams, editor of *The Daily Advertiser*, who sent four daughters to the Ursuline Convent, in *The Charlestown Convent*, pp. 90–91.

14. Kathryn Cavarly Hulme, *The Nun's Story* (Boston: Little, Brown, 1956); this best-seller was made into a popular movie starring Audrey Hepburn.

15. Quoted in Dan Herr, *Through Other Eyes* (Westminster, MD: Newman Press, 1965) 44. The travelers that Herr quotes are generally favorable to Ameri-

can Catholicism. Alexis de Tocqueville felt Catholicism had been "erroneously" identified as the enemy of democracy (p. 30). Alexander MacKay believed that both in St. Louis and New Orleans there were excellent seminaries for young ladies and "not a few of those who attend them become converts to the church" (p. 55). Harriet Martineau's 1837 statement that "The Catholic religion is modified by the spirit of the time in America; and its professors are not a set of men who can be priest-ridden to any fatal extent" was used to refute anti-Catholic charges of undue clerical interest (J. T. Ellis, *American Catholicism*, p. 73). A more critical view is noted in Max Berger, "The Irish Immigrant and American Nativism As Seen by British Visitors, 1830–60," *Pennsylvania Magazine* 70 (1946) 146–60. Andrew Greeley dismisses this evidence by saying that "Most of the foreign visitors, alas, did not know what they were talking about" (*The American Catholic: A Social Portrait* [New York: Basic Books: 1977] 48).

16. Ex-priest autobiographies began to be popular during the 1830s and had successive waves of popularity during the nineteenth century. The addition of "former priest of Rome" to an author's name seemed to give the required verisimilitude. William Hogan, who signed all his literature as "formerly Roman Catholic Priest," wrote *A Synopsis of Popery As It Is* (Boston: Saxon and Kelt, 1845). Hogan felt that, insofar as women were concerned, Catholicism should be compared to Mormonism for the perversion of the sexual ethic (D. B. Davis, *Fear of Conspiracy*, pp. 100–101); Vincent Philip Mayerhoffer had similar lurid tales to tell of the confessional (*Twelve Years a Roman Catholic Priest* [Toronto: Rowsell & Ellis, 1861]). The most widely published priestly recusant of the nineteenth century was Charles Pascal Chiniquy. His autobiographical work *Fifty Years in the Church of Rome* (New York: F. H. Revell Co., 1886) was a straightforward tale of increasing disillusionment with anti-democratic and jesuitical pressures. But his *The Priest, the Woman and the Confessional* (St. Anne, IL, 1884) was highly sensational. Chiniquy asked the inflammatory rhetorical question, "Do American men know what their wives tell the priests in the Confessional?" This putative tableau—the American wife telling her priest unmentionable sins—is invoked many times in the anti-Catholic literature; see, for example, Rev. Isaac J. Lansing, *Romanism and the Republic* (Boston: W. Kellaway, 1889).

Ex-nun books captured the public imagination infinitely more than did those tales of former priests. Although the genre can be traced to Diderot and eighteenth-century French anti-Catholicism, the first to receive wide circulation was Rebecca Reed's *Six Months in a Convent* (Boston: Russell, Odiorne and Metcalfe, 1835) which purported to be the story of an "inmate" of Charlestown's Ursuline Convent on Mt. Benedict for six months in 1831–32. Reed was the "simple Protestant girl" whose testimony was to be refuted by a series of persons, including the Mother Superior of her convent. According to her editors, Reed had written her story of misery at Mt. Benedict before the burning of the convent. Her supporters saw her as a Protestant Jeanne d'Arc, who had "escaped from Catholic superstition, in order to maintain the infallible purity of a secret community of foreign females, who have introduced among us for the imitation of the daughters of republicans, the ascetic austerities of a religious discipline destructive of all

domestic and social relations" (p. 6). The young woman did not wish to publish
her story; it was "committed to the press" only after "a long, deliberate and . . .
prayerful consideration" (p. 11). According to the "preliminary suggestions for
candid readers" which served as a preface, the purpose of publication was to de-
ter Protestants from educating their daughters in convents. The editor was indig-
nant at the "humiliations" practiced by the nuns, "unsuitable for the daughters of
a republic," especially the humiliations of one sister who, presumably because of
her rustic simplicity of speech, was frequently forced to kiss the floor in penance.
"As a test of humility," Reed herself was forced to eat the Mother Superior's ap-
ple parings. This volume charged no gross impurities (which may account for its
being less popular than Maria Monk's *Disclosures*), but stressed the priests' and
nuns' economic rapacity and their alien need of subservience and "austerities,"
equally repugnant to the American temper. Reed's work was answered by a pamphlet written by Mother Mary Edmund St. George (originally Mary Ursula
Moffat), exposing its falsehoods and manifold absurdities (*An Answer to Six
Months in a Convent* [Boston: J. H. Eastburn, 1835]). The "Lady Superior"
started by repeating the claim of Reed's publishers that no "innocent young Protestant girl" could make up such a story, which she refuted by saying, "If they had
any recollection of the history of mankind, they would see that nothing was more
easy." The Superior claimed that Reed came from desperately poor parents, that
she was too lazy to work in a way "commensurate with her humble origins," and
that she was "artful, suspicious, and a double dealer" whom the Superior had
long recognized as "a romantic and ignorant girl" (pp. xxxvii and 12). She refuted most of the specific charges, pointed out that the "flighty and unsteady"
girl had no real vocation, and that the nuns could not only "laugh very heartily at
recreation" but that they read the Bible too (pp. 19 and 31). Reed's final rejoinder was in her *Supplement to Six Months in a Convent* (Boston: Russell, Odiorne
and Co., 1835).

Reed was called upon to testify at the trial of the men accused of burning down
the convent and was described as "a delicate looking creature" whose "deport-
ment on the stand was modest and pensive." The trial reporter commented on the
spectators' "great curiosity" "to see the Convent ladies in the court room." Although the writer was very much opposed to the burning, he made much of the
appearance of Mother St. George who, in contrast to Reed, was "a woman of
masculine appearance and character, high-tempered, resolute, defiant, with stub-
born imperious will." Lending credence to the general air of strangeness and mystery, she arrived wearing a veil, "which she declined to remove, until it was suggested by the court that this would be necessary in order to understand her
testimony, then she unveiled" (*The Charlestown Convent*, pp. 42, 80, and 35).
The final document in the Reed case was a refutation of Mother St. George's refutation, which, as its subtitle promised, "was a vindication of Miss Reed" (*Review
of the Lady Superior's Reply to Six Months in a Convent* [Boston: W. Peirce and
Webster and Southard, 1835]).

Other "escaped nun" narratives, such as Rosamund Culbertson's *Rosamund*

(New York: Leavitt, Lord & Co., 1836), followed Monk's *Awful Disclosures.* This work had an introduction by Samuel B. Smith, "late a priest," and so was doubly authentic. Located in Cuba, an exotic touch, it tells the "sufferings of an American female under the popish priests. Josephine M. Bunkley's *The Testimony of an Escaped Novice from the Sisterhood of St. Joseph, Emmetsburg, Maryland* (New York: Harper, 1855) may be the volume advertised as *The Escaped Nun or Confessions of a Sister of Charity* in the 1855 *Know-Nothing Almanac.* The Mother House of the Sisters of Charity of St. Joseph, founded by Mother Elizabeth Seton, is at Emmitsburg, Maryland, and a misplaced "i" or "e" is of no great moment in these rather free-wheeling narratives. The *Almanac* quoted a review from the *Boston Daily Times* according to which *The Escaped Nun* was expected "to exceed *Uncle Tom's Cabin* in its circulation, and it certainly should do so, for it is far beyond the latter, in a literary point of view" (p. 49). Other examples of this genre were by Edith O'Gorman (*The Trials and Persecution of Miss Edith O'Gorman* [Hartford: Connecticut Publishing Co., 1871]), who claimed to have escaped from St. Joseph's Convent in Hudson City, New York, and Julia Wright (*Secrets of the Convent and Confessional* [New York: National Publishing Co., 1872]), who concentrated primarily on the unfortunate nature of papal infallibility (which had been announced as doctrine in 1870) and its incompatibility with republican institutions.

17. See "Interviews of Maria Monk with Her Opponents Held in This City on Wednesday, August 17th," Printed for the Author, presumably Ms. Monk (New York, 1836); and W. W. Sleigh, *An Expose of Maria Monk's Pretended Abduction and Conveyance to the Catholic Asylum in Philadelphia by Six Priests on the Night of August 15, 1837* (Philadelphia: T.K. and P.G. Collins, 1837). "The True History of Maria Monk," an "expose" by William L. Stone which appeared in the *New York Commercial Advertiser* on 8 October 1836, has been reprinted by the Paulist Press.

18. Thus even though through their vows nuns and priests opposed a "normal" domestic life, subservience and the lack of intellectual autonomy were the primary thrust of the argument against convents. This was emphasized in the many stories of "abduction" and imprisonment—the outward sign of the inward bondage. See, for example, Hiram Mattison's *The Abduction of Mary Ann Smith by the Roman Catholics and Her Imprisonment in a Nunnery for Being a Protestant* (Jersey City, NJ, 1868).

In his diatribes against papism, Robert J. Breckinridge interjects several case studies, of which he claims personal knowledge, of women being held against their will in the Carmelite Convent in Baltimore. One of them, "for the last nineteen years a prisoner called Sister Isabella," actually managed to escape but was forcibly returned by a priest (*Papism in the XIX. Century in the United States, being Select Contributions to the Papal Controversy, during 1835–40* [Baltimore: D. Owen & Son, 1841] 235–38). He points out that the Catholic authorities have responded in the same way to all the criticism ("Milly McPherson was mad," "Miss Harrison was mad," "Miss Reed was mad") and wonders at the possibility of so many deranged young females in the same kind of institution at a given time. His conclusion is that they were driven mad by being kept by priests "in a prison for women" (p. 236).

The importance of woman's free will and her ability to exert it for her religion meant that she could, if her cause was righteous enough, defy male authority. A good deal of popular literature is devoted to this theme. See, for example, Barbara Welter, "Defenders of the Faith: Women Novelists of Religious Controversy in the Nineteenth Century," in B. Welter, *Dimity Convictions: The American Woman in the Nineteenth Century* (Athens, OH: Ohio University Press, 1976) 103–29; and also such nativist fiction as that in William H. Ryder, *Our Country or The American Parlor Keepsake* (Boston. J. M. Usher, 1854), of which "The Heretic Wife: A Tale of Our Own Times" (pp. 104–25) is a good example: Mary Lee, a Protestant, is married to a wealthy, delightful Roman Catholic, Harry Stratton. Although he loves his wife, Harry is worked upon by his church, in the persons of a drunken Irish priest and a "wily young Jesuit" who perjures himself, claiming to have been Mary's lover. As a result, she is divorced by her husband and rejected by her family before she dies of a broken heart.

19. Some examples of child-rearing manuals are John C. Abbot, *The Mother at Home* (Boston, 1833); Lydia Child, *The Mother's Book* (Boston, 1831), and *Hints and Sketches by an American Mother* (New York, 1839). See also Anne L. Kuhn, *The Mother's Role in Childhood Education: New England Concepts* (New Haven: Yale University Press, 1947); Robert Sunley, "Early Nineteenth-Century Literature on Child Rearing," in *Childhood in Contemporary Cultures*, ed. Margaret Mead and Martha Wolfenstein (Chicago: University of Chicago Press, 1955) 150–67; and Philip Greven, *The Protestant Temperament: Patterns of Child-Rearing, Religious Experience and the Self in Early America* (New York: Alfred A. Knopf, 1977).

20. M. Monk, *Awful Disclosures*, p. 18.

21. Chapters 4 and 5 of William James' *The Varieties of Religious Experience: A Study in Human Nature* (orig. ed. 1902; reprinted New York: Modern Library, 1929) are the "Religion of Healthy-Mindedness" (pp. 77–114). James had definite views on the distinctive differences between Protestantism and Catholicism: "The two will never understand each other—their centres of energy are too different. Rigorous truth and human nature's intricacies are always in need of a mutual interpreter" (p. 450).

22. M. Monk, *Awful Disclosures*, pp. 49 and 69.

23. Samuel F. B. Morse, *Foreign Conspiracies against the Liberties of the United States* (New York: Leavitt, Lord & Co., 1835); this was originally published as a series of lectures in the *New York Observer* under the name "Brutus." While admitting that some critics believed that these inflammatory articles were responsible for the burning of the Ursuline Convent, Morse's biographer, Carleton Mabee, says that Morse had nothing against Catholic religious practices. Morse objected purely on the grounds of their incompatibility with the free will and independence required in a democracy (*American Leonardo: A Life of Samuel F.B. Morse* [New York: Knopf, 1943] 164). G. Myers, however, is less generous in his

assessment: ". . . a strange mixture of pliancy to new ideas in the realm of invention and imperviousness to any fresh ideas in the religious or social field" (*History of Bigotry*, p. 160).

24. For the rivalry between Catholic and Protestant missionaries see Barbara Welter, "She Hath Done What She Could: Protestant Women's Missionary Careers in Nineteenth Century America," in *Women in American-Religion*, ed. J. W. James, pp. 111–26.

25. John Murray Cuddihy, *No Offense: Civil Religion and Protestant Taste* (New York: Seabury Press, 1978). The question of taste and its related matter of caste, in which religions are ranked socially, has been explored by Digby Baltzell, *The Protestant Establishment: Aristocracy and Caste in America* (New York: Random House, 1964). Twentieth-century Catholics discussed the "taste" associated in the public mind with the church more freely. See, for example, *Catholicism in America: A Series of Articles from The Commonweal* (New York: Harcourt, Brace and Co., 1954), especially Walter Kerr's article on "Movies" (pp. 209–17). He remarks, "Bad taste is not one of the seven deadly sins. . . . The Church in this country has permitted itself to become identified with the well-meaning second rate" (p. 209).

26. Martha Finley and Isabella Macdonald Alden (writing as "Pansy") both used the convent to symbolize punishment and repression, a particular threat to the spiritual life and physical health of young women. The former's *Elsie Dinsmore* was published in 1867 and had twenty-seven sequels; the latter's work sold over a thousand copies annually from 1870 to 1919. See Paul R. Messbarger, "Isabella Macdonald Alden," in Edward T. James et al., eds., *Notable American Women 1607–1950: A Biographical Dictionary* (Cambridge, MA: Belknap Press, 1971) 1:31–33.

The permeation of English literature with anti-Catholicism is discussed in Edward Hutton, *Catholicism and English Literature* (Folcroft, PA: Folcroft Press, 1969); and Edward Norman, *Anti-Catholicism in Victorian England* (London: Allen & Unwin, 1968). Three English women novelists who wrote prolifically against the Catholic Church and were particularly opposed to the influence of Catholicism on women were very popular in the United States. "Charlotte Elizabeth" (Charlotte Browne Tonna) is typified in *The Convent Bell and Other Poems* (New York: S. J. Taylor & Co., 1845). The Presbyterian Board published prose works such as *The English Martyrology* (Philadelphia: Presbyterian Board of Publications, 1843) and *The Female Martyrs of the English Revolution* (1844). Martha Butt Sherwood's collected works, virtually all on anti-Catholic themes, were published in a special American edition of fifteen volumes in 1855. *The Nun*, published in America in 1834, ends with the pious hope, "trusting that those things respecting the Roman Catholic Church which I have faithfully recorded may tend to fill the inhabitants of this Protestant land with a sense of that gratitude to God who has liberated this country from the slavery of this great apostasy whose name is Mystery" (quoted in G. Myers, *History of Bigotry*, p. 149). The third is Catherine Sinclair, whose *Beatrice, or The Unknown Relatives* had its fourteenth edition in 1853 (New York: DeWitt & Davenport). The preface to this edition gave "the object of this narrative" as the portrayal for "consideration of young girls" of the "enlightened happiness derived from the religion of England, founded on the Bible, contrasted with the misery arising from the superstition of Italy." One of Mrs. Sinclair's prose works that was well received in the United States was *The Priest and the Curate* (London: R. Bentley, 1853), which had the diary of a wholesome Anglican curate on one side of the page and that of a bigoted, venal priest on the other, making the most of the contrasts.

27. Lizzie St. John Eckel, *Maria Monk's Daughter: An Autobiography* (New York: Published for the author by U.S. Publishing Co., 1874). It is hard to know how much of this long autobiography has any claim to truth. It is taken as historical statement by Leo L. Twinem in *Maria Monk's Daughter of Sharon and Amenia: The Story of Lizzie St. John Eckel Harper and Her Church on the Hill* (Flushing, NY: Privately printed, 1932). Twinem accepts her birth as Monk's second child in 1838 and thinks she died between October 1916 and October 1917. He quotes a review from *Brownson's Quarterly* which may have said it all: "her book bears on every page the stamp of rare genius. No novel is more entertaining" (p. 31). She later published *St. Peter's Bride* (New York: G. W. Carleton and Co., 1878), which is an attempt to discuss the church-state controversy as a dialogue between St. Peter (the Church) and his Bride (the State). She concludes that the match is hopeless and walks away.

28. Lizzie St. John Eckel, *Maria Monk's Daughter*, p. 95.

29. Ibid., p. 232.

30. Ibid., p. 602.

31. Ibid., p. 597.

32. Ibid., pp. 603-4.

33. Orestes A. Brownson, "The Worship of Mary," in *The Works of Orestes A. Brownson*, ed. Henry F. Brownson (Detroit: T. Nourse, 1882–1907) 8:83. For biographies (which do not discuss his feelings about women) see Arthur M. Schlesinger, *Orestes A. Brownson: A Pilgrim's Progress* (Boston: Little Brown & Co., 1939); and Theodore Maynard, *Orestes Brownson: Yankee, Radical, Catholic* (New York: Macmillan Co., 1943.)

34. Orestes A. Brownson, "Spiritism and Spiritists," in *The Works of Orestes A. Brownson*, 9:346.

35. Theodore Stanton and Harriot Stanton Blatch, eds., *Elizabeth Cady Stanton as Revealed in Her Letters, Diary and Reminiscences* (New York: Harper & Brothers, 1922) 2:195; and Elizabeth Cady Stanton, *Eighty Years and More: Reminiscences 1815–1897* (T. Fisher Unwin, 1898; reprinted New York: Schocken Books, 1971) 347, see also pp. 376–93 and her *The Woman's Bible*, originally published in two parts in 1896 and 1898 (reprinted New York: Arno Press, 1972).

36. Edward T. James et al., eds., *Notable American Women*, 3:715–16. The Catholics are Mathide Franziska Giesler Anneke, Kate Kennedy, and Hortense Sparks Malsch Ward; Mary Nichols is the convert.

37. See, for example, Sarah Josepha Hale, *Manners or Happy Homes and Good Society* (Boston, 1868); Eliza Leslie, *The Ladies Guide to True Politeness*

and Perfect Manners (Philadelphia, 1864); and Mary Elizabeth Wilson Sherwood, *Manners and Social Usages* (New York, 1884) as examples of the mentor literature.

38. See, for example, *Reports of the Magdalen Society of Philadelphia* (1800) and *The Magdalen Society of New York* (1813). The latter eventually became Inwood House, a home for unmarried mothers; see Annette K. Baxter and Barbara Welter, *Inwood House: One Hundred and Fifty Years of Service to Women* (New York: Inwood House, 1980).

39. John Courtney Murray's review in the *Catholic World* was typical of the way the book was received by the Catholic Press: "Mr. Blanshard . . . has given what is to date the most complete statement of the New Nativism. In the cold cultured manner of its utterance, it is unlike the ranting, red-faced mid-nineteenth century Nativism. Its inspiration is not Protestant bigotry, but the secularist position that deplores bigotry, at the same time that it achieves a closure of mind and an edge of antagonism that would be the envy of a Bible-belt circuit rider. At all events, despite the intellectualization, it is pretty much the same old article" (169 [June 1949] 233).

Blanshard's work had already appeared in *The Nation*, so his critics were ready for him. Two book-length studies by Catholics were in print within three years: Dale Francis, *American Freedom and Paul Blanshard* (Notre Dame, IN: Ave Maria Press, 1950); and James O'Neill, *Catholicism and American Freedom* (New York: Harper and Brothers, 1952). O'Neill devoted considerable space to combatting even the muted favor the book had found with some critics. For example, although the *Library Journal* recommended its purchase, the review ended with the caveat "local decision after careful reading against consideration of local temper required" (74 [1 May 1949] 736). The *New Yorker* believed the book to be interesting and free of invective but doubted it would persuade "any but the already persuaded" (25:27 [27 August 1949] 66). The reviewer in the *Christian Science Monitor* was impressed by the documentation which gave "substantial evidence" for the author's views (28 April 1949, p. 18). On the other hand, O'Neill cites with pleasure the unfavorable review of Will Herberg, although he also points out that "No one should expect non-Catholic reviewers to catch *all* the mis-statements and misinterpretations concerning Catholicism in Mr. Blanshard's text" (p. 235).

Herberg was opposed to the tone ("vulgar anti-Catholicism"), but even more to Blanshard's "perfervid nationalism and statism" with its inability to grasp the dictates of a "higher law," in which "the dictates of the state may be disallowed if they conflict with obedience to God" (*Commentary* 8 [August 1949] 180–200). Responding to critics of his review, Herberg repeated his condemnation, concluding, "To me bigotry is bigotry whether directed against Catholics or against Jews" (*Commentary* 9 [March 1950] 289). The issue of any similarity between the allegiance owed to the Vatican and a putative allegiance owed by Jews to Israel, with the potential for a conflict of priorities, was not discussed.

The review in the *New York Times* and that paper's refusal to allow the book to be advertised, predictably pleased its detractors and infuriated Blanshard. Replying to *My Catholic Critics* ([Boston: Beacon Press, 1952] 52), Blanshard included an open letter to the *Times* in which he complained about the "eulogy" which Theodore Maynard gave O'Neill's book: "But then, my view of the O'Neill work may be slightly jaundiced because of its subject matter. And that, when you stop to think about it, should qualify me as a *Times* reviewer for Cardinal Spellman's next novel! You may consider this letter an application."

The historiography of the book (it was reprinted in 1982 by Greenwood Press of Westport, Connecticut) is itself interesting. Besides being reviewed, the book was written about in the context of the controversy. *Time* captioned its article, "Trouble with U.S. Catholics" (55 [6 February 1950] 50). Evelyn Waugh wrote an article for *Life* entitled "American Epoch in the Catholic Church" (27 [19 September 1949] 134), and discussions of reviews, critical letters, and responses continued for months in the *Atlantic Monthly*, *Harper's*, and the *Saturday Review of Literature*. As G.L. Joughlin titled his piece in the *South Atlantic Quarterly* (40 [July 1950] 265–81), it was "The Catholic Problem Again."

40. Blanshard, who was born in 1892 in Fredericksburg, Ohio, and died in St. Petersburg in 1980, attended the University of Michigan, Harvard, Columbia, and Union Theological Seminary. He worked as a Congregational minister, a lawyer for Mayor LaGuardia in his effort to clean up Tammany Hall, and a consultant for the Caribbean at the State Department. As his obituary writer, Steven R. Weisman, pointed out, these diverse interests "had a common thread: controversy" (*New York Times*, 30 January 1980, p. B4). Although *American Freedom and Catholic Power* was his best-known book, he continued to explore the relationship between the church and the state in *Communism, Democracy and Catholic Power* (Boston: Beacon Press, 1951), *The Irish and Catholic Power* (Boston: Beacon Press, 1953), *God and Man in Washington* (Boston: Beacon Press, 1960), in which he wrote about the hazards of a Catholic presidency, *The Future of Catholic Power* (Washington, D.C.: Protestants and Other Americans United for Separation of Church and State, 1961), in which he spoke harshly about the reality of a Catholic president, *Freedom and Catholic Power in Spain and Portugal* (Boston: Beacon Press, 1962), and *Paul Blanshard on Vatican II* (Boston, Beacon Press, 1966). In this last book, apparently feeling that he might have mellowed, Blanshard found the "new" Catholicism very palatable. He attended the Council as an observer and (with remarkable charity) was "treated well." However, when questioned if he had changed his opinion about the Catholic Church he responded, "The answer is 'Yes,' but only to the extent that the Catholic Church has changed. I am as hostile as I ever was to the autocracy of its central power structure and to many of the family and church-state policies that flow from that clerical autocracy" (p. 10). In 1972, according to his obituary, he "came to the conclusion that Christianity is so full of fraud that any honest man should repudiate the whole shebang and espouse atheism."

41. Paul Blanshard, *American Freedom and Catholic Power*, p. 15.

42. W. S. Tisdale, *The Controversy between Senator Brooks and "John" the Archbishop of New York* (Albany: C. Van Benthuysen, 1858). This speech was occasioned by the correspondence and sermons in which Archbishop Hughes re-

sponded to Senator Brooks' speeches in the New York Senate on the Church Property Bill.

43. P. Blanshard, *American Freedom and Catholic Power*, p. 15.

44. Translated in *The Great Encyclical Letter of Pope Leo XIII* (2nd ed., New York: Benziger Brothers, 1903) 320–35). See also Leo's apostolic letter *Testem Benevolentiae* to Cardinal Gibbons, pp. 441–53. For a contemporary view of the Pope's "threat" to America, see Rev. Justin D. Fulton, *Leo XIII in American Politics* (Boston: Weekly American, 18— [probably 1899]. Also Edward T. Gargan, ed., *Leo XIII and the Modern World* (New York: Sheed and Ward, 1961); and Harold R. Rafton, *The Roman Catholic Church and Democracy: The Teachings of Leo XIII* (Boston: Beacon Press, 1951).

45. P. Blanshard, *American Freedom and Catholic Power*, pp. 59–60. The "School Controversy" has just as long a history and bibliography as that surrounding "Americanism." Ellis' *Life of James Cardinal Gibbons* devotes a full chapter to it (I:635–707) as does Moynihan's *Life of Archbishop John Ireland* (pp. 73–103). Some Protestant views are clear in their titles, for example, Rev. Jeremiah Crowle, *The Parochial School: A Curse to the Church, a Menace to the Nation* (Chicago: Printed for the Author, 1905); and Melancthon Jacobus, *Popery against Common School Education* (Philadelphia: Presbyterian Board of Publications, 1853). See also Daniel F. Reilly, *The School Controversy 1891–93* (Washington, DC: Catholic University of America Press, 1943). The Catholic University Press also published several dissertations on Catholic education in individual states. James Burns (*The Catholic School System in the United States* [New York: Benziger Brothers, 1908] and *The Immigrant Church: New York's Irish and German Catholics, 1815–1865* [Baltimore: Johns Hopkins University Press, 1975]) discusses the earlier years; Arthur J. Hope's *Notre Dame: One Hundred Years* (Notre Dame, IN: University of Notre Dame Press, 1943) is a good history of an important parochial school. See also Edward J. Power, *A History of Catholic Higher Education in the United States* (Milwaukee: Bruce Publishing Co., 1958). However the historical record is set straight, there is nonetheless a steady stream of rhetoric against these schools, of which Blanshard's work forms a part. For example, the complaints found in Rev. Edward McGlynn's *Public Schools and Their Enemies* (New York, 1889) are virtually the same as in Emmett McLoughlin's *American Culture and Catholic Schools* (New York: L. Stuart, 1960). McLoughlin's analysis of the schools takes their "threat" just as seriously as did the nativist of the 1890s, and much more so than does Blanshard. As an ex-priest, McLoughlin feels he speaks with special authority when he identifies "the steady movement to control education" as the "most serious present threat to American freedom and institutions (p. 263).

46. See J. T. Ellis, *The Life of James Cardinal Gibbons*, 1:664–65; James Cardinal Gibbons, *A Retrospect of Fifty Years* (2 vols., Baltimore: J. Murphy Co., 1916); and a pamphlet put out by the National Educational Association of the United States, entitled *The Two Sides of the School Question* (Boston: Arnold, 1890). This work summarized the speeches of Cardinal Gibbons and Bishop Keane "on the one hand" and Edwin D. Mead and the Hon. John Jay "on the

other." For Gibbons' own analysis of his church, see his immensely popular *The Faith of Our Fathers* (Baltimore: J. Murphy, 1904) which was in its seventy-third edition by 1904.

47. P. Blanshard, *American Freedom and Catholic Power*, pp. 65–66. John Cogley suggests that Catholics were quite surprised to see quotations from encyclicals like these. Al Smith, John Kennedy, and most of their co-religionists knew virtually none of the literature. Indeed, Cogley gives the impression that Blanshard may have been one of the very few people of any faith or any time who ever *did* read the encyclicals (see *Catholic America* [New York: Dial Press, 1973] 66).

48. P. Blanshard, *American Freedom and Catholic Power*, pp. 66–67.

49. This and equally specious material can be found in E. Hutchinson, *Young Sam, or Native Americans' Own Book* (New York: American Family Publishers, 1855) and *Pope or President: Startling Disclosures of Romanism as Revealed by Its Own Writers, Facts for Americans* (New York, 1859). For a wonderfully irrelevant comment on the degenerate nature of Catholicism, see the quotation attributed to Madam de Sevigné on Vincent de Paul: "He was an agreeable man—only he cheated at cards." Commenting on this, Catherine Sinclair says "And this is the kind of person who is now elevated to sainthood!" (*Popish Legends* [London: Longman, Brown, Green, and Longmans, 1852] vii). The double social bind also operated. In addresses to working persons and in much fiction, the Catholic Church was seen as the tool of the decadent European monarchies, presided over by Catholic kings and queens, advised by richly clad, undemocratic Jesuits. See, for example, "To the American Mechanics, Working Men, and Sewing Girls, Living in Cities and Towns," in *The Know-Nothing Almanac* (1856). The question is put to this audience, "Why are you poor?" and the answer is, of course, because of foreign competition and the lack of taxation of church property. See too such pieces as the Philadelphia firm of Barrett and Jones' 1846 advertisement for a forthcoming book entitled *The Bank and the Pope* addressed to the selling of indulgences (the Pope in question was Leo X, and the time the fourteenth century), which "the poor could not buy." The other argument of the double bind was about the tremendous number of poor illiterates, all of whom were Catholic. See, for example, A. W. Drury, *Romanism in the United States: The Proper Attitude toward It* (Dayton, OH: United Brethren Publishing House, 1894), and the presentation of Irish as "deliciously low" in even such otherwise benevolent works as those of Kate Douglas Wiggin.

50. In addition to Blanshard's Catholic critics cited in note 39, see also Daniel J. Callahan, *The Mind of the Catholic Layman* (New York: Scribner's, 1963), for an expression of honest bewilderment that Protestants should be so critical of ideas that no ordinary Catholic ever held. Also see the choices of Joseph Blaud, editor of *Cornerstones of Religious Freedom in America* (Boston: Beacon Press, 1949), for a traditionally liberal interpretation of American freedom. The book was published at the same time and by the same press as was Blanshard's. A strange historical footnote to Abraham Lincoln's reputation as a partisan of religious pluralism is found in Charles Granville Hamilton, *Lincoln and the Know-Nothing Movement* (Washington, DC: Public Affairs Press, 1954). He concludes

that "the Know-Nothings were clearly responsible for the election of Lincoln" (p. 20). Hamilton feels that Lincoln, however broadminded he was himself, did not repudiate the Know-Nothings and may have encouraged their support.

51. *Pastoral Letter of the Archbishops and Bishops of the United States, Assembled in the Third Plenary Council of Baltimore* (Baltimore, MD: Baltimore Publishing Co., 1884), reprinted in John Ireland, *The Church and Modern Society* (St. Paul, MN: Pioneer Press, 1905) 1:28.

52. P. Blanshard, *American Freedom and Catholic Power*, p. 17.

53. Ibid., p. 70.

54. Ibid., p. 67. Catholic nuns have been increasingly critical of their role and status in their church; see, for example, M. Albertus Magnus McGrath, *What a Modern Catholic Believes about Women* (Chicago: Thomas More Press, 1971). Sr. Albertus Magnus has a particular (and possibly justified) quarrel with the article on "Women" in the *Catholic Encyclopedia*, published in 1913-14 but not revised until 1967. Blanshard is in the tradition of nativist prose with his unappetizing physical descriptions and appeal to American women to assert themselves; see for example, the appeal to "The Ladies and the American Causes" in the *Know-Nothing Almanac* (1856); and Anna Ella Carroll, *The Great American Battle, or The Contest between Christianity and Political Romanism* (New York and Auburn: Miller, Orton and Mulligan, 1855). One element lacking in the twentieth-century attacks, so far as I know, is the vivid iconography of the nineteenth-century illustrations, many of which featured women in fairly advanced stages of undress, with headings like: "Lady After Torture, Before Tribunal of Holy Office" and "Sick Lady Confessing to Priest."

55. P. Blanshard, *American Freedom and Catholic Power*.

56. Ibid., p. 123.

57. See Emily Douglas, *Margaret Sanger: Pioneer of the Future* (New York: Holt, Rinehart & Winston, 1969); and David Kennedy, *Birth Control in America: The Career of Margaret Sanger* (New Haven: Yale University Press, 1970).

58. Although most writers on the theme of Catholic-Protestant tensions consider the issues quiescent, if not resolved, there are exceptions. See, for example, Andrew Greeley, *An Ugly Little Secret: Anti-Catholicism in North America* (Kansas City, MO: Sheed Andrews and McMeel, 1977). Greeley maintains that anti-Catholicism is "the last remaining unexposed prejudice in American life" (p. 1), more insidious than racism or anti-Semitism because it is unacknowledged and harbored mostly among "intellectual and cultural elites" (p. 2). He ends his book with a question apposite to this paper: "Do you now begin to wonder why American social science has for more than three decades virtually ignored the possibility that nativism might persist?" (p. 115).

4

Catholic Attitudes toward Protestants

JAY P. DOLAN

Ever since the Protestant Reformation of the sixteenth century Catholics and Protestants have not gotten along. Their mutual hostility toward each other took various shapes and forms over the centuries with armed conflict in the name of the one true God being quite common. When English Protestants settled in North America, they brought this legacy of the Reformation with them, and Massachusetts went so far as to outlaw Catholic priests in the colony.[1] The irenic spirit of the American Revolution and the call for religious freedom buried the spirit of anti-Catholicism for some time, but it surfaced again in the nineteenth century. Once again people were attacked verbally and physically simply because they were Roman Catholics; convents were burned, churches were stoned or destroyed, and school children were abused for refusing to recite Protestant prayers. The legacy of the Reformation was still very much alive in nineteenth-century America. But what about Catholics? Did American Catholics counterattack by stoning churches and parsonages and physically attacking those Lutherans and Congregationalists they met on the street? To the best of my knowledge they did not engage in such extreme anti-Protestant behavior. Some Catholics in Champlain, New York, burned Bibles in 1842, and this certainly caused harsh feelings. No doubt other Bible burnings took place, but I could not verify them. An incident that took place in Holyoke, Massachusetts, after the 1928 presidential election certainly qualifies as hostile. It seems that a

Protestant clerk in a local store loudly boasted that even though all the nuns voted for Al Smith, he still lost. A Catholic customer took exception to the remark and punched the clerk.[2] Undoubtedly, similar individual confrontations took place, but they do not reveal very much about the larger cultural issue of how Catholics viewed Prostestants.

The reason why Catholics did not engage in violent anti-Protestant behavior was that they were outnumbered. They were a minority group and perceived themselves as such; thus they avoided any extreme public actions that would weaken their already tenuous position in the United States. Catholics wanted desperately to be accepted as 100 percent American, and overt anti-Protestant behavior clearly was not conducive to such acceptance. For Catholics, then, religious hostility took on a different style than it did for Protestants. Rather than engage in mindless public acts of religious hatred that could be socially self-destructive, Catholics nurtured an attitude toward Protestants that was both deep-rooted and very hostile. This essay will examine such attitudes during the past 200 years and seek to explain why Catholics were so fundamentally anti-Protestant.

Two hundred years ago things were obviously quite different in the United States. An understanding of how great the difference was can be acquired from an incident that took place in the small town of Lebanon, Pennsylvania, in 1810. On July 23 of that year the Catholic church held a grand opening ceremony. A Jesuit priest, John William Beschter, presided at the ceremonies. "He preached, once in German and once in English, to a mixed congregation of Catholics and Protestants. Three Lutheran, three Reformed, and one Moravian minister listened attentively as Beschter spoke on Protestant misrepresentations of Catholicism and the solidity with which Christ had built his church. After the services, all of the clergy dined at the home of the local Lutheran minister."[3]

The American Revolution had unleashed a spirit of toleration unknown in earlier days, and a visible result of this was a prolonged period of cordial relations between Catholics and Protestants. What took place in Lebanon, Pennsylvania, was not unusual. Throughout the nation Catholics and Protestants were learning how to live together; mutual respect for one another had improved; they attended services in each other's churches, sometimes out of necessity, more often out of genuine interest and curiosity; Protestants gave money and land for the construction of Catholic churches and sent their children to Catholic schools; Catholics and Protestants were partners in politics and religiously mixed marriages were commonplace. Given the small number of Catholics and the modest size of most towns during the Republican era (1780 to 1820) such cordial social relations were not unexpected. In later years, where a similar environment prevailed, as in ante-bellum North Carolina or frontier Oregon, Catholics and Protestants enjoyed similar cordial relationships.[4]

To be sure many Catholics believed that Protestants were heretics and their churches were neither one, holy, Catholic, nor apostolic. This was a legacy of the Reformation, and it remained strong during the Republican period of Catholicism. But some Catholics, Bishop John Carroll of Baltimore being the most notable, were attempting to fashion a different theology of the church. Ever since the Reformation, Catholics described their church in such a manner that the one true church of God was exclusively identified with the visible institution centered in Rome and known as the Roman Catholic Church. Anyone not belonging to that Roman Catholic organization was judged to be outside of the true church and thus deprived of salvation. But for John Carroll and others the church was not solely identified with the visible institution of Roman Catholicism; they defined it more in terms of the people who made up the church. Such a view recognized the reality of religious pluralism and the salvation of those who were not Roman Catholics. Moreover, this school of thought recognized both the need and the legitimacy of the church adapting itself to the new age; concrete examples of such adaptation included a vernacular liturgy, an American-born clergy, a more democratic form of local church government, and a more modern definition of church.[5]

The significance of this is that during the Republican period of American Catholicism a new theology of church and a new view of history were emerging. Inspired by Enlightenment thought, this new definition of the church clearly articulated a more positive view of Protestantism than that developed during the post-Reformation period. Unlike the traditional classicist position that viewed church and theology as immune to change, untouched by history, the new historical consciousness allowed for change in the church and in theology. In the United States this meant a recognition of religious pluralism and a working out of its consequences for Catholic theology.

The point I want to make here is twofold. First, during the Republican period, 1780–1820, Catholics in general evidenced a very cordial, positive attitude toward Protestants. A partial explanation of this was the social situation in which very few Catholics lived alongside of large numbers of Protestants in small towns. The major reason, however, was not social but theological or intellectual, namely the surfacing of a historical consciousness that allowed for a new theology of church. This is the second point. The Catholic theology of church shaped Catholic attitudes toward Protestants. In the Republican period a broad definition of church had gained currency in the marketplace, and this fostered a positive view of Protestantism. The absence of explicit anti-Catholicism helped; so did the small size of the Catholic community. But in my opinion the key reason was the more irenic definition of church that was in the air.

The second period that I want to examine is the era of the immigrant church, from 1820 to 1920. We move now from Lebanon, Pennsylvania, to Jacksonville, Illinois. The date was 1860 and a new Catholic priest had just arrived in town. The local ministerial association "extended to him an unprecedented invitation to join." The priest refused on principle, and this unleashed a torrent of anti-Catholic abuse in the press and the pulpit; at the local college, students met to debate the question: "Resolved: Catholicism should be abolished by law." The priest counterattacked with his own defense of Catholicism before a large audience.[6] The social environment resembled Lebanon in 1810. Jacksonville was a small town with a population of five thousand people, and Catholics made up a small minority of the population. But religious hostility hovered close to the surface of public life, and it did not take much to ignite a controversy. Obviously much had changed in the previous fifty years.

The immigration of millions of Irish and German Catholics, and eventually of Italian, Polish, Slovaks, and other Eastern European people radically changed American society. People were quick to realize this and sought to stem the tide of immigration. Despite such efforts, America remained an asylum of nations. The heavy influx of Catholics put fear into the hearts of Protestants, and some even went to bed at night armed with guns in order to repel any sudden papal attack. Ministers mounted the pulpit and preached a Protestant crusade to save the nation from the papists. During the ante-bellum period this crusade enjoyed widespread support. After a lull in the 1860s and early 1870s, anti-Catholicism surfaced again and reached another high point in the 1890s with the emergence of the American Protective Association. The social environment had obviously changed. Catholics now were the single largest denomination in the United States; in some towns they made up one-half or more of the population; in some cities Irish Catholics controlled the local government. A segregated city replaced a cosmopolitan town; cultural barricades emerged to separate one group of people from the next, and religious differences reinforced these barriers. Such social and cultural developments were not conducive to friendly relations between Catholics and Protestants.

Another important development was the Catholic canonization of the church as the one perfect visible institution on earth. This definition of the church as a visible institution reached its zenith of popularity during the age of the immigrant church. It meant that the one and only true church was identified with the visible institution of Roman Catholicism;

as the first Vatican Council put it, "outside the church no one can be saved . . . what is not in this ark will perish in the flood."[7] For Catholics there was no question who was outside the ark. This theology of church had come to the forefront of Catholic thought during the Protestant Reformation and gave birth to a style of religion known as Tridentine Catholicism; the name, Tridentine Catholicism, is derived from the sixteenth-century Council of Trent which wrote the theological Magna Carta for Roman Catholicism in the modern period. In the nineteenth century Tridentine Catholicism was riding a crest of popularity and enjoyed the support of a militant papacy. Born in an environment of hostility and religious wars, Tridentine Catholic theology was mainly apologetics; in other words, theology consisted in proving that Catholics were right and everyone else, Protestants especially, were wrong. Thus, at its very core Catholic theology was anti-Protestant. Some people developed it in a virulent, hostile manner; others were more benign and civil. Regardless of the style, however, they agreed on one fundamental truth — Catholics were right and Protestants were wrong.

Tridentine Catholic theology, apologetic in nature, was defensive, militant, and supremely confident. It was the bedrock of the Catholic ethos and shaped the way Catholics thought about themselves and everyone else, especially Protestants. The American social environment, which put the Catholic minority on the defensive and separated them from other religious groups, was tailor-made for this type of theology. In a society segregated along racial, ethnic, and religious lines, Tridentine Catholic theology made eminent sense. With this basic understanding of religion and society in place, examination of the attitude of Catholics toward Protestants during the era of the immigrant church becomes more intelligible.

As a key agency in the formation of the Catholic ethos the parish school provided a good barometer of popular thought. Children in these schools not only learned the catechism, but they also studied church history. This was where they learned about the "so-called Reformation." One syllabus instructed teachers to "show that up to this period [the Reformation] none of the present heretical sects were in existence; that they, unlike our holy Religion, are the work of depraved men, not of God; that heresy was propagated by persecution, plunder and brute force." This syllabus, put together for the Catholic schools in New York, went on to suggest the goal of the course in modern church history:

> Outlining the History of the Church from the beginning of the so-called Reformation to the accession of the present Pontiff, taking special pains to impress upon the children's minds the solemn truth that God's Providence was visibly guiding, ruling and extending His Church during the

whole of that trying period, e.g., in spite of atrocious penal laws, Ireland held fast to the old religion; in spite of Luther, many Germans, and in spite of Calvin, most of the French remained Catholics, while in Spain, Portugal, Italy, and in much of Switzerland, the so-called Reformation found no footing at all.[8]

Numerous devotional guides circulated throughout the Catholic community and invariably they included instructions for young men and women. One popular guide gave the following counsel:

Let the young Catholic remember that his is the only true and divine faith; that the Catholic church alone has survived the changes and revolutions of 1800 years; that millions of martyrs have bled for it, and millions more have confessed it before persecutors, before ever the world had heard or dreamed of Protestants. He should look with charity and pity upon all the perishing and deluded multitude of heretics and infidels around him, but never give in to their false principles, never deny his faith, nor hide it, nor darken it, nor blush for it.[9]

One of the most popular books ever written by an American Catholic was *The Faith of Our Fathers* by James Cardinal Gibbons. It was a clear, well-written explanation of the Catholic religion. The aim of the author "was to bring home the truths of the Catholic faith to our separated brethren."[10] Typically Catholic, it developed each chapter by the point-counterpoint method; in other words, the Catholic position was always explained in reference to Protestantism. Gibbons did this in a very civil manner, and this was a partial explanation for the book's success among both Catholics and Protestants. Nevertheless, it illustrates a key point; the very definition of Catholicism included rejection of Protestantism as an erroneous and thus inferior religion.

Another barometer of Catholic opinion were the numerous essays and lectures written and delivered by leading figures in the community. Certain themes stood out as central to all of these essays. First, Protestantism was in a state of decay. The historian John Gilmary Shea analyzed an 1881 census that documented the decline of Protestant churchgoers. His conclusion was that because they had abolished true worship, namely the Catholic Mass, Protestants were no longer going to church. Bernard McQuaid, the bishop of Rochester and a noted Catholic leader, used Shea's data in an essay he wrote for *The North American Review* in 1883 entitled "The Decay of Protestantism." He wrote that when Protestantism

left the Catholic communion, it was much like a mariner going out to sea in a ship without a rudder, who, when the storm arises, casts out one bit of cargo after another, in the vain hope of saving the sea-tossed and foundering vessel. Protestantism went out to sea without Christ's appointed pilot, and has been discharging cargo ever since, to escape shipwreck. Now that there is little left to throw overboard, above all wrangling and contention the cry of distress is heard, that danger is imminent and disaster inevitable. In all its multitudinous forms Protestantism is decaying—is dying.[11]

Archbishop John Ireland, another national Catholic leader, believed along with others that "as a religious system, Protestantism is in process of dissolution; that it is without value as a doctrinal or a moral power, and it is no longer a foe with which we need reckon."[12]

The root of this decay could be traced back to the Reformation. For Catholics this was the root cause of all evil in the world, the so-called Reformation or what they liked to call the Protestant Revolt. Orestes Brownson, a Yankee convert to Catholicism, put it in very specific and harsh terms. For Brownson the real issue surrounding the controversy with Protestants was "between atheism and the Catholic church. The more logical and clear-sighted among Protestants see it and either return to the church and become Catholics, or draw from the principle of the Protestant Revolt its last logical consequences, and become downright atheists."[13] Brownson was more vitriolic than most. Others were more civil and also more cosmic as regards the effects of the Reformation. At one national Catholic congress clerical speakers blamed the Reformation for the evils of rationalism, materialism, evolution, socialism, as well as general social and moral anarchy.[14] School children learned the same history lesson. The Protestant Reformation was the root cause of religious, moral, and civil decay. It was a revolt against the authority of the church, and once this authority was rejected such decay was inevitable.

Another consequence of the Reformation was a spirit of indifferentism. A Catholic layman made this point in a very irenic manner:

> While we welcome with eager hearts the spirit of sane broadness, a spirit of Christian kindliness, we Catholics utterly repudiate any such idea or doctrine as "one religion is as good as another." [Applause] While we plead for a right understanding of what we believe and in doing so extend to our non-Catholic citizens the right hand of Christian fellowship, we instinctively shrink from yielding one iota of the "faith of our fathers."[15]

For Bishop McQuaid the "decay of Protestantism" resulted in "a transition to the ranks of indifferentism and infidelity."[16]

The social consequences of this attitude were evident. Catholics grew up believing Protestants were inferior. Deluded by Luther, Calvin,

Zwingli, and Henry VIII, Protestants were on a road destined for eternal damnation. Catholics learned to adopt a patronizing, condescending attitude toward Protestantism and its adherents. Associations with Protestants were discouraged because such associations were a clear danger to the faith of Catholics.[17] Marriages with Protestants were not only discouraged, they were also forbidden. The California hierarchy issued a typical pastoral letter on the topic in 1872 stating that religious marriages between Catholics and Protestants "besides committing a mortal sin, cause great scandal to religion and people in such marriages do great injury to themselves, living in a state of degradation, their matrimony being nothing else but a palliated concubinage, which will surely bring them to eternal condemnation, unless they repent and repair the scandal by redressing their steps." Those who ignored the teaching of the church were guilty of "not only exposing themselves to make a contract which has no force before God, and, consequently, does not prevent their intercourse from being a horrible concubinage, but, also, committing really a sin of sacrilege."[18] Despite such intense opposition the church did reluctantly grant dispensations to Catholics who wanted to marry Protestants, provided the children of such marriages were raised as Catholics. But these dispensations were relatively few in number. For immigrant Catholics a mixed marriage was when an Irishman married a German.

Even though the inherently erroneous nature of Protestantism was a major intellectual principle for Catholics, some Catholics did evidence a more irenic, positive view of Protestantism. The Paulist priest Alfred Young was one. A convert from the Episcopal Church, Young belonged to an order of priests, the Paulists, who sought to convert Protestant Americans to Roman Catholicism. In Young's mind there was no question that Protestantism was a flawed system. Nevertheless, he recognized that "what religion they [Protestants] have is Christian, and what acts of faith, hope, and charity they make are essentially acts of Catholic Christian religion."[19] The faith of those Protestants *who are in good faith* is identical with ours in its essential quality," he wrote, "and saving their pitiable ignorance, I am convinced that it would open the way to the conversion of many of them." Once converted they would realize that they were "never anything but a Catholic" all their lives.[20] Though condescending, Young's attitude was still quite removed from the general assessment that those not in the ark of salvation were destined for damnation. His position represented the standard Cathlic teaching about invincible ignorance which left the door of salvation open to Protestants. Though standard teaching, it was infrequently mentioned.

Much more common was a call for cooperation between Catholics and Protestants, not on a religious or theological level, but in the area of charity and reform. A national conference of Catholic laymen held in Baltimore in 1889 resolved that "Catholics could come together with non-Catholics and shape civil legislation for the public weal."[21] Laymen active in charity work also urged cooperation with Protestants on behalf of the common welfare of all people. The Progressive period witnessed a noticeable increase in such calls for cooperation on behalf of social reform. In the early twentieth century the Knights of Columbus, at the suggestion of Washington Gladden, mounted a campaign to reduce religious prejudice among Catholics and Protestants alike.[22] But such cooperation was to be limited to issues unrelated to "religion and right morals." This was the mandate of the Vatican after Catholic priests and bishops had taken part in the World Parliament of Religions in Chicago in 1893. Prior to Rome's decision Catholics and Protestants did gather together "from time to time" to discuss "religion and right morals," but henceforth, Rome said, Catholics could not participate in such gatherings. The reason for Rome's decision was the fear of religious indifferentism that such mixed assemblies allegedly fostered.[23]

By the early twentieth century the conservative wing of Roman Catholicism was in the ascendency both in Rome and in the United States. This precluded any possible breakthrough in Catholic-Protestant relations, and the best that could be hoped for was cooperation in the area of social reform. The prevalent Catholic view of Protestants remained essentially the same. Fundamentally erroneous, inherently weak, Protestantism was still on the road to decay.[24] The best that could be hoped for was that Protestant America would become Catholic; to achieve this goal Catholics mounted a vigorous crusade to convert Protestants to Roman Catholicism.

Cultural and religious barricades continued to separate Catholics from Protestants. Even though they might have lived on the same city block, Catholics and Protestants grew up in their own world. A woman raised on Chicago's South Side in the 1920s and 1930s recalled that her neighborhood "was an Irish neighborhood. Everybody was Irish," she said. As she remembered, "everybody" was also Catholic and belonged to St. Columbanus parish. But the hard data of the U.S. Census demonstrated how mythical her world was. The neighborhood was predominantly Protestant; for every one Catholic there were three Protestants. Over twenty-six different ethnic groups lived in the neighborhood, and the Swedes, not the Irish, were the largest group in the area. When confronted with this information, the woman said, "I really don't remember anything but Irish." Of course, she was right. Her social world was peopled with individuals who were mostly Irish Catholic. For her the neighborhood was Irish Catholic though statistically it was a melting pot.[25]

Studies of Middletown (Muncie, Indiana) and St. Louis reveal similar divisions between Catholics and Protestants. Geographically they were neighbors; culturally and socially they lived in two different worlds.[26]

The third and final historical vignette that I offer took place in Holyoke, Massachusetts, in 1940. Margaret Sanger, the famous advocate of birth control, was scheduled to speak at the First Congregational Church in early October. For Holyoke's Catholics, who made up two-thirds of the city's population, the appearance of Margaret Sanger in a Protestant church was an outrage. The Catholic church strongly opposed the practice of birth control, and Massachusetts was one of the two states in the United States where doctors were still forbidden by law to provide birth-control information to married persons. Thus, what began as a simple announcement of a birth-control lecture "became within a few days the subject of citywide conflict involving deep religious, economic, and political forces and the major leaders of the community." Sanger did speak, but in a union hall, not a Protestant church.[27]

Holyoke's Catholics had made a major power play by using the threat of economic boycott to persuade the city's Protestant leaders not to support the Sanger lecture. In 1940 Holyoke Catholics clearly viewed themselves as the moral guardians of the community. Since Sanger presented a serious threat to the community's moral integrity, they mounted an aggressive campaign that in the end was partially successful.

Holyoke in 1940 was quite different from Jacksonville, Illinois, in 1860. By the mid-twentieth century Catholics had acquired a sense of confidence about their place in American society. They viewed themselves as the true moral hope of American civilization, indeed of Western civilization. At a time when many Americans were disillusioned about the future of modern civilization, Catholics set out "to defend the values and promises of American idealism," and they did so in a confident and aggressive manner.[28] Church leaders campaigned vigorously against birth control, divorce, immoral books and movies, and the red plague of communism. According to Catholic thought all of these moral and social evils were the direct result of the Reformation and the decay of Protestantism. Catholics clearly viewed themselves as the moral guardians of the nation, sincerely believing that Protestants had abdicated this responsibility. Nothing since World War I had persuaded Catholics to change their opinion of Protestants. The rise of the Ku Klux Klan in the 1920s fueled the flames of religious hostility; Al Smith's unsuccessful campaign for the presidency in 1928 unleashed another torrent of anti-Catholic sentiment and once again demonstrated the intense degree of religious prejudice that people harbored against Catholics. When, in 1939, President Roosevelt appointed Myron C. Taylor as ambassador to the Vatican, Protestants protested loudly; a public debate between Catholics and Protestants ensued and the lines of conflict hardened. The issue of federal aid to private schools surfaced with periodic regularity, and this too deepened the chasm separating Catholics and Protestants. As in the Progressive period some cooperation between Catholics and Protestants on behalf of social reform was present during the New Deal era. In addition, the National Conference of Christians and Jews, founded in 1928, sought to promote religious tolerance. But the New Deal's promotion of reform ended with the outbreak of World War II, and the National Conference of Christians and Jews had very little impact in places like Holyoke, Massachusetts.[29]

As far as the Catholic theology of the church was concerned, not much had changed. Catholic textbooks articulated a theology of the church according to which Roman Catholicism was the only one, holy, Catholic, and apostolic church with all others being "false churches."[30]

At a more popular level the *Baltimore Catechism*, revised in 1941 after several years of discussion among bishops and theologians, featured a new addition, an appendix entitled "Why I am a Catholic." Its purpose was to help Catholics explain their religion to their "non-Catholic friends" and to demonstrate that "the only true Church of Christ is the Catholic Church." The twentieth-century successor to Gibbon's *Faith of Our Fathers* was Father John A. O'Brien's work, *The Faith of Millions*, published in 1938. Translated into numerous languages, millions of people bought this classic in Catholic apologetics. Like Gibbons, O'Brien's attitude toward Protestants was very civil, but once he began to write about the Reformation and Luther, the gentle person became a harsh critic. According to O'Brien, Luther had ushered in the principle of the supremacy of private judgment in religion, and this in turn led to religious indifferentism, one of the worst evils in American society.[31]

Protestantism was still decaying and the root cause remained the same, the so-called Reformation and its revolt against authority. Added to the long list of evils brought on by the Reformation were World War I and World War II; they "were the logical outcome of Luther's teaching . . . the line from Luther to Hitler was straight. Hitler brought the doctrines of Martin Luther to inevitable conclusion" wrote one Catholic journalist.[32] As Catholics became more acculturated, their association with Protestants increased and this heightened the Catholic fear of religious indifferentism; it was one of the evils of the age along with such other dogmas as secularism and communism. Church authorities especially feared religious indifferentism and for this reason did not favor the "so-called irenical spirit" among Catholics.[33]

The times were changing, however. By the 1950s the United States was no longer a Protestant nation. The walls of the immigrant ghetto were crumbling and Catholics were slowly but steadily moving into the mainstream of American life. Interethnic marriages were very commonplace by the mid-twentieth century. Religiously mixed marriages were also becoming more common even though Catholic church law still prohibited them except in unusual cases. In religiously pluralistic America, however, the unusual was becoming more normal. This was especially true in the rural South, in places like Florida and South Carolina, where about half of the Catholic marriages at mid-century were religiously mixed. In Louisiana the percentage was about 30. In the urban North the percentage was much smaller.[34] Despite the negative image of Protestants promoted by the church, many Catholics obviously felt comfortable marrying one. Environment and circumstance had a lot to do with this. The odds were that few Catholics married Protestants in Holyoke, Massachusetts, whereas in Charlotte, South Carolina, one of every two Catholics who applied for a marriage license had a Protestant partner.

While the social situation was changing slowly but perceptibly, the theological climate was also experiencing some change. Catholic theologians in Europe were sending out ecumenical signals, hoping to improve relations with Protestants. The foundation for this was a new theology of the church that had been developing since the post-World War I period. In the United States the issue of religious liberty served as a catalyst for interfaith cooperation. The pluralistic nature of American society clearly demanded such, and Catholic church leaders sought to persuade Rome of the need for interfaith cooperation. But Vatican authorities failed to understand the American situation and continued to prohibit such mingling of Catholics and Protestants. In 1954 the World Council of Churches met in Evanston, Illinois, but Catholics were forbidden to attend even as observers.[35] The chasm separating Catholics and Protestants appeared as wide as ever. Nevertheless, the times were changing; ecumenical programs were taking place and the hostility of the 1940s and early 1950s was disappearing. Then in October 1958 a pudgy, seventy-six-year-old dynamo was elected pope of the Roman Catholic Church. This marked the beginning of the end of Tridentine Catholicism as Pope John XXIII ushered in a new Reformation. Only then, with the emergence of a new theology of church, a sense of historical consciousness, and the desire for Christian unity, did the Catholic attitude toward Protestants substantially change. But it would take a long time to change the effects of 400 years of history. For those Catholics raised in the church of Vatican I the scars of religious prejudice are not easily removed; nor is it easy to erase the effects of decades of teaching about "poor, deluded Protestants." For those Catholics raised in the church of Vatican II the unity of all Christians still remains a hope, not a reality. That they could even hope for such a goal is the real revolution in Catholic thought.

Notes

1. John Tracy Ellis, ed., *Documents of American Catholic History* (Chicago: Henry Regnery Co., 1967) 1:111–12.

2. Daniel Dorchester, *Christianity in the United States* (New York: Phillips & Hunt, 1888) 554; and Kenneth Wilson Underwood, *Protestant and Catholic: Religious and Social Interaction in an Industrial Community* (Boston: Beacon Press, 1957) 159; my thanks to Robert Handy for the Dorchester reference. It should be noted that Catholics evidenced a good deal of overt hostility to Jews and blacks.

3. Joseph P. Chinnici, "American Catholics and Religious Pluralism 1775–1820," *Journal of Ecumenical Studies* 16:4 (Fall 1979) 727–28.

4. See Joseph Agonito, "Ecumenical Stirrings: Catholic-Protestant Relations During the Episcopacy of John Carroll," *Church History* 45 (September 1976) 358–73; also Stephen C. Worsley, "Catholicism in Ante-bellum North Carolina," *North Carolina Historical Review* 60:4 (October 1983) 399–430.

5. See Chinnici, "American Catholics and Religious Pluralism."

6. Don Harrison Doyle, *The Social Order of a Frontier Community: Jacksonville, Illinois 1825–1870* (Urbana: University of Illinois Press, 1983) 144–45.

7. Quoted in Avery Dulles, S.J., *Models of the Church* (Garden City, NY: Doubleday, 1974) 38.

8. *Report of the Reverend Superintendants of the New York Archdiocesan Schools, February 1905–July 1906* (New York: New York Catholic School Board, 1906) 16.

9. *The Mission Book of the Congregation of the Most Holy Redeemer* (Baltimore: Kelly and Piet, 1862) 321–22.

10. James Cardinal Gibbons, *The Faith of Our Fathers* (Baltimore: John Murphy & Co., 1876) vii.

11. Bernard J. McQuaid, "The Decay of Protestantism," *North American Review* 136 (February 1883) 135–36; John Gilmary Shea, "Protestant Churches and Churchgoers," *American Catholic Quarterly Review* 7:27 (July 1882) 427–86.

12. John Ireland, *The Church and Modern Society* (New York: D.H. McBride & Co., 1903) I: 81.

13. "Controversy With Protestants," *Brownson's Quarterly Review*, Last Series, 2:4 (October 1874) 481.

14. Alfred Juan Ede, "The Lay Crusade for a Christian America: A Study of the American Federation of Catholic Societies 1900–1919" (Unpublished Ph.D. dissertation, Graduate Theological Union, 1979) 114–15.

15. Ibid.

16. McQuaid, "The Decay of Protestantism," p. 151.

17. See *Pilot* (Boston), 15 January 1924 and 9 February 1924; also *Morning Star* (New Orleans), 25 January 1913.

18. Quoted in R. A. Burchell, *The San Francisco Irish 1848–1880* (Berkeley: University of California Press, 1980) 86–87.

19. "A Plea for Erring Brethren," *Catholic World* 50 (December 1889) 358.

20. Ibid., pp. 363 and 366.

21. Quoted in Aaron I. Abell, *American Catholicism and Social Action* (Notre Dame, IN: University of Notre Dame Press, 1963) 104.

22. Christopher J. Kauffman, *Faith and Fraternalism: The History of the Knights of Columbus 1882–1982* (New York: Harper & Row, 1982) 153–89.

23. Gerald P. Fogarty, *The Vatican and the American Hierarchy From 1870 to 1965* (Stuttgart: Hiersemann, 1982) 130–31; James F. Cleary, "Catholic Participation in the World Parliament of Religions, Chicago, 1893," *Catholic Historical Review* 55 (January 1970) 605–6.

24. The *Pilot* (Boston), 19 January 1924 and 23 February 1924.

25. Thomas Lee Philpott, *The Slum and the Ghetto: Neighborhood Deterioration and Middle Class Reform* (New York: Oxford University Press, 1978) 131–35.

26. See Robert S. Lynd and Helen Merrell Lynd, *Middletown* (New York: Harcourt, Brace & Co., 1929); and H. Paul Douglass, *The St. Louis Church Survey* (New York: George H. Doran Co., 1924).

27. Underwood, *Protestant and Catholic*, p. 22.

28. William M. Halsey, *The Survival of American Innocence* (Notre Dame, IN: University of Notre Dame Press, 1980) 2.

29. See Leonard Curry, *Protestant-Catholic Relations in America: World War I through Vatican II* (Lexington: University Press of Kentucky, 1972).

30. Richard McBrien, *Catholicism* (Minneapolis: Winston Press, 1980) II: 659–61.

31. Michael A. McGuire, *The New Baltimore Catechism and Mass* (New York: Benziger Brothers, 1949) 214–18; John A. O'Brien, *The Faith of Millions* (Huntington, IN: Our Sunday Visitor, 1938) 46–61.

32. Quoted in Underwood, *Protestant and Catholic*, p. 150.

33. Curry, *Protestant-Catholic Relations*, p. 94; see also Gustave Weigel, S.J., *A Catholic Primer on the Ecumenical Movement* (Westminster, MD: Newman Press, 1957).

34. Michael J. McNally, "A Peculiar Institution: Roman Catholic Parish Life in the South Atlantic Region 1850–1980" (Unpublished MS) 77–78; Joseph H. Fichter, S.J., *Southern Parish* (Chicago: University of Chicago Press, 1951) 108–9; Joseph B. Schuyler, S.J., *Northern Parish* (Chicago: Loyola University Press, 1960) 128, where he indicates level of mixed marriages to be 13 percent.

35. Fogarty, *The Vatican and the American Hierarchy*, p. 387; also Weigel, *A Catholic Primer*.

5

The Eclipse of Old Hostilities *between* and the Potential for New Strife *among* Catholics and Protestants Since Vatican II

MARK A. NOLL

The twenty-five years between the installation of Angelo Giuseppi Roncalli as Pope John XXIII in 1958 and the celebration of the 500th anniversary of Martin Luther's birth in 1983 made up a quarter century of unprecedented Catholic-Protestent rapprochement. In America, developments during this period were so extraordinary that it is now difficult to recapture empathetically the situation as it existed at mid-century. Merely to chronicle the extent and depth of the recent changes, however, is only part of the challenge, for the significant question remains what such a rapid rearranging of the landscape actually means. This paper attempts, first, to describe some of the more consequential events of the last quarter century and then to suggest ways of putting them into perspective. This latter effort should lead us to see more clearly that the reasons for a decline in traditional Protestant-Catholic antagonisms are the very reasons that, under altered circumstances, also account for newer forms of interreligious strife involving Catholics and Protestants.

I

By mid-century the grosser forms of religious hostility that had been described in Ray Allen Billington's superb study of ante-bellum nativism and John Kane's workmanlike survey of Protestant-Catholic strife had largely passed from the scene.[1] But interreligious tensions were not extinct. As Andrew Greeley put it, "While most overt violence has come to an end, discrimination against some religious groups continues . . . and religious prejudice and bigotry has by no means vanished from the scene."[2]

Two comments, two events, and two books suggest the extent of Protestant-Catholic disengagement that existed in the decade and a half after World War II. In 1945 the Presbyterian fundamentalist, Carl McIntire, who was then more centrally located on the religious spectrum than he would become, assessed the world situation in terms that some other Protestants would have shared: "As we enter the post-war world, without any doubt the greatest enemy of freedom and liberty that the world has to face today is the Roman Catholic system. Yes, we have Communism in Russia and all that is involved there, but if one had to choose between the two . . . one would be much better off in a communistic society than in a Roman Catholic Fascist set-up. . . . America has to face the Roman Catholic terror. The sooner the Christian people of America wake up to the danger the safer will be our land."[3] Three years later, the Protestant church historian Wilhelm Pauck, who moved in more liberal orbits than McIntire, took stock of the interreligious situation and concluded that "the difference between Protestantism and Roman Catholicism is so profound that it seems almost impossible to recognize them as two forms of one Christianity."[4]

These evaluations reflected a more general climate characterized by considerable mutual suspicion. In 1946 President Truman's reassignment of a formal representative to the Vatican was greeted with a frightening din from all along the Protestant spectrum. G. Bromley Oxnam, bishop of the Methodist Church in New York and president of the Federal Council of Churches, criticized the move as "encouraging the un-American policy of a union of church and state" which the Catholic church pursued.[5] Nor was suspicion all on one side. When the second General Assembly of the World Council of Churches met at Evanston in 1954, Chicago's Cardinal Samuel Strich issued a pastoral letter forbidding priests to attend even as reporters and urging Catholics in general to stay far away.[6]

Even the authors who attempted to write most sympathetically about Catholic-Protestant differences could at best describe a cordial antagonism. When Jaroslav Pelikan, a Lutheran, published *The Riddle of Roman Catholicism* in 1959, he admitted "that the prejudices and clichés of past generations continue to dominate the image of the Roman church current in America." His book, by contrast, was a charitable effort to dispel prejudice. Yet when Pelikan came to describe the current situation, he turned instinctively to metaphors of conflict—"unconditional surrender," "the great divide," "theological alienation." And he did not hold out high hopes for an improvement in "what we have now . . . on both sides, a picture of the other side that is part photograph, part old daguerreotype, and part caricature."[7] For Catholics the Newman Press translated Louis Bouyer's *The Spirit and Forms of Protestantism* for American readers in 1956, the year of its original French publication. Like Pelikan, Bouyer was eager to replace prejudice with sympathy; and he was most willing to concede a great deal to Protestantism. But also like Pelikan the point was reached when the language of antithesis took over, and Bouyer concluded that while the religion of Luther, Calvin, and Karl Barth contained insights that the Catholic church needed, it was "compromised . . . irremediably" by its fatal attachment to sixteenth-century nominalism.[8] In sum, on the very eve of John XXIII's pontificate, and one might add, of the American presidential election of 1960, there seemed no particular reason to expect a quantum leap in Protestant-Catholic good will.

But then the situation changed with lightning speed. The most visible public signal of a shift in the United States was the election of a Catholic as president in 1960. John F. Kennedy's victory was itself a milestone. It marked the culmination of a long process begun during the Revolutionary period by Charles Carrol's participation in the Continental Congress and George Washington's suppression of Pope's Day, sustained during the nineteenth century by a long line of public-spirited bishops, and approached through 150 years of intensive Catholic involvement in grassroots politics.[9] The circumstances of Kennedy's own career added even greater symbolic importance to the 1960 election. His campaign speech before Protestant ministers in Houston seemed to convince them, and many others, that a Catholic president would not imperil national integrity. Kennedy's scrupulous record on church-state matters, particularly his opposition to government aid for parochial schools, silenced many critics who feared that Catholics did not have proper national priorities. On this issue Billy Graham spoke for others by bestowing the indelicate praise that Kennedy had "turned out to be a Baptist president."[10] Moreover, the apotheosis that occurred after Kennedy's assassination left him, a Catholic, to this day the most revered American president among the public at large.[11] The "religious issue" in American politics, though not yet dead, had suffered a crushing blow.

In spite of its manifest importance, the Kennedy phenomenon was still less significant for long-term improvement in Protestant-Catholic relations than the more strictly religious events that, after having been set in motion in Rome, led to great changes in America. Ripple effects from

John XXIII's ecumenical spirit were not long in coming. Even before the convening of the Council, the pope had sent Catholic observers to the 1960 assembly of the World Council of Churches in New Delhi and had established a Secretariat for Promoting Christian Unity in the Vatican. In the wake of the Council's Decree on Ecumenicism, which "commends this work to the bishops everywhere in the world for their diligent and prudent guidance," the Conference of American Bishops in November 1964 set up its own Ecumenical Commission. This agency sponsored subcommissions that very soon were deep in discussion with the Orthodox Church in the United States and with several of the major Protestant traditions.[12] Of these meetings, that between Lutherans and Catholics has produced the richest fruit, with a series of agreements on the Nicene Creed, baptism, the eucharist, and, most recently, justification by faith.[13] Catholic entrance into ecumenical activity has continued on a broad level. Although the church does not belong to either the National Council or World Council of Churches, it takes an active observer's role in the deliberations of these bodies. Moreover, it has become a member of the National Council's Commission on Faith and Order, an agency whose executive director is now a Catholic.[14] And Catholic-Protestant discussions, instructions, debates, and dialogue appear at nearly all the major interfaith forums on almost every imaginable issue.[15]

Signs of the recent Catholic-Protestant reengagement also extend far beyond formal ecumenical circles. The charismatic movement has treated traditional stand-offs cavalierly, so much so that whether on small-scale local levels or in the large groups like the Word of God Community in Ann Arbor, Michigan, Protestant-Catholic differences have receded into the background.[16] Public taste in spiritual literature shows the same lack of respect for the great divide of the sixteenth century, with Protestants buying the books of Thomas Merton and Henri Nouwen, Catholics reading Richard Foster and Richard Lovelace, and American Christians of all sorts devouring the books from Britain's C. S. Lewis and G. K. Chesterton without being entirely sure which is the Catholic and which the Protestant. American publishers encourage the growing traffic between the traditions by publishing numerous books which treat interconfessional differences far more relatively than authors in the 1950s could have imagined. To sample almost randomly, it is possible to point to popular titles like Albert Boudreau's *The Born-Again Catholic* from Living Flame Press, and more serious studies such as George H. Tavard's *Justification* from Paulist Press, which argues that Luther's construction of this key doctrine is compatible with the theology of Trent, or T. F. Torrance's *Theology in Reconciliation: Essays Towards Evangelical-Catholic Unity in East and West* published in this country by William B. Eerdmans.[17]

Even on matters concerning the Bible, always a sensitive barometer of public sentiment in America, the last twenty-five years have witnessed a series of marvels. From rioting over Catholic desires to read the Douay-Rheims Bible in public schools during the nineteenth century, to the creation of mutually exclusive networks of professional biblical scholars in the first half of the twentieth, the study and reading of scripture has now become a nonsectarian free-for-all.[18] Catholics currently may read the Living Bible and the Good News Bible, both produced under strictly Protestant auspices, with the *imprimatur* and *nihil obstat*. Catholic scholars sit on the revision committee of the Revised Standard Version, and Protestant purchasers swell the sales of the Catholic Jerusalem Bible. Official delegates were exchanged between the Catholic Biblical Association and the Society of Biblical Literature for the first time only in 1959, yet by 1966 a Catholic had been elected president of the SBL.[19] So unpredictable had the times become that it was a Catholic group which set records in the distribution of scripture, with the Sacred Heart League placing record orders from the American Bible Society for 775,000 New Testaments in 1979 and 800,000 in 1983.[20]

The recent careers of two stars in the religious media suggest how much and how rapidly things have changed. Billy Graham, of southern fundamentalist extraction and nativist evangelical education, enjoyed less than cordial relations with Catholics early in his evangelistic career. During the 1950s Catholic officials in South American and the Philippines forbade their coreligionists to attend his meetings; in the same years local priests and bishops in the United States also often discouraged attendance at Graham crusades. During the presidential election of 1960, Graham only just succeeded in muting his enthusiasm for Richard Nixon and, again, just barely in hiding his apprehensions about a Democratic regime that would include not only a Catholic president, but also a Catholic Majority Leader in the Senate, Mike Mansfield, and a Catholic Speaker of the House, John McCormack. Very soon thereafter, however, Graham began to work at improved relations with Catholics. His efforts have been unusually successful. Catholics now make up a considerable portion of those who attend his meetings, record decisions for Christ, and watch the crusades on television. Tangible evidence of Graham's transcendence of interconfessional antagonisms has multiplied in recent years. In 1977 he was granted permission to hold a crusade in one of American Catholicism's most hallowed locations, the football stadium at the University of Notre Dame. In 1978 he became the first Protestant leader to be entertained by the abbot of the shrine of the Black Madonna in Częstochowa, Poland. In 1981 he sought and was granted an audience at the Vatican by Pope John Paul II, who short years before as Cardinal

Karol Wojtyla had made it possible for Graham to preach in Catholic churches during his evangelistic tour of Poland.[21]

If Billy Graham's growing friendliness with Catholics is remarkable, what may be said about the Catholic volte-face on Martin Luther? Although the antagonisms of centuries had cooled somewhat by the 1950s, Luther was still treated harshly or ignored entirely by the Catholic populace at large. Only two of thirty American Catholic periodicals in one survey provided reviews of Roland Bainton's life of Luther, the most compelling modern study, when it appeared in 1950.[22] Catholic reaction to the Martin Luther movie of 1953 was also decidedly unfavorable. One commentator in *The Priest* summed up his judgment by calling Luther "a lewd satyr whose glandular demands were the ultimate cause of his break with the Christian Church."[23] In the wake of the Council, an altogether different attitude filtered down rapidly into popular levels. By 1965, the pages of *The Priest* reflected a different attitude. According to one writer, "We'd feel quite silly today declaiming against Luther in the intemperate words of yesterday."[24] Scholarly and popular reassessment of Luther went on apace until 1980 when a series of meetings to celebrate the 450th anniversary of the Augsburg Confession heard from many Catholics about the usefulness of that symbol for their tradition.[25] The reevaluation reached a grand climax in the *Lutherjahr* itself. Local Catholic officials, anticipating the pope's own appearance in Rome's Evangelical-Lutheran Christ Church on December 11, 1983, accepted invitations to preach in Protestant services.[26] Catholic presses responded in kind to Protestant titles like *Martin Luther: Prophet to the Catholic Church* by publishing books like *Luther: A Reformer for the Churches*.[27] It encapsulates the startling changes wrought by the passage of only a few years to note that in the mid-1950s Chicago Catholics fought to keep the Luther film off local television, while in 1983 the Notre Dame alumni magazine devoted much of one issue, including an attractive cover portrait, to a discussion of "What Martin Luther Means to Us."[28] The dramatically altered position of Martin Luther in Catholic-Protestant relations testified eloquently to an unprecedented improvement in interconfessional attitudes.

II

As soon as we put this broader situation into perspective, however, we run headlong against both conventions of civility and complexities of analysis. In light of the respect, cooperation, and edification that have flowed so readily between Catholics and Protestants in recent decades, it seems churlish to probe beneath the surface, especially since such probing reveals the potential for more hostility affecting Catholics and Protestants. And in light of the many factors that now enter into questions of interreligious relations, it is tempting to wave a magic wand, whether contemporary like "secularization theory" or traditional like "the movement of the Holy Spirit," at the changed circumstances of our day and to leave it at that. But still more can be said.

Two clusters of considerations help explain both the complex changes in Catholic-Protestant relations and the potential for further hostility. The first of these concerns the nature of the religious communities themselves. The time is long past when responsible analysts could speak of Catholics and Protestants at homogeneous wholes. This has been a truism in the discussion of American Protestantism since the end of the last century, but only in recent decades have historians taken seriously the impossibility of lumping together, say, fundamentalists, liberals, Lutherans, Pentecostals, or any one of these families, into an undifferentiated unit. In spite of persistent efforts to speak of a unified Catholic this or that, such efforts are now as indefensible as similar generalities applied to Protestants. What Catholics have recently insisted concerning their own internal pluralism only echoes the situation for both groups. Richard McBrien from a theological perspective can say of the current scene, "that there are sometimes sharper divisions *within* the Roman Catholic Church than there are between certain Catholics and certain Protestants."[29] Andrew Greeley makes the same point as a sociologist: "Every generalization about values that begins with the word 'Catholic' is likely to be misleading, if not erroneous, precisely because the generalization will mask substantial differences in values that exist among the Catholic subpopulations."[30] One reason, then, for the decline of traditional Protestant-Catholic hostility is the growing awareness of how artificial it is to talk about denominational clusters as simple monoliths ranged over against each other as discrete entities.

A second reason is the passionate and tangled nature of contemporary public affairs where Christian faiths and civil religions collide in nearly every conceivable combination. The crucible effect wrought by this situation explains why some Catholic-Protestant barriers have fallen: committed toilers in the public vineyard have glanced up in surprise to find previously despised Catholics or Protestants laboring right alongside. And it helps explain why religious factors remain an important source of hostility, for the same toilers have not infrequently conjured up the ogres of traditional mythology when opponents present themselves as proponents of *the* Catholic or *the* Protestant position.

The complex controversies surrounding three of America's fundamental social concerns—sex, national self-defense, and the economy—have withered old interreligious antagonisms and created the potential for new ones. Political debates on these issues, particularly controversy on how convictions concerning these matters are to shape education, regularly reflect the passionate commitments of Americans from all points on the religious compass. Religiously infused arguments—whether on the morality of capitalism, governmental involvement in birth control and abortion, or the justice of American defense policies—fill the air. The significant fact for contemporary interreligious hostility in all of this is that allegiance to a general Protestantism or Catholicism is no longer a reliable indicator of commitments on public policy. Both theoretical questions and practical dilemmas, both theological applications and religious reflexes, are so diverse that whatever systematic differences still separate Catholics and Protestants are regularly lost in the public shuffle.

Intraconfessional pluralism and the complex character of contemporary public life are certainly related to religious events more narrowly conceived. The Second Vatican Council eased the way toward greater pluralism within Catholicism and made possible a whole range of new alliances between Catholics and Protestants. Changes within American Protestantism—such as the decline of liberalism and the resurgence of fundamentalism and evengelicalism—have also reshaped the nature of interreligious hostility. In short, developments within the last twenty-five years have made it almost possible to write finis over *traditional* forms of Protestant-Catholic strife. But that is only to begin to grasp the nature of ongoing friction in which Catholics and Protestants are deeply involved.

Before examining these modern forms of discord, however, it is necessary to admit that one type of contemporary Catholic-Protestant hostility remains very much as it has been for centuries. This is an atavism that lives on in the changed conditions after the Council, but which owes its inspiration to earlier periods. Some of the anti-Catholic prejudices chronicled by Andrew Greeley in *An Ugly Little Secret* illustrate this phenomenon.[31] Greeley's evidence is persuasive that a residual willingness to perpetuate cultural and ethnic stereotypes and to tolerate inequities based on religious persuasion continue to exist in modern America. The survival of these biases is an embarrassment. Not only have they lost whatever basis in fact they may once have had, but they also contradict the civilized sensibilities fostered by an era of civil rights.

Another example of atavistic hostility appears in more expressly religious categories among a few Protestant fundamentalists and evangelicals where the reflexive religious bigotry of an earlier era lives on. Two recent comic books, *Alberto* and *The Double Cross*, produced by a California publisher named Jack Chick, illustrate the lingering force of this hostility. The books purport to tell the story of a former Spanish Jesuit, who was trained to subvert Protestantism through a number of ingenious schemes, and of his sister, who endured the terrors of Maria Monk in an English convent. They use a language every bit as unreserved as John "Bilious" Bale in the sixteenth century or Lyman Beecher in the nineteenth to denounce the sins of Rome. The fairly wide sale of the comic books suggests that latent antagonisms remain in Protestant circles which the well-publicized Catholic-Protestant reengagements of recent years have not affected. As an indication of changing times, however, Protestants from very many backgrounds joined Catholic spokesmen in denouncing the books; the Christian Booksellers Association, which represents largely a conservative Protestant constituency, expressed its regret over the publications; and evangelical journalists contributed much of the hard information that exposed the comic books as fraudulent.[32]

The hostilities that Greeley describes and Jack Chick markets would have been well at home in the 1840s or 1890s. While it is unwise to treat them now as if they had nothing to do with contemporary forms of Catholic-Protestant tension, it is difficult to find spokesmen recognized in either the most WASP-ish social circles or the most conservative religious circles who are willing to sanction the open expression of these traditional prejudices.

III

Distinctly modern forms of interreligious hostility involving Catholics and Protestants come into sharper focus if we arrange members of these groups not so much along lines of denominational allegiance as along the lines that create the pluralism within each communion. Two matters stand out above the rest for these distinctions. First, Catholic and Protestant Christians divide among themselves concerning the historical conditioning of the Christian faith. The conviction is now often expressed that the historical origins of Christianity and the historical circumstances of Christian communities make it impossible to speak of religious fixities that are equally applicable in all times and in all cultures. The Protestant historian Brian Gerrish, thus, speaks of "a pluralistic world of continued change" and of the way in which "historical modes of thought are inescapably relativizing" in order to describe the evolving nature of religion.[33] The Catholic Bernard Lonergan talks of two religious modes, one "classicist, conservative, traditional," the other "modern, liberal, perhaps historicist." According to Lonergan, "the old dogmatic theology

... thought not in terms of evolution and development, but of universality and permanence." By contrast, the new mode recognizes that "meanings differ from nation to nation, from culture to culture, and that, over time, they develop and go astray."[34] While the historicist mode is represented, and is probably dominant, among professional students of religion, "unhistorical modes of thought," in Gerrish's phrase, "are far more tenacious in the churches, both Protestant and Roman Catholic." As just one illustration of that tenacious commitment to "unhistorical modes," Gerrish points to the 1965 encyclical, *Mysterium Fidei*, in which Paul VI affirmed the church's ability to formulate doctrine that is valid for everyone in all times and places.[35] Other illustrations could be heaped up easily from Protestants believing something of the same thing on the basis of scripture and confessions. Even those who now stand in the middle on this matter, who have gone beyond Paul Riceour's "primitive naïveté" and who yet do not give up hope in the possibility of a second naïveté,[36] usually sort themselves out to one side or the other on this issue—coming down either as historicists who respect the older absolutist stance, or as absolutists who acknowledge the immense, but ultimately penultimate force of historical conditioning. The divide on this most basic attitude toward the faith opens up great potential for religious hostility, both on matters of the faith itself and on matters of public policy related to the faith.

A second variable that cuts across both Catholics and Protestants, whether historicists or absolutists, is the degree to which Christians have assimilated habits of mind distinctively characteristic of American experience. At this point the question is not one of political left or right, but merely the ordering of values. Ideal types clarify the discrimination. First are those who picture some variation of American values as the fulfillment, or the equivalent of, Christian values. In contrast are those for whom everything uniquely valuable about American experience is still in principle subordinate to the Christian faith. Even more than with the historicist variable, it is obvious that many Catholics and Protestants stand somewhere between the ideal types. Yet to speak of an Americanist appropriation of the Christian faith makes it possible to describe more intelligently interreligious hostilities involving Catholics and Protestants over the last quarter century.[37]

With historicist and Americanist discriminations we can identify three different kinds of both Catholicism and Protestantism in the recent history of the United States. First, to borrow Brian Gerrish's term, are *New Catholics* and *New Protestants* who believe ultimately in the historically conditioned character of Christianity and who generally believe that one or another vision of American values points the way to a better future.[38] These New Catholics and New Protestants may be regarded as both historicists and Americanists.

Next we may speak of *Old Catholics* and *Old Protestants* who believe in the fixity of dogma, however that belief may be qualified, and who profess a higher allegiance to Christian principles than to any possible expression of American values.

Finally we may talk of *Americanist Catholics* and *Americanist Protestants* whose attitudes toward the historically conditioned character of Christianity may differ, but who testify by belief and practice to their foundational commitment to the unique superiority of aspirations, values, and institutions that arise from modern American culture. These Catholics and Protestants come closest to embodying a generalized version of what Sidney Mead has called "the religion of the Republic," or to believing, in Martin Marty's phrase, in "the self-transcendence of the nation."[39] Such may, however, differ quite dramatically among themselves as to which values American experience has revealed as uniquely superior.

Catholic-Protestant tension since the Second Vatican Council has been *most visible* for issues involving Americanist Catholics and Americanist Protestants. It has been *most antagonistic* where Old Catholics and Old Protestants square off against New Catholics and New Protestants. And it has been *most fruitful* where Old Catholics and Old Protestants enter into theological discussion with each other.

IV

Recent hostility involving Americanist Catholics and Americanist Protestants is capable of endless and entertaining analysis. But it more properly belongs to considerations of civil than religious strife. To be sure, both the breakdown of traditional Catholic-Protestant antagonisms and the formation of new sources of Catholic-Protestant hostility seem intimately involved. This, however, is mostly an optical illusion. Such developments betray their character as inter-Americanist problems when we observe the common tendency for religious convictions to sanction commitments to some ideal of American experience. The key is predictability. If a person can be identified with a particular socioeconomic, educational, geographical, or ideological position that owes its distinctive shape to American experience, and if that person's pronouncements on public issues fully reflect that position, then regardless of the Christian words employed, the public statement probably expresses more an American than a Christian value.[40]

This phenomenon explains some of the alliances of the last quarter century. Catholic and Protestant writers for the *National Review* may hold Christian values very dearly, but that commitment is not nearly as visible as the commitment to economic and political conservatism. Similarly, when the radical evangelical Sojourners community in Washington, D.C., opens its periodical to Catholics, what is most obvious is that the Catholic writers express variations of the Sojourners' political and economic views. Writers for both periodicals often invoke compelling Christian warrants for their opinions, but the unifying framework in both cases is a vision of goodness that can be explained in terms of American cultural history as well as of basic Christian conviction. Since this is the case, discussion of either journal—whether in creating Catholic-Protestant alliances or in providing a forum for selective criticism of Catholic or Protestant actions—belongs as much to a history of recent ideologies in American life as to a history of Protestant-Catholic relations.

In disentangling Americanist loyalties from Christian convictions it is helpful to identify the contrasting sets of basic American values that intermingle with, or coopt, Christian beliefs in the discussion of public issues. One set involves visions of public order in which the United States looms as either the salvation of the world or its curse.[41] Another set involves a selective absolutization of freedom. The libertarianism of the Right speaks apocalyptically about tyranny in public schools, that of the Left with similar apocalypticism about tyranny over a woman's body. A final set concerns economic systems, with capitalistic, socialistic, and mixed versions providing seemingly absolute points of reference. In the advocacy of these various positions, a great amount of interchange, mutual support, and encouragement now passes between Catholics and Protestants. That such interchange is not, however, directly pertinent to the question of Catholics and Protestants *as* Catholics and Protestants is suggested by the fact that comparatively little interchange occurs within the communions across the grain of these loyalties.

One result of the close conjunction between civil and religious convictions on these matters is confusion in the media and a promiscuous mingling of analytical categories. Recent reactions to the Catholic bishops' letter on nuclear arms is a case in point. The letter was a comment on public affairs rooted quite self-consciously in religious reflections. It is possible, therefore, to examine the religious underpinnings of the opinion or its policy implications.[42] Americanist-religious confusion occurred, however, both when the foundational religious discussion was read as thinly veneered ideological propaganda and also when responses to the policy proposals were perceived as an attack on the bishops' religious integrity. Congressman Henry Hyde, himself a Catholic who enjoys considerable support from the hierarchy for his efforts to prohibit federal funding of abortions, encouraged the first kind of confusion by reading the letter as something which merely "reinforces the liberal Left."[43] Columnist James Reston furthered the second by calling the Reagan administration's reaction to the letter an assault on "the right of the church to challenge official policy."[44] In making these assessments, Hyde allowed his Americanist views on nuclear arms to foreclose the possibility of considering the bishops' religious case on its own terms. Reston, on the other hand, allowed his doubts concerning the Reagan administration, doubts arising from Americanist beliefs in how best to fulfill national aspirations, to fashion a religious issue out of a debate over public policy. In both cases there appears to be interreligious hostility, but in neither do commentators escape the domination of Americanist loyalties.

As the Reston comment on the bishops' letter illustrates, confusion concerning interreligious hostility surrounds especially the quintessential American commitment to separation of church and state. All Americans are of course for it. But approval is also almost always selective. Right-wing Americanists worried about the violation of this principle during the Vietnam era when clergymen gave their voices to the antiwar effort. Left-wing Americanists now worry about its violation when antiabortionists, creationists, and advocates of a voucher system for public education present their proposals to the public. On each of these issues the air is filled with pious language. But in each case as well, at least some of that religious language represents defense of values rooted in Americanist rather than Christian loyalties.

A qualification is in order when describing the confusion between Americanist disharmony and interreligious tension. This has to do with the complexity of motives that can underlie public pronouncements. Catholics and Protestants in this country are prone, as perhaps all people are in similar situations, to regard support for their public positions as something rooted in Christianity and expressing the finest American traditions, while opposition is an affront to the faith and a violation of national ideals. It may not be as easy, however, to disentangle Americanist and religious motives as I have been suggesting.[45] What religious critic of Michael Novak, for example, is fully qualified to say that he is more a practicing Americanist than a practicing Catholic when, in his *Confessions of a Catholic*, he faults his church for resisting artificial contraception and for slighting the virtues of democratic capitalism?[46] Or what religious defender of Jimmy Carter can be sure that his inconsistencies in foreign policy were really the product of Christian striving rather than the outworking of unrealistic Americanist ideals? The analytical problem here involves the tight bond between motives and conceptual tools. Motives may be Christian, but the arguments actually employed Americanist, or vice versa. In either case, and in the more complicated situations where Christian and Americanist impulses have actually merged into each other, simple judgments are impossible.

Such considerations mean that all conflicts with Catholic-Protestant overtones are not merely disguised civil strife. But they should not obscure the fact that essentially nonreligious issues occupy a good bit of the terrain regularly treated as interreligious hostility.

V

A second kind of modern hostility involves controversies setting New Catholics and New Protestants over against Old Catholics and Old Protestants. This face-off involves not only the clash of religious values but also a large intermixture of Americanist loyalties. Thus, combatants square off on public issues from motives derived from both religious and national values. While the agreements between New Catholics and New Protestants, as well as between Old Catholics and Old Protestants, are never exact, they are sufficient for the creation of working alliances. Old Catholics may believe in the fixity of truth because of a conception of the magisterium, Old Protestants because of a stance toward scripture, but both are united in principle against merely contextual analyses of public values. New Protestants may lean to the Left or Right politically for different reasons than New Catholics, but both will place greater weight on the possibility of sure guidelines arising from within the modern world itself than their Old counterparts. Such conditions define a different kind of religious hostility than that which prevailed until the mid-twentieth century, but still a potentially potent one.

Langdon Gilkey's book, *Catholicism Confronts Modernity: A Protestant View*, presents a succinct account of the picture from a New or historicist perspective. To Gilkey, modernity means to experience "the radicality of historical *change*," which "engulfs and relativizes each historical embodiment, even the ecclesial embodiments of the faith that transcends history." In such a world the Christian message must itself be adaptable. "If the *kerygma*, the gospel, is to speak to our age, it must do so in relation to the modes and forms of modern self-understanding."[47] Catholics and Protestants who share Gilkey's assessment are willing to countenance the possibility that technological change, new discoveries in ethics, politics, or theology, and the evolution of human needs may essentially alter the inherited faith. Old Catholics and Old Protestants, on the other hand, may concede that the Christian faith opens out to meet the changes of the modern world, perhaps on the model of Newman's *Development of Doctrine* or through more simple intuitions, but they still hold that contemporary faith is substantially identical, and not merely continuous with, the original sources of scripture and tradition. Contrasting attitudes to the faith itself, when intermingled with Americanist loyalties, are portents of hostility.

Where Americanist loyalties confuse the issues, however, the hostility is reduced. Both New and Old Christians have strong views on governmental involvement in education, on the economic system, and on nuclear arms. But in each of these cases, Americanist factors diffuse the sharp clash between New and Old religious perspectives. The Americanist damper is perhaps most obvious for education. Southern Baptists usually are Old Protestants theologically, yet they often also have an Americanist commitment to public education and an Americanist opposition to governmental support of private schools. On the other hand, Old Protestants like the members of the Christian Reformed Church or the Lutheran Church–Missouri Synod believe that government aid for private education is a matter of simple justice to taxpaying parents. Across the historicist divide, New Catholics may have no objection to the idea that an evolutionary cosmology should be a part of all education, yet still retain a commitment to inherited traditions of parochial schools. New Protestants, for their part, may have little sympathy with the sectarian motives of any sort of private education, whether fundamentalist Protestant, confessional Protestant, or Catholic. In such a case Americanist loyalties disperse rather than reinforce convictions concerning the fixity or relatively of Christian teaching. And it is much the same for questions of the economy and military preparedness. Moral absolutists differ among themselves when they apply ethical standards, because they approach these issues with greatly different cultural baggage. Historicists differ among themselves when they read the signs of the times, because of the different lenses that American experience has provided them.

A different situation exists on the question of abortion where there is more potential for interreligious hostility now than for any other issue. Unlike the situation with education, Americanist factors do not cancel out theological divisions. In fact, public debate on the question usually unites the opposing forces more tightly among themselves. Pro-choice forces defend their position on the basis of the unique character of twentieth-century society: new medical capabilities, modern definitions of "the quality of life," contemporary conclusions about social, educational, economic, racial, and class realities. Pro-life forces may concede a great deal to these modern factors, but they continue to insist that the supreme reality must still be the sanctity of human life as defined by the church directly, by the church's interpretation of natural law, or by a traditional interpretation of scripture.

The national media, unfortunately, still tend to treat this matter as "a Catholic issue," after the fashion of nineteenth-century Bible reading in the schools. Actual research shows a more complex story. Americanist influences—like respect for individual rights or tendencies toward pragmatic resolution of differences—seem to exert a great influence on the majority of both Catholics and Protestants. Polling data are often contradictory, but it appears as if church attendance correlates better with strong opposition to abortion than does denominational affiliation. In some polls, Protestants identified as evangelicals express stronger opposition to liberal abortion laws than Catholics in general. Among Catholics, ethnic origin seems to affect attitudes on this subject a great deal. In general, polling shows that people with absolutist views in religion, whether Catholic or Protestant, are more likely to oppose abortion than those who do not have them, again whether Catholic or Protestant.[48]

Whether these affinites will lead to a mobilization of Old Catholics, Old Protestants, and their allies that succeeds in changing the laws or their administration is not clear.[49] Nor is it possible to say whether New Protestants, New Catholics, and their allies could successfully combine to roll back such a triumph. Clearly, however, this issue contains the potential for great interreligious hostility—Catholics acting combatively on the basis of Catholic beliefs, Protestants acting combatively on the basis of their beliefs—even if the crucial line of division now runs among rather than between the Catholic and Protestant communities.

VI

A final source of Catholic-Protestant tension over the last quarter century has been confrontation between Old Protestants and Old Catholics.[50] This tension has neither the potential for public hostility as the debate over abortion nor the attraction for the media involved with many Americanist issues, but it is still an interesting phenomenon and the most distinctly theological discussion between Catholics and Protestants in recent years. This interchange is a far cry from the atavistic hostilities left over from the nineteenth century, for those who engage in it are largely free of the unreflective bigotries of the past. Rather, tension continues to exist because some take seriously the fixed character of religious truth and do not quail before the realization that other Christians construe that truth differently than themselves.

This kind of interaction has been related to the recent Protestantizing of Old Catholics and the Catholicizing of Old Protestants. The Second Vatican Council encouraged both a concentration upon scripture and a concern for collegiality that were more nearly Protestant than any major actions of the church since the Reformation.[51] For their part, a considerable number of Old Protestants have been busy refurbishing confessional heritages and mining more assiduously the resources of the Christian past. Still other more strictly Americanist Protestants are even in the process of rethinking the limits of inherited professions to be following "no creed but the Bible."[52]

The context for Old Catholic—Old Protestant discussions is much more relaxed than previously, not only because of the Council but also because of shared Americanist loyalties. Old Christians of noncapitalistic inclination cooperate across the Catholic-Protestant boundary in journals like the *New Oxford Review* or *Sojourners*, as do those of a culturally conservative tendency on ventures like the Center for Christian Studies and its *Center Journal*.[53] The initiative of the Bishops' Ecumenical Commission has already been mentioned as a major stimulus toward face-to-face meetings between Old Catholics and Old Protestants.

The recently published Lutheran—Roman Catholic statement on justification by faith illustrates the potential and remaining problems for this Protestant-Catholic relationship. After working together for nearly six years, the team of twelve Lutherans and nine Catholics concluded that members of their communions could agree on the substance of the doctrine, that "it is not through our own initiative that we respond [to the call of the gospel], but only through an undeserved gift which is granted and made known in faith, and which comes to fruition in our love of God and neighbor, as we are led by the Spirit in faith to bear witness to the divine gift in all aspects of our lives." The committee acknowledged that the passage of time, especially involving "developments in the study of Scripture," had made it easier to reach this accord.[54] But they did not subscribe to the historicist assumption that altered circumstances alter the faith, only that altered circumstances might clarify the faith once delivered.

The most intriguing part of the report, however, may be its isolation of matters that still divide Lutherans and Catholics. The committee acknowledged these to include "the papacy and magisterial infallibility," "official teachings on Mary and the cult of the saints," and "disagreements about structures of thought in relation to the proclamation of the gospel."[55] These disagreements will probably not be sources of hostility in the future, but they are continuing points of theological friction dividing Catholics and Protestants who retain the goal of approaching a single faith for Christians in all times and places.

Less formal discussions have also echoed the concerns of the Lutheran-Catholic dialogues. Considerable debate now occurs among evangelical Protestants, and between evangelicals and Catholics, on the traditional theological disagreements of the sixteenth century. The trend is clearly toward a franker and less judgmental assessment of these issues, but not necessarily toward a closer unity. Old Catholics have the example of their pope who, when commenting positively on the ecumenical implications of the Council's documents, still warned against "that false irenicism which gives the impression that practically nothing divides us."[56] American evangelicals number several spokesmen who are as charitable, but also as cautious, as John Paul II. David Wells, a theologian at Gordon-Conwell Seminary, is one of these who recently expressed his concern in a comment on efforts by an evangelical (Clark Pinnock) and a Catholic (Avery Dulles) to define a procedure in theology that took the best from both traditions. To Wells the goal was praiseworthy, but the theological sacrifices were too great: "The structure and function of authority in Pinnock's though and in Dulles' are as different as night and day. Pinnock believes in an authoritative Scripture that exclusively contains God's special revelation; Dulles does not. Dulles believes in the unfolding of revelation with the people of God; Pinnock does not. Pinnock and Dulles both want something that is authoritative and in this both are anti-liberal. And both employ tradition to secure the proper functioning of this authority. They do it so differently, however, that it would be true to say that in this Pinnock is not catholic. And on the matter of revelation, Dulles is not evangelical."[57] Cautious strictures of this sort from either Catholics or Protestants will not grab headlines in the public media nor receive more than passing interest in the religious press. They are, nonetheless, the concerns that may have the greatest ultimate significance for those Catholics and Protestants who, while recognizing the shaping force of American experience and twentieth-century culture, still give highest allegience to the ideal of an eternal Body of Christ.

Religious hostility involving Catholics and Protestants now looks very different than it did immediately after World War II. For one thing, interreligious antagonism is far less respectable than has ever been the case in the history of the United States. All who follow or respect "the Prince of Peace" should be deeply grateful for this development. At the same time, sources of friction have by no means passed away. Lines of demarcation within the communions have become every bit as important as traditional sectarian antagonisms. Alliances across the Catholic-

Protestant divide testify to the altered circumstances, but also to the continued potential for tension. Those whose faith is in "the stone of stumbling" and who have taken up "the offense of the cross" should not be surprised at the continuation of religious hostility. But they, and commentators on American public life, will serve themselves and future generations better by discriminating more clearly among the kinds of strife that pass under the banner of Catholic-Protestant hostility and by looking more closely into the tangled civil and religious roots of those hostilities that remain.

Notes

1. Ray Allen Billington, *The Protestant Crusade, 1800–1860* (New York: Macmillan, 1938); John J. Kane, *Catholic-Protestant Conflicts in America* (Chicago: Regnery, 1955). Also helpful is James H. Smylie, "Phases in Protestant Anti-Roman Catholic Relations in the United States: Monologue, Debate, and Dialogue," *Religion in Life* 34 (Spring 1965) 258–69.

2. Andrew Greeley, *The Denominational Society* (Glenview, IL: Scott, Foresman, 1972) 206.

3. Quoted in James Morris, *The Preachers* (New York: St. Martins, 1973) 199.

4. Wilheim Pauck, "The Roman Catholic Critique of Protestantism," in *The Heritage of the Reformation* (New York: Oxford, 1968) 231, originally published in *Theology Today*, 1948.

5. Quotation from "Controversies Aroused in U.S. by Taylor Mission to Vatican," *U.S. News and World Report*, 28 June 1946, 21.

6. John B. Sheerin, C.S.P., "American Catholics and Ecumenism," in *Contemporary Catholicism in the United States*, ed. Philip Gleason (Notre Dame, IN: University of Notre Dame Press, 1969) 75.

7. Jaroslav Pelikan, *The Riddle of Roman Catholicism* (New York: Abingdon, 1959) 12, 176, 189, 219, 201.

8. Louis Bouyer, *The Spirit and Forms of Protestantism*, trans. A. V. Littledale (Westminster, MD: Newman, 1956) 223.

9. The historical background is well illustrated in John Tracy Ellis, ed., *Documents of American Catholic History* (2d ed., Milwaukee: Bruce, 1962); and well told in James Hennesey, S.J., *American Catholics: A History of the Roman Catholic Community in the United States* (New York: Oxford, 1981).

10. Theodore C. Sorensen, *Kennedy* (New York: Harper & Row, 1965) 188–95, 357–65; Marshall Frady, *Billy Graham: A Parable of American Righteousness* (Boston: Little, Brown, 1979) 446.

11. James Giglio, "JFK: From Camelot to the 1980s," *OAH* [Organization of American Historians] *Newsletter*, February 1984, 23–24.

12. Sheerin, "American Catholics and Ecumenism," in *Contemporary Catholicism*, ed. Gleason, pp. 75–78.

13. The first six "Dialogues" were published by Augsburg Press in Minneapolis: *The Status of the Nicene Creed as Dogma of the Church* (1965), *One Baptism for the Remission of Sins* (1966), *The Eucharist as Sacrifice* (1967), *Eucharist and Ministry* (1970), *Papal Primacy and the Universal Church* (1974), and *Teaching Authority and Infallibility in the Church* (1980). The most recent on justification is discussed below at note 54.

14. "Faith and Order U.S.A.," pamphlet from the National Council of the Churches of Christ in the U.S.A. (n.d.).

15. In 1978, James Gustafson wrote that Catholic-Protestant exchange followed patterns of social and theological commitment, with radicals talking to radicals and moderates talking to moderates. He also said that "the most conservative Catholic and Protestant theologians do not relate to each other at all." Recent events have verified the correctness of Gustafson's remarks for radicals and moderates, but also show that a great deal of interchange takes place among conservatives. See below at note 53. James M. Gustafson, *Protestant and Roman Catholic Ethics: Prospects for Rapprochement* (Chicago: University of Chicago Press, 1978) 30.

16. For a brief survey of the results that the charismatic movement has had on Catholic-Protestant connections, see Donald Bloesch, *The Future of Evangelical Christianity: A Call for Unity Amid Diversity* (New York: Doubleday, 1983) 38–42.

17. An indication of the speed with which Catholic-Protestant relationships have changed comes in a review of Boudreau's book by the evangelical Anglican J.I. Packer, writing in the evangelical monthly *Eternity* (December 1983, p. 92): "If when I was a student you had told me that before old age struck I should be reviewing a popular Roman Catholic book on the new birth which used Campus Crusade material, carried an official *nihil obstat* and *imprimatur*, and was already in its fourth printing, I doubt whether I would have believed you. But that is what I am doing now. Again, if at that time you had predicted that one day an Anglican bishop would tell me how the last Roman Catholic priest to whom he talked quizzed him hard as to whether Anglicans really preached the new birth as they should, I would probably have laughed in your face. But this month it happened. Things are not as they were!"

18. For background, see Nathan O. Hatch and Mark A. Noll, eds., *The Bible in America* (New York: Oxford, 1982) 4, 8, 16 n.36, 17 n.43, and 165–66.

19. Ernest W. Saunders, *Searching the Scriptures: A History of the Society of Biblical Literature, 1880–1980* (Chico, CA: Scholars Press, 1982) 84.

20. As reported in *Presbyterian Journal*, 6 July 1983, p. 3.

21. Frady, *Billy Graham*, pp. 326, 441–46; John Pollack, *Billy Graham: The Authorized Biography* (New York: McGraw-Hill, 1966) 218–20; Pollock, *Billy Graham: Evangelist to the World* (San Francisco: Harper & Row, 1979) 129–30, 290–91, 307–10; Richard V. Pierard, "From Evangelical Exclusivism to Ecumenical Openness: Billy Graham and Sociopolitical Issues," *Journal of Ecumenical Studies* 20 (1983) 428.

22. Survey conducted by Cy Hulse, "Luther's Changing Image Among Catho-

lics," prepared for a course at Trinity Evangelical Divinity School, ca. 1978. This fine paper is also the source for the quotations below.

23. "Should We Speak or Hold Our Tongue?" *The Priest* 12 (February 1956) 134.

24. Perplexus (pseud.), "The Charm of Melody," *The Priest* 21 (July 1965) 585.

25. For a good review of this discussion, see Avery Dulles, S.J., "The Catholicity of the Augsburg Confession," *The Journal of Religion* 63 (October 1983) 337–54.

26. For full coverage, with text, of the pope's sermon, *New York Times*, 12 December 1983, pp. 1, 4.

27. James Atkinson, *Martin Luther: Prophet to the Catholic Church* (Grand Rapids: Eerdmans, 1983); Mark Edwards and George H. Tavard, *Luther: A Reformer for the Churches* (Ramsey, NJ: Paulist Press, 1983).

28. Pelikan, *Riddle of Roman Catholicism*, p. 219. Kenneth L. Woodward, "Luther in Excelsis," *Notre Dame Magazine*, October 1983, pp. 11–15. Similar attitudes prevailed in Protestant circles at the 800th anniversary of the birth of St. Francis. See, as examples, the appreciative essays in *Sojourners*, December 1981, pp. 3–5, 13–22.

29. Richard P. McBrien, "Roman Catholicism: *E Pluribus Unum*," in *Religion and America: Spirituality in a Secular Age*, ed. Mary Douglas and Steven M. Tipton (Boston: Beacon, 1983) 181.

30. Andrew M. Greeley, *The American Catholic: A Social Portrait* (New York: Basic Books, 1977) 252.

31. Andrew M. Greeley, *An Ugly Little Secret: Anti-Catholicism in North America* (Kansas City: Sheed Andrews & McMeel, 1977).

32. Gary Metz, "Jack Chick's Anti-Catholic *Alberto* Comic Book Is Exposed as a Fraud," *Christianity Today*, 13 March 1981, pp. 50–52. "Bookseller's Group May Expel Chick," *Christianity Today*, 23 October 1981, p. 62.

33. B. A. Gerrish, *The Old Protestantism and the New* (Chicago: University of Chicago Press, 1982) 265, 266.

34. Bernard J. F. Lonergan, S.J., "The Transition from a Classicist World-View to Historical-Mindedness," and "Theology in Its New Context," in *A Second Collection*, ed. William F. J. Ryan, S.J. and Bernard J. Tyrrell, S.J. (Philadelphia: Westminster, 1974) 2, 59, 61.

35. Gerrish, *The Old Protestantism and the New*, p. 267. In discussing recent Catholic social theory, Peter Hebblethwaite phrases this another way by speaking of "the conviction, or the presumption, that something of universal validity can actually be said": Hebblethwaite, "The Popes and Politics: Shifting Patterns in 'Catholic Social Doctrine,'" in *Religion and America*, ed. Douglas and Tipton, p. 201.

36. Paul Ricoeur, *The Symbolism of Evil* (New York: Harper & Row, 1967).

37. An objection at this point could be raised by either Catholics or Protestants who feel that the history of the United States has in fact resulted in the complete fulfillment of some Catholic or Protestant value. In such a case, it would be im-

possible in principle for Christian and Americanist values to diverge. This is a serious objection, but I have nonetheless written the paper under the assumption that such an identity is in principle not possible. Reasons for my assumption are set out in Mark A. Noll, George M. Marsden, and Nathan O. Hatch, *The Search for Christian America* (Westchester, IL: Crossway Books, 1983), especially chaps. 1 and 2.

38. Gerrish, *The Old Protestantism and the New*, pp. 264–67.

39. Sidney E. Mead, "The 'Nation with the Soul of a Church,'" and Martin E. Marty, "Two Kinds of Two Kinds of Civil Religion," in *American Civil Religion*, ed. Russell E. Richey and Donald G. Jones (New York: Harper & Row, 1974) 60, 151. I avoid the phrase "civil religion" here, since in the usage of Robert N. Bellah, whose work has been the center for discussion of this concept, a "civil religion" embodies moral and religious values that transcend the merely parochial or nationalistic values of any one nation. See Bellah, "Civil Religion in Ameria," *Daedalus*, Winter 1967, as reprinted in *American Civil Religion*, ed. Richey and Jones, and *The Broken Covenant: American Civil Religion in Time of Trial* (New York: Seabury, 1975), especially p. ix, where Bellah spells out clearly the potentially supranational character of "civil religion."

40. In this paragraph and what follows, I assume that "religion" involves an idea of God, and that it is not just a "symbol system" establishing "moods and motivations" for ordering existence as described by Clifford Geertz, "Religion as a Cultural System," in *The Interpretation of Cultures* (New York: Basic Books, 1973).

41. For a general discussion of this Manichaean tendency, see C. Vann Woodward, "The Fall of the American Adam: Myths of Innocence and Guilt," *The New Republic*, 2 December 1981, pp. 13–16; and for specifically religious interpretations of American history, Nathan Hatch, "The Search for a Worthy Past," in *The Search for Christian America*, pp. 107–24.

42. The unsigned editorial in the *New York Times* concerning the bishops' letter was exemplary in keeping its discussion of policy implications unencumbered by extraneous religious confusions: "Bishops and the Bomb," 6 May 1983, p. A30. It had been a different story several years earlier when the *Times* editorialized on the encyclical *Humanae Vitae*, at which time moralistic quasireligious ejaculations and pragmatic policy evaluations mingled with little discrimination: "'Of Human Life,'" *New York Times*, 30 July 1968, p. 38.

43. Bruce Buursma, "Archbishop's Opinions Echo Across Nation," *Chicago Tribune*, 12 February 1984, sect. 4, p. 1.

44. James Reston, "'Render Unto Reagan,'" *New York Times*, 4 May 1983, p. I, 27.

45. A particularly interesting case of historical revision and contemporary reflection interacting with each other on this subject concerns the changing reputation of the nineteenth-century founder of the Paulists, Isaac Hecker. Interest in Hecker earlier in this century concentrated on a debate whether or not he really advocated the "Americanist" positions which Pope Leo XIII condemned in *Testem Benevolentiae* (1899). In the wake of the Council, however, a number of

scholars have been working, both as historians and participants in modern discussions, to see if Hecker was both a thoroughly American and a thoroughly Catholic member of the church. See the perceptive discussions in John Farina, ed., *Hecker Studies: Essays on the Thought of Isaac Hecker* (Ramsey, NJ: Paulist Press, 1983), especially William L. Portier, "Isaac Hecker and *Testem Benevolentiae*: A Study in Theological Pluralism."

46. This question is raised in a sensitive way by Christopher Derrick, "Michael Novak's Neoliberal Catholicism," *New Oxford Review*, December 1983, pp. 17–19.

47. Langdon Gilkey, *Catholicism Confronts Modernity: A Protestant View* (New York: Seabury, 1975) 5, 12.

48. Greeley, *American Catholic*, pp. 245–58; The Gallup Organization and Christianity Today, *Evangelical Christianity in the United States: National Parallel Surveys of General Public and Clergy* (Princeton: Princeton Gallup Organization and Princeton Religion Research Center, 1979) 55, 160–61, and 228; *Religion in America* (Princeton: Princeton Religious Research Center, 1982) 161; David A. Roozen, *The Churched and the Unchurched in America* (Washington, DC: Glenmary Research Center, 1978) 42; Corwin Smidt and James M. Penning, "Religious Commitment, Political Conservatives, and Political and Social Tolerance in the United States: A Longitudinal Analysis," *Sociological Analysis* 43 (Fall 1982) 231–45.

49. The conservative evangelical publicist Franky Schaeffer calls for such a coalition with specific reference to the need to combat abortion in *Bad News for Modern Man* (Westchester, IL: Crossway Books, 1984).

50. Disagreements between New Catholics and New Protestants seem to lie in the area of pragmatic negotiation rather than principled opposition, and so are omitted from discussion in this paper.

51. Cf. Jaroslav Pelikan's comment that the Council's "Constitution on the Sacred Liturgy" was "bound to evoke the enthusiastic approval of anyone who believes that the Reformation was the work of the Holy Spirit": *The Documents of Vatican II: With Notes and Comments by Catholic, Protestant, and Orthodox Authorities*, ed. Walter M. Abbot, S.J. (New York: Guild Press, 1966) 180.

52. As examples of this Old Protestant literature, see M. Eugene Osterhaven, *The Faith of the Church: A Reformed Perspective on Its Historical Development* (Grand Rapids: Eerdmans, 1982); Robert E. Webber, *Common Roots: A Call to Evangelical Maturity* (Grand Rapids: Zondervan, 1978); Donald G. Bloesch and Robert Webber, eds., *The Orthodox Evangelicals* (Nashville: Thomas Nelson, 1978).

53. The winter 1983 number of *Center Journal*, for example, listed on its masthead as "editorial consultants" ten Catholics and sixteen Protestants. The Protestants were about evenly divided between those from evangelical institutions and from older confessional ones.

54. "U.S. Lutheran–Roman Catholic Dialogue: Justification by Faith," *Origins: NC Documentary Service*, 6 October 1983, p. 298 (par. 161), p. 293 (par. 122).

55. Ibid., p. 293 (par. 119), p. 297 (par. 154).

56. Karol Wojtyla (John Paul II), *Sources of Renewal: The Implementation of Vatican II* (San Francisco: Harper & Row, 1980; orig. 1972) 323.

57. The entire discussion was an illuminating one for these concerns: Clark H. Pinnock, "How I Use Tradition in Doing Theology," *TSF* [Theological Students Fellowship of InterVarsity Christian Fellowship] *Bulletin* 6 (September-October 1982) 2–5; Avery Dulles, S.J., "Tradition and Theology: A Roman Catholic Response to Clark Pinnock," ibid., 6 (January-February 1983) 6-8; David F. Wells, "The Role of Tradition for Pinnock and Dulles: A Response," ibid., 6 (May-June 1983) 5–6 with quotation p. 6. Wells's *Revolution in Rome* (Downers Grove, IL: InterVarsity Press, 1972), expressed the same sort of evaluation concerning the Council, which for Wells showed too many tendencies toward "New" principles and too much determination to hold onto the wrong kind of "Old" ones.

III

LIBERAL-CONSERVATIVE TENSIONS

A resurgence of conservative, even extreme religious thought and behavior has occurred within almost every religious community in recent years. Secular Jews are shocked to find their college-educated children studying Talmud at ultra-Orthodox yeshivot[1] at the same time that evangelical churches seem to represent the wave of future Protestantism. Many liberals, who once took leadership roles for granted, now find themselves a minority, if not altogether unwelcome within their own denominations. The rise of the Ayatollah Khomeini in Iran suggests that this may not be an exclusively American phenomenon.

Internal tensions may have become prominent only recently, but they are hardly new. It is worth remembering that the colony of Rhode Island was founded 350 years ago after Puritan Roger Williams was forced to flee Massachusetts when his efforts to keep the church free from the taint of secular society brought him into conflict with the Puritan theocracy.

Although the tensions within separate communities are inevitably different from one another, comparison of their dynamics demonstrates that along with their idiosyncrasies they have much in common. For although expressed in language appropriate to the communities within which they occur, the issues that underlie these debates are very much the same. Among evangelicals, for example, creationism has become a source of conflict particularly as a result of that community's commitment to biblical inerrancy. Orthodox Jews, on the other hand, must determine whether one can participate in the larger society and still remain Orthodox, a formulation that recalls the older controversy of whether Reform Jews' willingness to compromise with modernity had resulted in the loss of their Jewishness. Meanwhile, even Roman Catholicism, long regarded as monolithic by those outside it, embraces a variety of competing views, reflecting fundamental differences as to the nature and proper role of the church.

Must one choose between evolution and the Bible, or can the findings of modern science be incorporated into classical religious systems? Does American culture pose a lethal threat or offer boundless opportunities? Is the church a refuge from a difficult world or the root of a new society? By examining these questions—or, perhaps, they are different facets of the same question—we can identify a theme that seems to be a function of modernity itself: What is religion's relationship to society and what is the religious community's proper role within it? Many religious communities find themselves divided over how to handle such issues, suggesting again that religious hostility is often but the external expression of far deeper tensions.

Notes

1. Cf. Joseph Berger, "Children Embrace Ancient Faiths," *New York Times*, 3 April 1985, pp. 15–16.

6

Orthodox Jews:
An Open or a Closed Group?

SAMUEL C. HEILMAN

> With us Jews the individual doesn't
> exist; it's the community that counts.
> —*Chaim Grade*

Survival Versus Integration?

Since the late eighteenth century and particularly after the Congress of Vienna, Western societies began to open themselves to Jewish participation. After generations of life during which Jews by and large lived in separate and isolated communities, they were gradually transformed from barely tolerated individuals and communities into full-fledged citizens. The process was variously called Jewish naturalization, reform, civic betterment, amalgamation, assimilation, or emancipation. Among the specific changes this process required were changes in education, appearance, and the right to mobility. The state often demanded that Jewish communities establish schools for their civic education; where this was not feasible, Christian schools were obliged to take in Jewish pupils. Furthermore, after emancipation, the distinctive dress that Jews had often been required to wear in public could now be discarded. The body tax Jews had to pay on going from one place to another was abolished. A Jew would be permitted to learn handicrafts and encouraged to open factories. Jews were free to seek apprenticeships with Christian masters if they could find masters willing to take them on. In general, the parochial community found exits into the outside host society.[1]

This paper is based upon research carried on with Steven M. Cohen and written with his assistance.

To be sure, these developments in the life of the Jews were achieved more as a result of a general public sentiment in the countries of the West in favor of equality for all people than by the victory of those who championed the case of the Jews. It was simply the case that where a "transformation from a semifeudal to a constitutional state was achieved, there Jewish emancipation, too, became a legally secured fact."[2] Yet whatever the reasons, the result has been, as Joseph Blau has put it, that "These last two hundred years might be described as the time in which the Jews have come out of the ghetto and into the world."[3]

This coming out, while providing many Jews with great material, social, and political benefits, also brought home to them new cultural realities. "As soon as the Jewish people realized that its road was not a by-path removed from the beaten track of world history but belonged and, what is more, had to belong to that history, the changes that took place in the Jewish pole coincided with those in the non-Jewish pole."[4] Along with changes in civil society and the host culture came parallel changes in Jewish life. As the world moved increasingly toward secularization and universalism as ideals, so too did many Jews. In the practice of Jewish life this often meant "omitting parts that seemed irreconcilable with the new position of Jews and introducing, or at least reemphasizing, tenets that seemed appropriate to the new situation."[5]

Jews faced a particular dilemma: How were they to enter society on an equal footing with others and yet still preserve some aspects of their group ties and cultural differentiation? The dilemma was sharpened by many European thinkers and policymakers who made the dissolution of Jewish group ties an explicit condition of admission into the larger society. Others, perhaps more tactful or tolerant, supposed that admission of Jews as full participants in the larger society would promote the eventual disappearance of many, if not all, aspects of Jewish group distinctiveness—in particular those elements most alien to Western (European or American) culture. And thus the Jew had to decide if he should succumb to the temptation of acculturation, if it involved accepting Christianity or some secularized variation of it, or if he should remain a member of a socially inferior minority.

Several Jewish ideologies or worldviews arose in response to this new challenge which, in effect, appeared to offer acceptance in return for assimilation. One path followed acceptance and led to great waves of people who sought emancipation by liberating themselves from their Jewish identity, which they found to be "too narrow, too archaic, and too constricting."[6] They believed, as one man put it, "that it is better to be a Christian professor in St. Petersburg than to be a Jewish *melamed* in the shtetl."[7]

Another path of Jewish response moved in the direction of rejection, eschewing assimilation. One group traveling this path was the classical Zionists, who maintained that Jewish continuity was indeed threatened both physically and spiritually in the Diaspora (lands outside of Israel), and only the removal of the essential bulk of Jews from "foreign" countries to an independent Jewish homeland in Palestine could assure Jewish survival in the face of the twin threats of virulent anti-Semitism and advancing assimilation.

Others, and more central to our discussion here, were those Orthodox Jews who rejected some of the cultural demands and social consequences of emancipation and argued that isolation was necessary for Jewish survival. "To perpetuate ourselves in spite of the tremendous forces making for the disintegration of the Jewish type," ran one such argument, "we need the consolidating, strengthening, vitalizing influence of the Jewish environment."[8] Simply put, these people claimed that "a Jew is a Jew when he is with other Jews," because assimilation meant "the suicidal extinction of Jewish being."[9]

According to those who followed this path, not only did Jews as a people have to be segregated, but so too—some of the rejectionists suggested —did Judaism. They rejected the concept of a "Judeo-Christian culture," of a continuity between what they considered to be polar opposites, and argued instead—in the words of a contemporary version of this position —that "to view Judaism within a foreign context is to strip Judaism of its vital force, if not completely to castrate it."[10]

In America, these isolationists tended, as much as possible, to keep themselves separate from the surrounding culture. They established many of their own institutions and neighborhoods; they often spoke among themselves in Yiddish rather than in the English vernacular. And when they built their academies of higher Jewish learning, their yeshivas, they made "a deliberate attempt to isolate their students from American life."[11] It was, for example, no accident that the Lakewood Yeshiva, perhaps the preeminent such institution in America, was located in a rural New Jersey town far from any indigenous Jewish community. The basic premise among the isolationists thus remained that "if the Jewish community is to survive, it must become more explicit and conscious about the incompatibility of integration and survival," and that in order to perpetuate itself in America it must "reject the value of integration."[12]

Between these extremes were those who rejected the validity of a forced choice between group survival or integration into the larger society. Although more conservative in their approach than others who embraced the contemporary surrounding culture and society, modern Orthodox Jews represented this trend. Modern Orthodoxy's principal social thinkers (primarily rabbis in nineteenth-century Europe and twentieth-century United States) argued in favor of a principle that became known as "*Torah im derech erets.*" This ideology did "not look upon the mingling of Judaism with European [read: non-Jewish] culture as a deplorable and unalterable condition."[13]

The modern Orthodox very simply took an optimistic view of the survival-versus-integration dilemma and argued that they should get out of the ghetto. "But we should get out as Jews, with our own spiritual treasures."[14] In their relative unwillingness to admit that they were making changes or compromises with the modern world, even the most modern among the Orthodox, however, differed from proponents of other Jewish worldviews—primarily those which became known as Reform and Conservative—that were also optimistic about the feasibility of reconciling the twin impulses to survive as a group and integrate into society. Indeed still today, even the modernists among the Orthodox often argue that contemporary Reform and Conservative Jews have broken from the authentic Jewish tradition by granting contemporary, secular culture equal legitimacy and authority with sacred Jewish law. In principle, the modern Orthodox from the beginning have believed, as one of their great nineteenth-century ideologues, the German Rabbi Samson Raphael Hirsch, put it, "that were our Torah to demand that we abstain from everything going under the name of civilization and enlightenment, then, without vacillation should we honor this demand since our Torah is our faith."[15] (Of course, few among the mainstream of the modern Orthodox believed things would ever have to come to that; they remain convinced instead that they can be in and of the modern world without sacrificing their rootedness and attachments to Orthodox Jewish life and its strict demands.)

Not only have the non-Orthodox perpetrated what their Orthodox counterparts consider heretical (or, at best, overly compromising) approaches to Jewish survival in the modern world, they have also courted the danger of assimilation by failing to preserve those aspects of the tradition the modern Orthodox see as necessary not only for authenticity and legitimacy, but for the maintenance of social borders between themselves and others as well. In fact, the mainstream modern Orthodox have for a long time hung between their Orthodox counterparts on their traditionalist right and their non- or nominally Orthodox coreligionists on their modernist left. They have seen the former as too insular, and hence too ready to surrender the shaping of modern Judaism to those with less than adequate commitments to the true religious heritage. And they have seen the latter as, at best, well-intentioned, but also misguided, heretical, and inadequately committed to Jewish authenticity and distinctive group survival in the modern, open society.

The two alternative polar approaches to the survival/integration dilemma—one demanding near-total self-segregation; the other allowing for complete integration—have exerted competing influences upon American modern Orthodoxy. Both the community and individuals have resolved the dilemma differently over the years.

In the late 1950s, the 1960s, and even into the early 1970s, for example, many modern Orthodox rabbis, institutions, and thinkers advocated an open approach tolerant of Jewish pluralism that at the same time allowed those Orthodox who wished to to make their way into contemporary American society. This laissez-faire attitude encouraged a kind of Jewish cultural pluralism and discouraged sectarian divisions. Some rabbis who took this point of view cautioned their followers not to accuse their non-Orthodox counterparts of "heresy." Said one such rabbi: "The use of [such] epithets and the leveling of sanctions [against the non-Orthodox] are counter-productive." And he added, "such words and actions are tantamount to an admission of intolerant mindlessness at worst and religious insecurity at best."[16]

Thus, modern Orthodox rabbis frequently joined their Reform and Conservative counterparts in such interdenominational bodies as the Synagogue Council of America and local boards of rabbis. Several modern Orthodox day schools that emphasized high achievement in secular studies along with commitment to religious studies gained prominence in modern Orthodox circles. And many modern Orthodox made their way into walks of life that had heretofore been considered beyond the pale of their existence.

At the same time, the modern Orthodox also retained links and a concomitant rapport with traditionalists on their right wing. Sir Immanuel Jakobovits, chief rabbi of the United Kingdom and for many years spiritual leader at the modern Orthodox Fifth Avenue Synagogue in New York, explained the connection as follows: "The perimeters of both circles [the modern and the traditionalist Orthodox] intersect to provide a considerable area of common agreement and joint endeavor, ideologically as well as organizationally."[17] Indeed, the Orthodox modernists sought not only a modus vivendi with their traditionalist counterparts, but also "a recognition that both schools of thought may be needed, together with the rivalries between them, to maintain the momentum of Orthodox ascendancy."[18]

By the late 1970s, however, that "momentum" had resulted in a change in the posture of modern Orthodox officialdom and laity. Cooperation between modern and non-Orthodox waned. In the face of the chaotic 1960s, some Orthodox rabbis and their congregants began to argue against openness. In the words of one: "Tolerance, acceptance, and the opportunity to join as equals in an alien society have proven to be dangerous and debilitating, eroding Jewish observance and destroying Jewish identity as time passes."[19] Openness seemed to offer less in the way of advantages and threaten more in the way of erosion. By the mid-1970s, the period of the liberal swing in Orthodoxy seemed to be coming to an end.

Several theories have been advanced for this shift, real or apparent, to a more insular or segregationist stance. Some have argued that it was a part of the general "resurgence of ethnic consciousness of the early 1970's . . . [which] helped to give [traditionalist] Orthodox Judaism a certain legitimacy, an aura of glamour and authenticity lacking in other Jewish religious expressions which, by the emerging standards of the times, seemed to many to be hopelessly . . . bland."[20] Against the background of that notion, there seemed no point in making peace with those who would dilute the genuine Judaism (which the Orthodox always believed was in their safekeeping). The idea that the preservation of ethnicity could act as a barrier against alienation and anomie was easily translated by some Orthodox Jews into the argument that adherence to a strict, aggressively contra-acculturative and Jewishly observant life was a bulwark against the ills of alienation and anomie that were the legacy of the 1960s.

Another contributing factor, no doubt, was the institutional maturation and growing affluence of Orthodoxy. At one time, Orthodox Jews had few institutions whose success in America they could point to with pride. By the late seventies, many of those institutions, particularly those of the post–World-War-II era when a large immigration of Orthodoxy to America occurred, had a generation of success. In addition, the once substantially less-affluent Orthodox were now richer, and a generation of them was university educated like their Reform and Conservative Jewish counterparts. Using their newly acquired resources and ethnic pride, Orthodox Jews built large numbers of yeshivas, synagogues, *mikvehs* (ritual baths), and other highly visible institutions. These were tangible symbols of their success that simultaneously fostered a sense of self-sufficiency. The more affluent Orthodox community began to support thousands of full-time Talmud students, young men who would spend a few years of intensive study in yeshivas or *kollels*—postgraduate academies of higher Jewish learning. After their studies, these men returned to Orthodox communities as highly learned laymen as well as religious virtuosi and exercised a significant influence on the tenor of their congregations and communities. As a result of their exposure to traditionalist rabbinic instructors in an isolated setting, their views often tend to theological conservatism and social insularity.

Finally, and in some measure as a result of these developments, the Orthodox developed a self-image and reputation as being largely exempt from the demographic problems commonly thought to endanger the survival of non-Orthodox Jews. With regard to intermarriage, divorce, birthrates, and assimilation, the Orthodox appeared to themselves and others as far more vital and secure. That made them look to others and to themselves like havens from the storm of modernity. The fact that visible numbers of nonobservant Jews were choosing to "return" to the Orthodox way of life only served to reinforce these feelings of triumphalism.[21] Thus, insularity and separation once again seemed to grow and create boundaries not only between Jew and gentile, but also between the Orthodox and other Jews as well.

Boundaries

But what is the nature of these boundaries? Where are they drawn and how sharply defined are they? In our analysis below we try to assess the extent to which Orthodoxy today is associated with insularity and segregation or with openness and tolerance. A previous paper has demonstrated that three broad subgroups can be distinguished among American Orthodox on the basis of ritual practice.[22] Those who are most punctilious in their observance we call the "traditionalists." Those who observe a minimum of observances (although more than the general Jewish population) but who still call themselves "Orthodox" we call "nominally Orthodox." Finally, those between these two extremes, who make up the bulk of the population of American Orthodox Jews, we call the "centrists." It is this last group, those in the center of Orthodoxy, upon whom we focus most of all in hopes that through them the lines of fracture in the social existence of Orthodox Jews can more clearly be seen. We seek to understand the tensions they experience in connection with their participation in a community set apart to some extent from both the larger American society of Jews and gentiles and from the insular traditionalist Orthodox community. By comparing them with their counterparts to their right and to the left, we can learn, if only by inference, about the competing attractions that pull at them.

Our analysis will revolve around three kinds of orientation toward a reference group: the cognitive, the affective, and the behavioral. In common parlance, these correspond to three broad questions: What do I think of and how do I perceive the group? How do I feel toward the group? What do I do (or think should be done) with, to, or for the group?

Applying this taxonomy to a stratified sample of approximately eleven hundred persons, three-quarters of whom identified themselves as Orthodox and the rest of whom constituted a non-Orthodox control group of Jews, we expect that more traditionally observant Orthodox should think of themselves as more similar to Orthodox Jews, that they should feel closer to them, and that they should be more actively involved in the Orthodox formal and informal community. Similarly, those who are only nominal in their Orthodoxy might be expected to have an opposite reaction; while those in the center would, as a group, be divided on these matters.

We also look at the rhetoric surrounding issues of parochialism and cosmopolitanism. The more modern Orthodox have argued that involvement both in the Orthodox community and in the larger society are theoretically reconcilable, that there is such a creature as a "cosmopolitan parochial," someone who can live in the local parish or particular community but still be a cultural citizen of a far more encompassing reality. In contrast, as already noted, traditionalists have suggested that integration would inevitably promote assimilation and the concomitant erosion of group survival, rhetorically describing emancipation as a mistake because it led the Jews to renounce their special status as eternal strangers and to secularize and thus undermine their lives as Jews. Thus, we want to see if rhetoric coincides with reality.

Rhetoric and Reality:
Intergroup Friendship as a First Testing Ground

Although there are undoubtedly several ways to assess the extent and nature of identification, commitment, and involvement with the Orthodox community as against non-Orthodox Jewish and non-Jewish alternatives, one of the most crucial areas is that of friendship relations.

Modern Jewish rhetoric declares that Orthodox Jews can be friends with any non-Orthodox, be they Jew or gentile.[23] Asking our respondents whether they agree with this sentiment (see table 1), we found that large majorities of Orthodox and non-Orthodox Jews agreed that: "An Orthodox Jew can be a close friend with Jews of all degrees of observance." At least three-quarters of the non-Orthodox (78 percent), nominally Orthodox (85 percent), and centrist Orthodox (88 percent) agreed or strongly agreed as did 70 percent of the traditionalists. But, much as we would anticipate, the two groups at the extremes—the non-Orthodox and the traditionalists—were least likely to support this optimistic view. Not only were relatively fewer of them ready to agree in any way with the statement, but they were substantially less likely to "agree

TABLE 1

FRIENDSHIP MEASURES BY ORTHODOXY

		ORTHODOXY			
	Response	Non-Orth.	Nom-inal	Cen-trist	Tradi-tional
An Orthodox Jew can be close friends with Jews of all degrees of observance.	Strongly Agree	33	39	41	24
	Agree	45	46	47	46
An Orthodox Jew can be close friends with non-Jews.	Strongly Agree	22	23	24	9
	Agree	43	50	46	35
How many of your close friends are Orthodox?	All	0	7	13	46
	Most	3	29	62	50
How many of your close friends are not Jewish?	None	27	26	46	67

Figures are given in percentages.

strongly." While roughly 40 percent of the nominally and centrist Orthodox strongly agreed they could be close friends with all types of Jews, no matter what their observance, only 33 percent of the non-Orthodox and a mere 24 percent of the traditionalists answered with such conviction.

To be sure, at least with regard to the traditionalists, people were responding on the basis of their experience. After all, 96 percent of these people admitted that all or most of their friends are Orthodox. What room was there then left in their lives for other friends? As for those who are only nominally Orthodox, their attitude is supported by their experience too; only a bit over a third of them claim that all or most of their friends are Orthodox.

In fact, the proportions who reported that "all" of their friends were Orthodox rises dramatically from 0 percent among the non-Orthodox to 7 percent among the nominally Orthodox, 13 percent among the centrists, and fully 46 percent among the traditionalists. Similarly, the proportions who reported having mostly ("all" or "most") Orthodox friends increases dramatically as we moved from the non-Orthodox left to the traditionalist right (i.e., 3, 36, 75, and 96 percent). In other words, speaking of the extremes, hardly any (3 percent) of our largely Conservative, non-Orthodox control group reported that most of their close friends were Orthodox; they contrast sharply with the traditionalists, almost all of whom had predominantly Orthodox friendship circles.

Among the Orthodox respondents, the centrists reveal perhaps the most interesting responses. Although 88 percent of them agreed in some way with the proposition about friendship, 75 percent admitted that all or most of their friends were Orthodox. One can only suggest that their attitude is more open than their reality. That, of course, is precisely why they are in the center. They are divided between an open attitude—a sense that they can be friends with any kind of Jew—and a closed reality—the fact that for the most part they are not close friends with non-Orthodox. The division between parochial and cosmopolitan—in this case as demonstrated in the split between attitude and reality—is the hallmark of these Jews. We shall see it again.

As for the non-Orthodox, their attitude and reality are also at odds. They say the idea of friendship is possible, but for the most part (nearly half of them) have no such friends, and only 3 percent claimed that most of their friends are Orthodox. The non-Orthodox are slightly less confident than the nominal and centrist Orthodox about the permeability of the Orthodox community. Undoubtedly, they too have fewer contacts with Orthodox Jews and are therefore likely to be holding on to ideas embedded in the popular impressions about the clannishness and insularity of the Orthodox. They can temper these feelings, however, with a certain open-mindedness either because they may have had contact with at lest the modernists among the Orthodox or because in general modern American culture ideologically holds on to the belief that integration and friendship is conceivable among all people. And thus they, more than the traditionalists on the other extreme, believe ties are possible.

Looking at these groups, then, one must conclude that rhetoric in most cases exceeds reality. Except for the traditionalists, who were insular and admitted it, and those marginally Orthodox who were in touch with groups beyond the one with which they are identified, more was claimed than was in fact the case.

We asked a similar question about the potential for friendship with non-Jews. Overall, somewhat fewer respondents in each category of Orthodoxy assented than did with respect to the previous question on friendship with nonobservant Jews. Except for the traditionalists, about two-thirds agreed or strongly agreed that "an Orthodox Jew can be close friends with non-Jews." However, only a minority (44 percent) of the traditionalists could uphold such a view. Moreover, when we examine only the "strongly agree" answers, the difference between the traditionalists (9 percent) and the other three groups (22, 23, and 24 percent) is even more striking.

Again when we examine the reality, we discover patterns similar to those seen earlier. The traditionalists' rhetoric corresponds to their reality. They claim and have few ties with non-Jews. (To be sure, even among the traditionalists in our sample, ties exist, even some close friendships, with outsiders. Whether these are the beginnings of a new network of ties, the residues of waning ones, or simply the signs of both modernity and Diaspora existence is, however, impossible to conclude from our data. Only the future will tell whether these figures change in one direction or the other.)

All the other groups, however, seem more optimistic than the reality would seem to warrant, asserting greater ties possible than what is in fact found. But at least with regard to non-Orthodox Jews, that should come as no surprise. At least since the period of emancipation, such Jews have assumed that the non-Jewish world would be as happy to accept them as they were to accept it—even when the reality denied this assumption.

It is the optimism of the Orthodox that seems a bit more surprising. They *know* they have relatively few close non-Jewish friends. After all, Orthodoxy—with its many restrictions on life style and adherence to rituals that as part of their deep structure imply and foster segregation from the rest of the world—would seem to militate against openness. Nevertheless, beyond the traditionalist fringe, a majority of the other Orthodox (70 percent for the centrists and 73 percent for the nominally Orthodox) agreed in some way with the proposition that an Orthodox Jew can be close friends with non-Jews. But the centrists stand out particularly because although they share the same open attitude as those to their modernist left (including the non-Orthodox), in fact nearly half of them have no close friends who are not Jewish. Again they turn out to be divided and ambivalent.

And why? One might argue that their modern attitude of cosmopolitanism, a product of their being neither remote from nor untouched by contemporary America, encourages cultural contact while the realities and restraints of their Orthodoxy, along with the separation it fosters in domicile, eating habits, and worldview, discourage the very same cultural contact. A bit of that is true for the nominally Orthodox who nevertheless suffer less segregation by virtue of their minimal Orthodox practice. So their rhetoric more closely approaches the reality. But even the nominally Orthodox still have practices and life styles that keep them, if not totally, at the very least partially insulated from those who are unlike them. Hence, only about a quarter of them claim that they have no close non-Jewish friends.

Identification with American Orthodoxy

What about identification with and a feeling of closeness to other Jews in general and other Orthodox Jews in particular? Will that show the same pattern of response? Will those in the middle (the mainstream and the nominally Orthodox) be divided in their sense of attachment and loyalties to other Orthodox as they were with regard to the non-Orthodox and non-Jewish? And will the two groups on the extremes—the traditionalists and the non-Orthodox—again be less equivocal?

Earlier we noted that the affective and cognitive dimensions are two important aspects of orientation to a reference group. That is, the extent to which people identify with a particular group can be understood partially by the extent to which they feel *close* to the group and to the extent to which they feel close to those outside the group. But not only do we want to know about affect (feelings), but also about cognition (images): To what extent do people feel *similar* to other members of their group, and to what extent do they feel they are like those outside the group? Obviously, this too will take us toward an answer to the question of whether Orthodox Jews are an open or a closed group.

We asked respondents to tell us how close they felt both toward most Orthodox Jews and toward most non-Orthodox Jews. In addition, we also asked them a second, parallel pair of questions on the extent to which they thought they were similar both to most Orthodox and to most non-Orthodox Jews. The responses (in table 2), although in some respects predictable, are interesting.

Louis Wirth once suggested: "The ghetto is not only a physical fact; it is also a state of mind," corresponding to "attitudes of social distance and of . . . group consciousness."[24] As we might well expect, proportions feeling "very close" toward most Orthodox Jews rise dramatically from the non-Orthodox through the three Orthodox groups. Only 9 percent of the non-Orthodox, 29 percent of the nominally Orthodox, 43 percent of the centrists, and almost three-quarters (73 percent) of the traditionalists felt "very close" toward other Orthodox Jews. That is, there appears to be a direct relationship between degree of Orthodoxy and affective ties.

Put simply, those who hold the most Orthodox beliefs, who are most stringent and punctilious in their observance, also admit to feeling closest to other Orthodox Jews (who, as we saw in the previous table, make up

TABLE 2

SELF-PERCEPTIONS OF CLOSENESS AND SIMILARITY TO ORTHODOX
AND NON-ORTHODOX JEWS BY ORTHODOXY

ORTHODOXY

	Response	Non-Orth.	Nom-inal	Cen-trist	Tradi-tional
How close do you feel toward most . . .					
Orthodox Jews?	Very Close	9 ⎱	29 ⎱	43 ⎱	73 ⎱
		⎰ 52	⎰ 88	⎰ 92	⎰ 99
	Somewhat Close	43 ⎰	59 ⎰	49 ⎰	26 ⎰
American Jews?	Very Close	24 ⎱	15 ⎱	12 ⎱	17 ⎱
		⎰ 75	⎰ 71	⎰ 59	⎰ 50
	Somewhat Close	51 ⎰	56 ⎰	47 ⎰	33 ⎰
Orthodox Closeness Index*		−19	15	32	51
How similar do you think you are to most . . .					
Orthodox Jews?	Very Similar	4 ⎱	9 ⎱	27 ⎱	57 ⎱
		⎰ 33	⎰ 61	⎰ 85	⎰ 89
	Somewhat Similar	29 ⎰	52 ⎰	58 ⎰	32 ⎰
American Jews?	Very Similar	25 ⎱	8 ⎱	4 ⎱	4 ⎱
		⎰ 70	⎰ 48	⎰ 43	⎰ 29
	Somewhat Similar	45 ⎰	40 ⎰	39 ⎰	25 ⎰
Orthodox Similarity Index*		−29	7	33	57

*Orthodox Closeness/Similarity Indices = (percent feeling "very close/similar" to Orthodox Jews – percent feeling "very close/similar" to non-Orthodox Jews) + ½ (percent feeling "somewhat close/similar" to Orthodox Jews – percent feeling "somewhat close/similar" to non-Orthodox Jews).

the bulk of their friends). To be sure, we cannot say whether the beliefs and practices stimulate the friendships or whether there is an interaction among all these factors.

But there is more to be said here. If we total those who answered both "very close" and those who said they felt at least "somewhat close" —that is, those who in some way or another felt close to other Orthodox Jews—we see an even clearer picture of the affective ties. There is clearly a threshold, or large gap, that separates the Orthodox (even those only nominally Orthodox) from the rest. Many fewer non-Orthodox felt "somewhat" or "very close" to most American Jews (52 percent) than did members of the three Orthodox groups (88, 92, and 99 percent). Thus, in spite of their open attitude toward the possibility of being close friends with Orthodox Jews as reflected in the figures in table 1 (recall that 78 percent agreed that it was possible for an Orthodox Jew to be close friends with Jews of all degrees of religious observance), our sample of non-Orthodox did not feel equally disposed toward the Orthodox Jews. This suggests perhaps that the non-Orthodox are less open toward Orthodox Jews than they believe the Orthodox Jews are capable of being toward them.

The results from the companion question on closeness toward non-Orthodox Jews parallel those of the previous question, although in the opposite direction and in a somewhat more muted fashion. Feeling close to the non-Orthodox diminished with traditionalism; the more observant felt less close to the non-Orthodox. Here, however, the threshold "break" lies between the nominally Orthodox and the centrists. About three-quarters of both the non-Orthodox (75 percent) and the nominally Orthodox (71 percent) said they felt at least "somewhat close" toward "most non-Orthodox American Jews." And, indeed, in their practices they are probably closer to such Jews; so their concomitant feelings should come as no surprise.

In contrast, only about half of the centrists (59 percent) and the traditionalists (50 percent) felt that way. Clearly, the extent of their involvement in ritual practice, to say nothing of their beliefs, seem to be enough to keep almost half of the centrists and traditionalists from feeling close to non-Orthodox Jews. Part of this undoubtedly comes from the experience that many Orthodox Jews have had with their non-Orthodox counterparts. One Orthodox informant encapsulated this feeling as follows: "You know the non-Orthodox Jews are the worst when it comes to tolerating my Orthodoxy. They always say 'You observe that? You don't really have to; I don't.' Gentiles are often more tolerant. They make no claims about knowing what Jews can and can't do."

In general, differences between groups were less dramatic here than they were in the case of the closeness to Orthodox Jews question. Traditionalist observance, apparently, is more consequential for feeling close to the ingroup (the Orthodox) than it is for feeling remote from the outgroup (non-Orthodox Jews). Add to that a general principle among all Jews, regardless of the orientation of their Judaism, to feel an ethnic loyalty to Jewish peoplehood and the small range of variation here becomes more easily understood. The idea of *knesset Yisrael*, the community of the Jewish people, apparently still holds.

The two other questions on perceived similarity to the Orthodox and to the non-Orthodox largely recapitulate patterns found in the answers to the two closeness questions. The more observant more often said they thought they were similar to other Orthodox Jews. And, indeed, looking around at their friends, they were right. Most of those around them were practicing a kind of life like theirs.

The two thresholds—between the nominally Orthodox and those on either side of them—might be explained by the fact that in practice the nominally Orthodox are quite different from most other Orthodox Jews yet still not part of the large mass of the non-Orthodox. They are on the margins and—judging from their affective ties—they know it.

Correlatively, the more observant were less likely to say that they felt similar to non-Orthodox Jews. Here, too, they were right. Relatively more involved in a ritual life that set them apart from other Jews, these Orthodox Jews were not like others in enough ways to allow for a self-image of being different. Again, the more intensive answers ("very similar") most clearly display threshold effects. Very few non-Orthodox and nominally Orthodox thought they were "very similar" to "most Orthodox Jews"; they knew they were on the margins at best. On the other hand about a quarter (27 percent) of the centrists and most (57 percent) of the traditionalists felt that way, proportions which probably reflect the nature of their ideological and practical ties with Orthodoxy accurately. Similarly, it is only among the non-Orthodox that we find either a substantial number (25 percent) who felt "very similar" to "most non-Orthodox American Jews" or a majority who felt at least "somewhat similar" to the non-Orthodox.

Two indices reported in table 2 summarize the feelings of closeness and similarity to the Orthodox and the non-Orthodox. The indices for both sentiments (closeness and perceived similarity) award "credit" for feeling closeness or for perceiving similarity to the Orthodox, and they subtract credit for parallel feelings toward the non-Orthodox. We gave twice as much credit (or deficit) for the stronger feelings or perceptions ("very . . . ") as the weaker responses ("somewhat . . ."). The indices could range from -100 (signifying total remoteness and dissimilarity from the Orthodox) to $+100$ (signifying total closeness and similarity to the Orthodox).

Within each of the four groups, the scores on the two indices are remarkably alike. The non-Orthodox score − 19 (for closeness) and − 29 (for similarity perceptions); in both respects they clearly leaned away from the Orthodox and inclined toward the non-Orthodox. The nominally Orthodox (25 and 7) tilted slightly toward the Orthodox. The centrists (32 and 33) were solidly identified with the Orthodox. The traditionalists (51 and 57) clearly saw themselves as much closer to and much more similar to most Orthodox Jews than to most non-Orthodox Jews.

In sum, greater ritual observance is closely associated with a sharper and more distinct definition of group boundaries. The more observant more often saw themselves as set apart from the larger world of American Jews, while they more often closely identified with a separate and distinct community of Orthodox Jews.

Conclusion

Looking at the data against the backdrop of recent Jewish history, one discovers that Orthodox Jews—precisely because they are not a monolith—are in fact both an open and closed group. Indeed, the internal boundaries between the various types of Orthodox Jews are reflected in the external boundaries. Those who have largely rejected the host society, who see themselves *in* but not *of* it, are tied up in a web of relationships with others like them, while those modernists who feel themselves neither remote from nor untouched by contemporary America have relatively greater ties with it. The traditionalists clearly feel that only the most rigid boundaries between themselves and others and who are not like them will protect their identity, practice, and the Jewish future. The others look forward to other more contemporary salvations. But all Orthodox Jews, whatever their persuasion or life style, have some links with America. Whether those who emphasize the boundaries or those who stress the ties represent the essential character of Orthodoxy in America is difficult if not impossible to say from the present data. Both the traditionalists and the modernists (both centrists and nominally Orthodox) have every intention of perpetuating their way of life in the next generation. Only time will tell if they succeed.

Notes

1. Jacob Katz, *Out of the Ghetto* (Cambridge: Harvard University Press, 1973) 162–63.

2. Ibid., p. 199.

3. Joseph Blau, *Judaism in America* (Chicago: University of Chicago Press, 1976) 303.

4. Natan Rotenstreich, "Emancipation and Its Aftermath," in *The Future of the Jewish Community in America*, ed. David Sidorsky (New York: Basic Books, 1973) 548.

5. J. Katz, *Out of the Ghetto*, p. 208.

6. Isaac Deutscher, *The Non-Jewish Jew and Other Essays* (New York: Oxford University Press, 1968) 26.

7. Irving Howe, *World of Our Fathers* (New York: Harcourt Brace Jovanovitch, 1976) 23.

8. Leo Jung, "What Is Orthodox Judaism?" in *The Jewish Library*, second series (New York: Bloch, 1930) 129.

9. N. Rotenstreich, "Emancipation and its Aftermath," p. 56; and Horace Kallen, "The Foundations of Jewish Spiritual and Cultural Unity," *Judaism* 6 (1957) 34.

10. Moshe Meiselman, "Women and Judaism: A Rejoinder," *Tradition* 15:3 (1975) 53.

11. Charles S. Liebman, *The Ambivalent American Jew* (Philadelphia: Jewish Publication Society, 1973) 78.

12. Ibid., p. viii.

13. M. Auerbach, "Survey of Jewish History," in *The Jewish Library*, first series, ed. L. Jung (New York: Bloch, 1943) 307.

14. Y. L. Peretz, *Stories from Peretz*, trans. and ed. Sol Liptzin (New York: Hebrew Publishing Co., 1947) 245–46.

15. M. Breuer, "Samson Raphael Hirsch," in *Guardians of Our Heritage*, ed. L. Jung (New York: Bloch, 1958) 291.

16. Shlomo Riskin, "Orthodoxy and Her Alleged Heretics," *Tradition* 15 (1976) 42.

17. Immanuel Jakobovits, letter in *Commentary* 58:5 (November 1974) 22.

18. Ibid.

19. Ralph Pelcovitz, "America's Bicentennial: A Torah Perspective," *Jewish Life*, Fall 1976, p. 13.

20. David Singer, "Voices of Orthodoxy," *Commentary* 58:1 (July 1974) 54.

21. See Janet Aviad, *Return to Judaism* (Chicago: University of Chicago Press, 1983).

22. Samuel C. Heilman and Steven M. Cohen, "Ritual Variation among Modern Orthodox Jews in the United States," in *Studies in Contemporary Jewry*, vol. 2, ed. P. Medding (Bloomington: Indiana University Press, 1986) 164–87.

23. Samuel C. Heilman *Synagogue Life* (Chicago: University of Chicago Press, 1976) 14.

24. Louis Wirth, *The Ghetto* (Chicago: University of Chicago Press, 1928) 8.

7

A Case of the Excluded Middle: Creation Versus Evolution in America

GEORGE M. MARSDEN

I n the United States during the past century "evolution" has sym-
bolized some of the nation's most bitter religious and cultural conflicts. In a widely held view that seems to be gaining in popularity, biological evolution is regarded as an opposite of divine creation and hence
incompatible with traditional Christian belief. So widespread is this belief that in 1981 the so-called "creationist" movement persuaded two
state legislatures to adopt laws that purport to ensure "balanced treatment" of the subject of origins in public schools by countering any treatment of "evolution science" with equal treatment of "creation science."[1]
The very appropriation of the name "creationist" for the movement that
promotes such legislation reflects a belief in, and even an insistence on,
the absolute antithesis between faith in a Creator and biological evolution. In fact the creation-science movement does not advocate creationism in the general sense of any belief in a Divine Creator or even in the
more limited sense of belief in creation by the God of scripture; rather it
defends only one view of creation, that based on a literal reading of the
first chapters of Genesis.[2] In this view, the six days of creation are literal
twenty-four-hour days so that the Earth can not be more than some thousands of years old. Evolution of any species, accordingly, is absolutely
precluded. So in response to suggestions that there are many other crea-

An abbreviated version of this paper appeared in *Nature* 305 (13 October 1983) 571–
74. Copyright © 1983 Macmillan Journals Limited. The portions reprinted here are used
with permission.

tionist positions that allow for an older Earth and for the possibility of at least some evolution, the typical response is "creation scientists maintain that there are only two basic explanations—creation and evolution—all explanations can be included within one or the other of these two basic positions."[3]

This insistence that there are only two polarized positions contradicts the facts concerning the views of Christians and other believers on the relation of creation to evolution. Even among American evangelical Protestants alone, to say nothing of liberal Protestants, varieties of Catholics, Jews, Mormons, Moslems, and so forth, there long have been distinguished advocates of mediating positions, usually designated "theistic evolution" or "progressive creation." Immediately upon the announcement of Darwin's theory some conservative Bible-believers had a ready answer to the suggestion that evolutionary doctrine must undermine faith in a Creator. God controls all natural processes through his providential care. The questions raised by biological evolution are therefore not in principle different from those suggested by other natural phenomena, such as photosynthesis. A fully naturalistic account of the process does not preclude belief that God planned or controlled it. So God may have used evolutionary processes as his means of creating at least some of Earth's species. Whether the creation of humans involved some special divine intervention has been a matter of some debate among evangelical theistic evolutionists. A strict reading of Genesis, they agreed however, does not preclude evolutionary developments. After all, already by the mid-nineteenth century most American evangelical scholars concurred that the "days" of Genesis One could mean long eras sufficient to allow for the enormous amounts of time demanded by geological theories. Evolutionary doctrine as such, therefore, need contradict neither any theological dogma nor a faithful reading of scripture.[4]

Such mediating views have a distinguished heritage within American evangelicalism itself. Asa Gray, America's first great proponent of Darwinism, remained an orthodox Congregationalist even though teaching at Unitarian Harvard. He argued in correspondence with Darwin that nothing in the new biological theories entailed lack of divine planning and hence guidance of the processes (unlike Darwin, Calvinists were not distressed by the idea of a God who permitted considerable cruelty and wastefulness in his universe). Gray's protégé and closest collaborator in demonstrating the compatibilities of biological evolution and orthodox belief was George Frederick Wright. Wright's orthodox evangelical credentials were so impeccable that he was asked to contribute an essay on evolution to *The Fundamentals* (1910–15), the publications that signaled the rise of organized fundamentalism. While criticizing extravagant philosophical and scientific claims of evolution, Wright insisted that the Bible "teaches a system of evolution" and that any demonstrated evolutionary developments would illustrate how God had designed life so to evolve. In fact, Wright held, to believe that all development of species happened sheerly by chance without divine guidance and even intervention was "to commit logical 'hara-kiri.'"[5]

Equally striking are the statements made at about the same time by Benjamin B. Warfield of Princeton Theological Seminary. Warfield, a formidable intellect, was an inventor of the term "inerrancy" and a leading proponent of that key fundamentalist doctrine that scripture did not err in any of its assertions. Despite such conservativism, Warfield made a point of observing that evolution and creation were not opposites. The discussion, he said, "can never sink again into rest until it is thoroughly understood in all quarters that 'evolution' cannot act as a substitute for creation, but at best can supply only a theory of the method of divine providence."[6] Warfield was clear on the distinctions. Creation might entail supernaturalism; but evolution did not therefore entail anti-supernaturalism.

The historical question we are faced with then is why, even when such illustrious leaders of the early fundamentalist movement pointed out the viability of mediating positions, did opposition to all biological evolution become for so many a test of the faith? The mediating positions have, of course, survived and even are dominant among evangelical academics who are heirs to the fundamentalist movement.[7] Nonetheless in the current American discussions these positions are either widely ignored or unknown. Not only does the immensely successful creation-science movement claim that theistic evolution is literally of the devil,[8] but whole state legislatures have also adopted the "balanced treatment" laws that assume that creation and evolution are opposites and the only two views worth considering. Certainly the popular press has done little to dispel this impression of a life-or-death struggle for survival of two wholly irreconcilable views.[9] The historical issue I propose to explore is two-fold. Why have creation scientists insisted on this polarization, and why have such dichotomized views been so popular in America?

The Role of the Bible

Central to the rejections of evolution as incompatible with the Christian faith in creation is the belief that "the Bible tells me so." Henry Morris, founder of the most prominent of the current creation-science organizations, says directly that "if man wishes to know anything at all about

Creation . . . his sole source of true information is that of divine revelation. . . .This is our textbook on the science of Creation!"[10] In recent court cases this theme has been obscured to avert constitutional difficulties. Nonetheless, Morris, his close followers, and his many pious admirers agree that it is obvious that Genesis One refers to twenty-four-hour days of creation and so absolutely precludes evolution. One question is, then, why do such principles of biblical interpretation persist with such strength in America? First we must consider the convergence of two powerful traditions of biblical interpretation in America. These, in turn, lead to a number of factors in the American religious and cultural heritage that have inclined some substantial groups of people toward accepting such views.

Millenarianism

The modern premillennial views that have flourished in America since the nineteenth century have often been based on exact interpretations of the numbers in biblical prophecies. The Bible, such millenarians assume, is susceptible to exact scientific analysis, on the basis of which at least some aspects of the future can be predicted with some exactitude. Seventh-Day Adventists, Jehovah's Witnesses, and the influential dispensational premillennialists among fundamentalists all treat the prophetic numbers in this way. For such groups it is accordingly important to have a biblical hermeneutic that will yield exact conclusions. Moreover, the hermeneutical principle that applies to prophecy ought to be consistent with those applied to scriptural reports of past events. Dispensationalists have often used the formula "literal where possible" to describe this hermeneutic. While they do not wish to apply literal interpretations to statements obviously poetical or figurative ("the mountains shall clap their hands") they do think that, unless we are compelled otherwise, we should interpret scripture as referring to literal historical events that are being described exactly. It is not surprising, therefore, that such groups who derive some of their key doctrines from exact interpretations of prophecy should be most adamant in interpreting Genesis One as describing an exact order of creation in six twenty-four-hour days. Fundamentalists, often with dispensationalist ties, have been among the most ardent supporters of the recent "creation-science" movement that insists on a young Earth, and hence on an entirely antievolutionary view of creation.

The influence of these prophetic views goes beyond the bounds of their immediate fundamentalist constituents, as is suggested by the fact that the dispensationalist prophetic volume by Hal Lindsey, *The Late Great Planet Earth*, was the best-selling book in America during the 1970s.[11] The principal creation-science organization, the Institute for Creation Research in San Diego, has close ties to this prophetic movement. Henry Morris, its founder, for instance, is author of a "literalist" commentary on the book of Revelation.[12] George McCready Price (1870–1963), the main precursor of Morris's young-earth flood-geology approaches, was a Seventh-Day Adventist. Price's whole career was dedicated to confirming the prophecies of Ellen G. White, who claimed divine inspiration for the view that the world-wide flood accounts for the geological evidence on which geologists built their theories.[13]

Protestant Scholasticism

Not all creation-scientists are millenarians, however. Another formidable tradition in American Protestantism that often has supported interpretations of Genesis One and has influenced both American fundamentalism and popular American conceptions of scripture is Protestant scholasticism. This tradition has been articulated most prominently by the Princeton theologians, such as Benjamin Warfield, who popularized the concept of the "inerrancy" of scripture. The Princetonians, however, were by no means the inventors of this concept nor the only major purveyors of it in America. The substance of the inerrancy view—that because the Bible is God's Word it must be accurate in matters of science and history as well as in doctrine—was already held in much of the scholastic Protestantism of the seventeenth century and was common in many quarters of nineteenth-century American Protestantism.[14] Belief in the inerrancy of scripture did not entail that it always be interpreted as literally as possible, as demonstrated by the allowance for long "days" of creation by some Princetonians. Nonetheless, the emphasis on scientific exactness of scriptural statements was conducive to views of those who insisted that Genesis One referred to literal twenty-four-days.

A good example is the Lutheran Church–Missouri Synod. For reasons no doubt related both to their Protestant scholastic tradition and to determination to resist infection by modern American theologies, the leading Missouri Synod theologians in the first half of the twentieth century insisted on a view of scripture perhaps even more conservative than that of the Princeton theologians. In their view the Holy Spirit dictated or suggested to the writers the very words of scripture. God therefore is properly the author of scripture. Moreover, the words of scripture have divine properties[15] according to the Missouri Synod interpreters. These considerations led to the conclusion that the days of Genesis One were twenty-four-hour periods, a point they insisted on. This conclusion, they said, was necessitated by the words of scripture itself (such as referring to the "evening and the morning" of the days). Evolution, accordingly, was necessarily "atheistic and immoral" and theistic evolution inconsistent with both scripture and true evolution.[16] Missouri Synod spokesmen argued that evolution itself was unscientific and a threat to civilization and to church doctrine.[17] No doubt the general cultural conservatism and defensiveness in the Missouri Synod contributed to a conservative hermeneutic that precluded all evolution. The central argument, however, was the appeal to scripture itself. In any case, when Henry Morris first organized the Creation Research Society in 1963, out of which grew most recent creation science, one-third of the original steering committee were Missouri Synod Lutherans.[18]

Rational and Scientific Christianity

Common to the prophetic-millennial and the scholastic traditions and relating them to each other has been a desire to establish a firm rational basis for Christian belief. Both traditions have emphasized conventional proofs for the existence of God and the truth of Christianity.[19] Since the seventeenth century many Christian apologists have considered it important to demonstrate that Christianity is a properly scientific belief. Especially in the eighteenth and the nineteenth centuries, defenders of Christianity assiduously collected evidences from natural sciences to confirm truths revealed in scripture. Nineteenth-century American apologists, whether scholastic or millenarian, typically based their apologetics on explicitly Baconian principles. They insisted that their arguments were based on cautious examination of evidence that everyone could observe through common-sense procedures. Speculative hypotheses would be avoided, so that arguments would be limited to careful induction. Evidences either from the physical sciences or evidences analogous to those in the physical sciences were preferred. The book of nature and the book of scripture were fully harmonious and to be understood, as Bishop Butler had so persuasively argued, in analogous ways.[20]

Crucial to the creation-science movement is the desire to restore this harmony of science and scripture which the twentieth-century intellectual climate seemingly had shattered. In the wake of the derision heaped upon William Jennings Bryan and fundamentalists generally after the Scopes trial, some literal-minded Bible believers set out to demonstrate that, contrary to popular opinion, science still supported scripture.

Henry Morris made this point explicitly in his first book, *That You Might Believe* (1946). While acknowledging that Christian truths must ultimately be based on faith and that he would accept the Bible "even against reason if need be," Morris emphasized that the Bible "in no way does violence to common sense and intelligence." The twentieth-century problem was that many people regarded Christianity "as outmoded beliefs, conceived in superstition and nurtured by scientific and philosophical illiteracy." Morris, by contrast, was sure that biblical beliefs would satisfy even his engineer's habit "of requiring satisfactory evidence and proof of all that they accept as fact."[21]

Buoyed by this confidence in the Bible, Morris proceeded to illustrate "the great number of scientific truths that have lain hidden within its pages for thirty centuries or more, only to be discovered by man's enterprise within the last few centuries or even years." These facts included evidences such as that the stars "cannot be numbered," or that the psalms directly described evaporation, wind, and electrical discharges as the cause of rain (Psalm 135:7). "He causeth the vapor to ascend from the ends of the earth; He maketh lightnings for the rain; He bringeth the wind out of His treasuries." The creation-science movement grew out of this impulse. While not claiming actually to prove that Christianity must be true, it seeks decisive evidences confirming biblical statement. So, not only do creation scientists assemble scientific evidences pointing to a world-wide flood, they sponsor expeditions searching for Noah's Ark.

The whole enterprise relates to a distinctive view of scripture itself. Fundamentalists and their allies regard the Bible as filled with scientific statements of the same precision as might be found in twentieth-century scientific journals.[22] God, they assume, would not reveal himself any less accurately. In the seminal *Genesis Flood*, Morris and John C. Whitcomb affirm "the complete divine inspiration and perspicuity of Scripture, believing that a true exegesis thereof yields determinative Truth in all matters with which it deals."[23] By "Truth," they mean the scientifically accurate facts that scripture contains. In the fundamentalist and the scholastic traditions the Bible is regarded as a book of "facts." So Charles Hodge in an often-quoted statement observed, "If natural science be concerned with the facts and laws of nature, theology is concerned with the facts and the principles of the Bible."[24]

In such traditions, the principal goal of biblical study was to classify the facts in Baconian fashion. "The methods of modern science are applied to Bible study," said dispensationalist spokesman Reuben Torrey, "thorough analysis followed by careful synthesis."[25]

Perhaps most importantly, this assumption that scripture speaks with scientific accuracy has invited the literalist hermeneutic that allows scriptural language as few ambiguities as possible. For instance, one of the most common arguments against evolution of species is that Genesis One repeatedly says that plants and animals should produce "after their kind." This phrase is usually regarded as precluding one species ever producing another. Similarly, a well-known dispensationalist argues against any compatability of evolution and the Bible by quoting Genesis 2:7, which states that man was created "out of the dust of the ground." But why, he asks, can this not allow a gradual evolution from the primordial dust? "This could not refer to or include a former animal ancestry, since it is to dust that man returns—and this is not a return to an animal state (Gen. 3:19)." Neither will this author allow that the first chapters of Genesis might be allegories that "still retain the 'thrust' of the Bible." Such a solution would dishonor God because, if evolution were true, the allegory would be "an entirely inaccurate one" so that "in giving it God was either untrue or unintelligent."[26] Even allegory, in this view, has to point directly toward the literal facts.

Common Sense

Scholars from other traditions might find such thinking incredible and surely to involve applying linguistic standards of one age to another. Nonetheless, there can be no doubt that in our age such thinking is widely regarded as common sense. Fundamentalists and kindred religious movements have made strong claims to stand for common sense. Such popular appeals reflect the nineteenth-century American evangelical heritage where Scottish common-sense realism was long the most influential philosophy.[27]

The Bible, according to the democratic popularization of this view, is best interpreted by the naïve readings that common people today give it. "In ninety-nine out of a hundred cases," wrote Reuben Torrey, "the meaning that the plain man gets out of the Bible is the correct one."[28] In modern America common sense is infused with popular conceptions of straightforward empirical representations of what is really "out there." Mystical, metaphorical, and symbolical perceptions of reality have largely disappeared. Instead, most Americans share what sociologist Michael Cavanaugh designates an "empiricist folk epistemology."[29] Things are thought best decribed exactly the way they appear, accurately with no hidden meanings. Such folk epistemology, it happens, is close to that which works best for engineers—straightforward, consistent, factual, with no nonsense. In fact, there are an unusual number of engineers in the creation-science movement.[30] Henry Morris, an engineer himself, connects his engineering standards to his standards for biblical hermeneutics. "Probably for no class of people more than engineers do common sense and reason have their greatest value, and I hope that these qualities have not remained completely undeveloped in me."[31] Many of his readers will agree, Morris correctly observes, that such "common sense and reason" must be applied to biblical interpretation.

Most contemporary scientists have difficulty understanding the degree to which the alleged scientific arguments of creation science also appeal to popular common sense. Evolution may have scientific experts on its side, but it simply strains popular common sense. It is simply difficult to believe that the amazing order of life on earth arose spontaneously out of the original disorder of the universe. Perhaps a common sense deeper than any culturally conditioned beliefs invites people who look at "the starry skies above and the moral law within" to believe that a personality, rather than blind chance, must have arranged these. The development of specific mechanisms, such as the eye, through blind chance also stretches common credulity. Could everything appear so ordered just by accident? The odds against a monkey at the typewriter producing an organized sentence by random typing is a favorite example. The length of time it would take for the present order of life to arise from disorder is staggering and stretches popular conceptions of probability.[32] As a common-sense argument, an antisupernaturalistic evolutionary outlook is far less compelling then the old argument from design.

As to the fact that so many experts agree on the truth of evolution, experts have often been wrong. Besides, the experts contradict one another, so the layperson has no obligation to believe them. Creation scientists, moreover, can produce their own experts, as creation-science organizations emphasize. In addition, however, people should be "deciding for themselves in a reasonable way." Audiences in church basements are told to go "see for themselves" fossil evidence that supposedly undermines evolution. "Let's decide upon a method by which we can resolve the controversy," says a typical appeal, "set up definitions, then examine the evidences."[33]

The American folk epistemology, then, is by no means antiscientific in principle. Rather it is based on a naïve realism plus popular mythology concerning proper scientific procedure and verification. These procedures are essentially Baconian, favoring simple empirical evidence.[34] The view of science is essentially optimistic and progressive; true science will eventually reach the truth, though it may be led off the track by prejudice. Neither are true science and Christianity in any conflict. True science can and will confirm Christian revelation. Michael Cavanaugh has suggested the marvelous characterization for this widespread American demand for empirical support of the faith as "doubting Thomism."[35]

The Sense of Cultural Crisis—The South after the Civil War

The popular appeal of uncompromising antievolutionists results not only from the coincidence of their hermeneutical and apologetic assumptions with much of American folk epistemology but also from their ability to convince their followers that antievolution is crucial to the future of civilization. In ethnoreligious terms, militant antievolutionists are almost all Northern European Protestants. Many of them have emphasized vigorously America's Christian (Protestant) heritage.[36] A sense of cultural crisis, typically described as a turning from Christian to secular civilization, seems an important factor in raising the stakes of the antievolution effort and hence reducing the likelihood of compromise.

This combination of beliefs seems more characteristic of the United States than of other countries[37] and more characteristic of the South than of the rest of the nation. Antievolution legislation and the recent creation laws have far better records in the states of the former Confederacy than elsewhere in the nation. Moreover, the irreconcilability of evolution and the Bible is a widely popular belief in the South not resting on the specific arguments or organizations of the recent creation-science movement, but antedating these.[38] It seems then that one clue to understanding the nature of militant antievolutionism is to look at some circumstances in which evolutionism has become for a substantial group of people identified with cultural decay.

The easy answer to explaining the strength of antievolutionism in the South is the prevalence of the "old-time religion" and relatively low levels of education of many Southern Bible-believers.[39] These factors are certainly important, although they do not explain why a particular belief (the dangers of evolution) gained an elevated status in Southern folk religion.[40] An interesting question is why antievolution became a standard test of the faith among Southern evangelicals earlier than it did among Northern fundamentalists.

A brief look at one incident in Southern antievolution history—the dismissal of James Woodrow from Columbia Theological Seminary in 1886—is instructive in answering these questions. Although this episode took place among the Presbyterian elite, it nonetheless was paralleled in other Southern denominations and received the widest coverage and popularization in the religious press. In the South, where an elite remained influential, the intellectual leadership successfully signaled to their constituency that acceptance of any form of biological evolution was a grave danger to the faith. For the popularizers this was easily translated into the question of whether one's ancestors were monkeys and the evangelists could take over from there. As the *Texas Presbyterian* put it, " 'The Lord formed man of the dust of the ground.' Man was born of an ape by ordinary generation. If these are not logical contraries, it would, in ordinary circumstances, be accounted a very strange use of language."[41]

The case of James Woodrow is a classic instance, arguably *the* classic instance, of the American and Southern tendency to draw a false dichotomy between creation and every form of biological evolution. In 1861 Woodrow was appointed to a chair "Professor of Natural Science in Connexion with Religion," at Columbia Theological Seminary, a leading institution of the Presbyterian Church in the United States (Southern Presbyterian). The establishment of this rather unusual theological chair reflected optimism among some Southern theologians as to the positive value of demonstrating the harmonies of science and scripture. Others, notably the famed Robert L. Dabney, were less ready to concede that the Bible needed any help from the scientific quarter.[42] James Woodrow's stance on science and the Bible involved basically conservative harmonizations, such as between the long "days" of Genesis One and the old Earth suggested by modern geology. Although he taught about evolutionary views during the first two decades of his tenure at Columbia, he inclined against the theory. Gradually, however, he was swayed by some of the scientific arguments and in 1884 publicly acknowledged his acceptance of a limited form of theistic evolution. Woodrow was, however, a proponent of what had recently become known as the "inerrancy" of scripture.[43] In fact he was so conservative on the question of the need to harmonize science with the direct statements of scripture that he held that, while God could have created the body (not the soul) of Adam "mediately" by evolution from the dust of the ground, the body of Eve was created immediately from Adam's rib.

Such literalism was not sufficient to satisfy either the Presbyterian hierarchy or the popular religious press. After a complicated controversy in various Presbyterian judicatories, the General Assembly of the denomination in 1886 finally declared that "Adam and Eve were created, body and soul, by immediate acts of Almighty power," and that Adam's body was created "without any human parentage of any kind," and that any method of biblical interpretation that led to denial of these conclusions would eventually "lead to the denial of doctrines fundamental to the faith."[44] On this basis Woodrow was dismissed from his professorship.[45]

Why did Southern Presbyterians thus try to bolt the door on even the most modest accommodation between creation and evolution? A number of factors converged. First are the dynamics of Southern white church and religious life after the Civil War. The war brought the restoration of the Union but not the reunion of the churches. Southern Christians had to justify this continued separation from their former brethren. The most likely principal explanation was that their Northern counterparts had been infected by a liberal spirit, evidenced in the first instance in their unbiblical attacks upon slavery. Southerners were thus alert for, and no doubt even eager to notice, any other trends toward laxity in Yankee religion. The continued separation was justified by the mounting conviction in the minds of Southerners that theirs were the only pure representatives of their denominations left. As one church paper declared, "the glory and the strength of our Southern church" is "that there are very few, if any" advocates of change.[46]

Such justifications of separation from the Northern churches were an integral part of the Southern glorification of the lost cause in the half-century after the War Between the States. Although Southerners had lost the war on the battlefield, they were determined to win the war of ideas.[47] The effect of this determination was to preclude change in any area and to celebrate whatever had been dominant in the ante-bellum era. This Southern determination arose almost simultaneously with the rapid spread of evolutionary ideas at all levels of the rest of Anglo-American thought. So the widespread belief in the value of change became particularly anathema in Southern thought. In theology the Southern conservatives focused on the issue clearly. As John L. Girardeau, one of the principal opponents of Woodrow put it, "There is a specious and dangerous form of this theory of development of doctrine that threatens, at the present day, to invade the supremacy of the written Word."[48] Moreover, from the perspective of the Southerners' romanticized self-image, evolution, or change of any sort, could be only a decline.

Such circumstances may have been sufficient to ensure some opposition to any evolutionary doctrine at the popular level. In addition, the theologians' stance on the issue of Genesis and biological evolution was reinforced by a firm commitment to a scholastic literalist hermeneutic. The Southern Presbyterians had been closely connected with the Old School Presbyterians at Princeton before the war, and so retained the essentials of that conservative-scientific approach to scriptural interpretation. This Presbyterian stance, especially in its Baconian tendencies to view the Bible as a collection of factual propositions, was at one with most biblical interpretation in the South.[49] Perhaps most importantly for the Southerners, however, was that they had been committed both to a literalistic hermeneutic and a nondevelopmentalism by the slavery controversy. The Bible condemned slavery only if one foresook the letter of the text for the alleged spirit. Committed to the letter of scripture regarding slavery, Southerners were hardly in a position to play fast and loose with other passages that might be reinterpreted in the light of alleged modern progress.

Fundamentalism after World War I

The rise of the fundamentalist campaigns against evolution in the 1920s is far better known and need only be summarized here. As we have already seen, outside the South before World War I, antievolution does not appear often to have been a test of the faith, except among sectarians. Probably most conservative Protestants had the impression that evolution and the Bible were irreconcilable opposites, but enough of their leaders saw the problems in this stance to prevent it from becoming a test of fellowship.

As we have seen, even *The Fundamentals* of 1910 to 1915 did not absolutely preclude all evolutionary views. During the 1920s, however, antievolution became increasingly important to fundamentalists and eventually became an essential hallmark of the true faith.[50]

The rise of the antievolution issue in fundamentalism was related to the convergence of several forces that took their exact shape when precipitated by the catalytic action of the American experience in World War I. The war exacerbated mounting liberal-versus-conservative Protestant tensions, especially as modernists turned on premillenialists for their failure to identify the kingdom with present efforts for the advance of world-wide democracy. Premillenialists and other Protestant conservatives, on the other hand, made the most of the extravagant anti-German propaganda by pointing out that German theology was the source of much modernist thinking. German theology and German "*kultur*," they said, had in common evolutionary philosophies. This "might is right" ideology had led to disaster for that civilization, which had lost all sense of decency. Evolution, moreover, had turned Germans away from faith in the Bible. The same thing that happened to Luther's Germany could happen to Protestant America. When the war ended, some of the American spirit to solve the world's problems through a crusade turned to the home front. For fundamentalists antievolution could serve as an important unifying principle, giving their version of the crusade wide import for civilization itself. The single concept of the threat of evolution explained the connections among the fundamentalist defense of conservative readings of scripture, their battles to combat modernist theology, and the entire destiny of America.[51]

The campaign needed only a leader to become a national sensation. William Jennings Bryan played that role as no one else could have. In estimating the reasons for the rise of an idea one must not underestimate the role of a charismatic personality. The battle for antievolution, the Bible, and civilization was a cause whose time had come; but it is doubtful that it would have become such a deeply engraved line of American thought had it not been for the colorful leadership of Bryan. If nothing else, Bryan's presence ensured wide press coverage, which of course always invited further simplifications of the issue.[52]

Bryan's own understanding of the connection between biological evolution and the dangers of evolutionary philosophies to society was an unusual one. In his view, evolutionary social views led to social Darwinism and hence to anti-Progressive politics and glorification of war. His followers, however, were not especially concerned with the details of the threat of evolution to civilization. They were convinced there was a threat to traditional beliefs posed by the spread of naturalistic, evolutionary-developmental philosophies. This supposition was not entirely fanciful. Bryan and his cohorts were aware in a general way of the same secularizing trends associated with evolutionary naturalism in philosophy that their intellectual contemporaries, such as Carl Becker and Joseph Wood Krutch, were also pointing out.

The beauty of the fundamentalists' position was that they could relate this threat to civilization directly to the abandonment of the Bible as a source of authority and truth. This linkage was most clear concerning the question of biological evolution. Here again, the fundamentalists were pointing to a real phenomenon of major cultural significance. American young people, especially those who were attending colleges, were forsaking traditional faith in the Bible in droves. Bryan was especially impressed by the 1916 study by Bryn Mawr professor James H. Leuba who demonstrated the dramatic erosion of traditional beliefs among American college students from their freshmen to their senior years. Science courses, especially those that taught naturalistic evolution, were leading contributors to this revolution. In fact, nearly two-thirds of the nation's biologists professed not to believe in a personal God or in immortality for humans.[53] The teaching of evolution was, then, a real contributor to a trend that many considered to have ominous implications for the future of civilization.

The perception of such stakes invited the sort of polarization of the issue that we have been discussing. Bryan's appeal to quasi-populist rural resentments against experts, especially in the South, added to the oversimplifications. Bryan's own case is especially revealing, since the private Bryan and the public Bryan of the 1920s seem to have disagreed on how simple the issue was. Bryan himself held to a somewhat moderate interpretation of Genesis One. As Darrow elicited from him at the Scopes trial, Bryan believed that Genesis One might allow for an old Earth,[54] a belief that was not unusual among fundamentalist leaders.[55] Bryan even confided just before the trial to Howard A. Kelly, a prominent Johns Hopkins physician and one of the contributors to *The Fundamentals*, that he agreed that one need have no objection to "evolution before man."[56] Yet in his public speeches Bryan had been allowing no compromise. "The so-called theistic evolutionists refuse to admit that they are atheists," he argued. Theistic evolution, he added, was just "an anesthetic administered to young Christians to deaden the pain while their religion is being removed by the materialists."[57] Bryan explained this inconsistency of his stances in his letter to Kelly: "A concession as to the truth of evolution up to man furnishes our opponents with an argument which they are quick to use, namely, if evolution accounts for all the species up to man, does it not raise a presumption in behalf of evolution to include man?" The impact of a skilled popular leader in polarizing issues is evident here. Convinced that the issues were of unparalleled importance, Bryan was not going to allow his constituency to be distracted from the warfare by the fine distinctions of mediating positions.

The Warfare Metaphor

Exacerbating the tendencies to polarization, arising from the convergence of all the above factors, has been the sheer power of military metaphors. For over a century warfare has been the dominant popular image for considering the relationships between science and religion, evolution and creation. Journalists, and historians only somewhat less, relish reporting a good fight. Reports that there is a war, moreover, can help ensure that hostilities continue.

In the historiography of the relationship between Darwinism and religion, argues James R. Moore in the most extensive treatment of this theme, the military metaphor was first promoted by the opponents of religion. In fact, ever since the famed Bishop Wilberforce–T. H. Huxley encounter of 1860, there was something of a warfare between churchmen and antisupernaturalist Darwinists. Given the many suggestions that the two outlooks might be reconciled, however, these conflicts might easily have been resolved or confined. Militant opponents of the whole Christian cultural and intellectual establishment, however, made the most of the conflict. Darwin's personal difficulties in seeing how theism could fit with his theories lent aid to their cause. Accordingly, Victorian polemicists like T. H. Huxley and historians such as John William Draper and Andrew Dickson White reinforced the idea that the whole history of the relations between science and religion was a "warfare."[58] As the statistics on the low number of traditional theists among early twentieth-century American biologists show, the weapon of Darwinism was indeed taking a heavy toll in this warfare on Christianity.

Given this actual hostility of many Darwinists toward traditional Christianity, it is not surprising that some Christian groups replied in kind. Particularly this was true of groups that already saw most of reality through warfare imagery. Sects are notorious on this score. Immigrant groups and Southerners each had their own reasons to view themselves as at least being in a cold war with the surrounding culture. Antievolution hostilities, however, did not reach nationwide proportions until the rise of fundamentalism in the 1920s. Fundamentalism was a peculiar blend of sectarianism and aspirations to dominate the culture. A coalition of conservative Protestant traditions, its most conspicuous unifying feature has been militancy. As Richard Hofstadter observes, "The fundamentalist mind . . . is essentially Manichean; it looks upon the world as an arena for conflict between absolute good and absolute evil, and accordingly it scorns compromises (who can compromise with Satan?)."[59] William Jennings Bryan's refusal to admit publicly the possibility of limited evolution for fear of giving a weapon to the enemy illustrates this tendency. In later fundamentalism, which has provided most of the leadership for the recent creation-science movement, compromises have been even less welcomed. The 1981 Arkansas creation-science law, for instance, in requiring the teaching of "a relatively recent inception of the Earth and of living kinds" to counterbalance antisupernaturalistic "evolution-science" would have excluded Bryan's own position that the "days" of Genesis could represent aeons.[60]

The Mythological Powers of Evolutionary Explanation

William Allen White said of Bryan that he was never wrong in political diagnosis and never right in prescription.[61] We might say the same thing of the creation-science movement that has been heir to his work. They have correctly identified some important trends in twentieth-century American life and see that these trends have profound cultural implications. Basically, they point to the revolution that has brought the wide dominance in American academia and much other public life of antisupernaturalistic relativism. Evolutionary theory has been, as we have seen, often used to support such an outlook. Carl Sagan's immensely popular *Cosmos* furnished a telling example. "The cosmos is all there is, there was, or ever will be," he states in his opening sentence.[62]

Such views are, of course, philosophical premises rather than conclusions of scientific inquiry, since no conceivable amount of scientific evidence could settle such an issue. Nonetheless, the fundamentalists of both sides make the same mistake in debating such questions. Both fundamentalistic antisupernaturalists, such as Sagan, and their creation-scientist opponents approach the issue as though it could be settled on the grounds of some scientific evidence. In each case, the oversimplification of the issue reflects widespread overestimation in American culture of the possible range of scientific inquiry.

Beyond such overestimation of the prowess of science in general is the peculiar role that "evolution" has come to play in the antisupernaturalist cultural and intellectual revolution. Both antisupernaturalists and their creation-scientist opponents have reflected common parlance when they have spoken of "evolutionary science" as equivalent to "naturalism" —that is, a view that the universe is controlled by natural forces insusceptible to influence by any ultimately supernatural plan or guidance.

Moreover, it seems correct to argue, as does David N. Livingstone, that evolution has become an all-explanatory metaphor in modern culture. It has become, Livingstone suggests, a "cosmic myth—a worldview which purports to provide, for example, guidelines for ethics and a coherent account of reality." All aspects of being and experience are explained according to evolutionary, developmental, or historicist models. Often these are presented as complete accounts of the phenomena involved or as the only meaningful accounts that humans have available. Evolution is, of course, a model with valuable explanatory powers; but it is worth asking, as Livingstone does, whether we have any adequate basis for making this metaphor the foundation for an all-comprehensive worldview.[63] In any case, creation scientists are correct in perceiving that in modern culture "evolution" often involves far more than biology. The basic ideologies of the civilization, including its entire moral structure, are at stake. Evolution does sometimes function as a mythological system, sometimes as the key element in a worldview that functions as a virtual religion. Given this actual connection with a philosophy antithetical to traditional Christianity, it is all the more difficult for many to see that the biological theory is not *necessarily* connected with such a worldview. Dogmatic proponents of evolutionary antisupernaturalistic mythologies have been inviting responses in kind.

Conclusion

What does the story of the polarization of the creation-evolution conflict tell us about religious conflict in general? First, it tells us something of the rich complexity of human thought processes and cultural developments that may lie behind such conflicts. Traditions, mythologies, assumptions, and experiences of a group help dispose it toward certain beliefs. Focusing on the creation-science side of the creation-evolution polarization, we have seen that in this instance at least the following are involved: (1) specific religious traditions; (2) epistemological, hermeneutical, and apologetic commitments important for preserving those traditions; (3) folk epistemologies congruent with these traditions, providing a basis for a popular appeal; (4) specific cultural experiences or crises of religious groups holding these traditions, exciting militant defenses; (5) effective leadership and organization; (6) popular metaphors and mythologies that amplify or simplify the issues, leading to parallel oversimplifications by the other side and in popular accounts; (7) a tendency, as the warfare proceeds, to make affirmation of a simple and unqualified statement of one's position a test of membership in the group, thus driving out equivocators; (8) perceptions, however imperfect, of substantial religious and cultural issues really at stake. A parallel list of factors could be used to help explain the reasons why some other groups have found the opposite positions compelling. Such analysis, however, should not be used to reduce the conflicts to only their cultural dimensions and hence trivialize the ideologies involved. Real and important issues may be at stake. The differences between creation scientists and wholly naturalistic evolutionists, for instance, derive largely from opposed starting points that organize the two worldviews. One group starts with the assumption that a Creator-God exists; the other assumes there is no such being. Whatever the cultural factors leading them to their respective conclusions, one group is closer to the truth than the other.

A related general issue is that as conflicts develop over such fundamental issues, coreligionists are likely to split among themselves between extremists and moderates. Some in the group, who perceive most clearly the gravity of the fundamental issue, will in the heat of controversy tend to spurn all who see complexities. Ideological commitments and traditions at this point combine with tactical considerations to invite branding as traitors those whose zeal for the cause is at all tempered by perceptions of its ambiguities. Traitors are as bad or worse than the enemy itself. Hence this secondary intrareligious conflict may be as severe as that over the primary question and the issues at stake may become confused with each other.

Our cultural analysis suggests also that such ideological conflicts, at either level, are not likely to be settled by mere argumentation. The beliefs and the assumptions on which they are grounded are too deeply rooted in the traditions and experiences of their communities to be dislodged by a logic that can merely chop off this or that ideological flower. Nonetheless, argumentation is not irrelevant to religious belief. It is, after all, one of the few implements we have to cut through the thick overgrowths of religious nonsense that surround us. Moreover, even if argument can not by itself solve religious problems, it still can help. It might be particularly helpful if included in such argumentation were some cultural-historical analysis. If we are willing to expose the roots not only of our opponents' beliefs, but also of our own, we have better possibilities of distinquishing that which is nourished by a healthy spirituality and that which is fertilized only by more transiently based sources.

Such enterprises, to which historians have a special calling, are important for reducing needless conflicts both between conflicting communities and within communities where extremists and moderates disagree. Since in the late twentieth century we are particularly alert to the extent to which the structures of thought are influenced by the experiences of communities, analysis of those experiences may be an important contribution to being able to translate the thought forms of one community or subcommunity into those of their competitors. To be constructive, such analysis and translation must not involve an abandonment of the questions of truth and error as though a bland "understanding" were the only goal of discourse. As the present paper presumes, trying to understand a community does not demand abandoning pointing out what we see as their errors. In fact the peculiar errors of a community may be important clues to understanding their entire outlook. By the same token, however, we must concede that even the more eccentric belief systems are, like perhaps all belief systems, based on the overemphasis or distortion of some truth. So, for instance, with respect to creation scientists, if one is a theist, one ought to credit them with being willing to a take a firm stand on some central issues. Unless other theists are willing to concede and to appreciate that, there is little hope that we will contribute anything to moderating their extremism.

Notes

1. Act 590 of 1981, State of Arkansas, 73rd General Assembly, Regular Session, 1981. Cf. a similar Louisiana law of 1981. The Arkansas law was declared unconstitutional in Federal District Court, 5 January 1982. The disposition of the Louisiana law remained pending at the time of this writing.

2. Duane Gish, one of the leaders of the creation-science movement, simply defines creation as "the bringing into being of the basic kinds of plants and animals by the process of sudden, or fiat, creation described in the first two chapters of Genesis": *Evolution: The Fossils Say No!* (San Diego: Creation Life Publishers, 1973) 24.

3. "ICR Scientist at Westminster College," *Acts & Facts* 119 (May 1983) 4.

4. These developments are discussed in many places. The history of Christian discussion of the age of the earth is summarized by Davis A. Young, *Christianity and the Age of the Earth* (Grand Rapids: Zondervan, 1982) 13–67. James R. Moore, *The Post-Darwinian Controversies: A Study of the Protestant Struggle to Come to Terms with Darwin in Great Britain and America 1870–1900* (Cambridge: Cambridge University Press, 1979), presents an impressive account of orthodox Protestant theologians' reconciliations with Darwinism during this period.

5. Moore, *Post-Darwinian Controversies*, pp. 269–80; George Frederick Wright, "The Passing of Evolution," *The Fundamentals* (Chicago: Testimony Publishing Co., c. 1912) VII: 5–16.

6. Benjamin B. Warfield, "On the Antiquity and the Unity of the Human Race," *Studies in Theology* (New York: Oxford University Press, 1932) 235. Cf. Warfield, "Calvin's Doctrine of the Creation," *Calvin and Calvinism* (New York: Oxford University Press, 1931) 31, where he goes out of his way to point out that "Calvin's doctrine of creation is, . . . for all except the souls of men, an evolutionary one."

7. By the 1970s most evangelical scientists teaching at Christian colleges accepted some form of theistic evolution or "progressive creationism," as they often preferred to call it: *Christianity Today* 21 (17 June 1977) 8. This view was advocated by most of the members of the evangelical American Scientific Affiliation: Ronald M. Numbers, "The Dilemma of Evangelical Scientists," in *Evangelism and Modern America*, ed. George Marsden (Grand Rapids: Eerdmans, 1984) 159. Roland Mushat Frye, "So-Called 'Creation-Science' and Mainstream Christian Rejections," *Proceedings of the American Philosophical Society* 127:1 (January 1983) 61–70, documents some mainline views.

8. For example, Henry M. Morris, "The Spirit of Compromise," *Studies in the Bible and Science or Christ and Creation* (Philadelphia: Presbyterian and Reformed, 1966 [1963]), says "the idea of an evolutionary origin must have had its first beginnings in the mind of Satan himself" (p. 98). Theistic evolution is accordingly precluded (p. 196). Cf. "The Bible and Theistic Evolution" (ibid., pp. 89–93). Among other things, Morris thinks God would not have invented a system involving the extermination of the weak and unfit (p. 92). He also suggests that "it seems incomprehensible that He would waste billions of years in aimless evolutionary meandering before getting to the point": Henry M. Morris, ed., *Scientific Creationism* (General Edition, San Diego: Creation-Life Publishers, 1974) 219. Darwin himself objected to theistic evolution on similar grounds (see note 4 above). The views of Darwin and Morris both reflect post-Calvinist conceptions of what God must be like.

9. Even *Christianity Today*, a journal close to the "progressive creationist" camp, published a major story about the Arkansas trial that included no intimation that there were such mediating positions: Jack Weatherly, "Creationists Concerned about Court Test of Arkansas Law," *Christianity Today* 25 (September 1981) 40–41.

10. Morris, "The Bible *Is* a Textbook of Science" (1964–1965), *Studies in the Bible and Science*, p. 114.

11. Grand Rapids: Zondervan, 1970.

12. Henry Morris, *The Revelation Record: A Devotional Commentary on the Prophetic Book on the End Times*, forewords by Tim LaHaye and Jerry Falwell (Wheaton, IL: Tyndale House, 1983). Such views on prophecy are not, however, the official views of the Institute for Christian Research: Henry Morris, ICR letter, February 1983.

13. Ronald L. Numbers, "Creationism in 20th-Century America," *Science* 218 (5 November 1982) 539. Numbers, here and elsewhere, has done valuable work in documenting the rise of creation-science organizations and ideas.

14. John Woodbridge, *Biblical Authority: A Critique of the Rogers/McKim Proposal* (Grand Rapids: Zondervan, 1982), by collecting counterinstances, counterbalances suggestions that the concept originated in the late nineteenth century. Ian Rennie, "An Historical Response to Jack Rogers" (Unpublished paper, 1981), clarifies the development of emphasis on something like "inerrancy" which seems to have received emphasis among some Protestants primarily since the seventeenth century.

15. John Mueller, based on lectures of Francis Pieper, *Christian Dogmatics* (St. Louis: Concordia Publishing Co., 1934) 104 and 120. Benjamin Warfield says: ". . . this conception of co-authorship implies that the Spirit's superintendence extends to the choice of the words by the human authors (verbal inspiration), and preserves its product from everything inconsistent with a divine authorship . . . thus securing, among other things, that entire truthfulness which is everywhere presupposed in and asserted for Scripture by the biblical writers (inerrancy)": "The Real Problem of Inspiration," in *The Inspiration and Authority of the Bible*, ed. Samuel Craig (Philadelphia: Presbyterian and Reformed Publishing Co., 1948) 173.

16. Ibid., 181. Cf. Theodore Graebner, *Essays on Evolution* (St. Louis: Concordia Publishing House, 1925).

17. Cf. Graebner, *Essays*, p. 16 and passim.

18. Numbers, "Creationism," *Science*, 5 November 1982, p. 542.

19. For example, Theodore Graebner, *God and the Cosmos: A Critical Analysis of Atheism* (Grand Rapids: Eerdmans, 1932), especially pp. 31–36; Charles Hodge, *Systematic Theology*, 1 (New York: Charles Scribners, 1871); Arthur T. Pierson, *Many Infallible Proofs: The Evidences of Christianity* (New York: Fleming H. Revell, 1886).

20. Two helpful evaluations of the assumption that the evidences for the truths of scripture will be similar to the evidences for natural science are Roland Mushat Frye, "Metaphors, Equations, and the Faith," *Theology Today*, April 1980, pp. 59–67; and Langdon Gilkey, "Creationism: The Roots of the Conflict," *Christianity and Crisis*, 26 April 1982, pp. 108–115.

21. Henry M. Morris, *That You Might Believe* (Chicago: Good Books, Inc., 1946) 4.

22. As Eileen Barker observes, "Those rejecting the values and consequences of a scientific world view are nonetheless children of the age of science": "In the Beginning: The Battle of Creationist Science against Evolutionism," in *On the Margins of Science: The Social Construction of Rejected Knowledge*, ed. Roy Wallis, *Sociological Review Monograph* 27 (Keele, England: University of Keele, 1979) 183.

23. John C. Whitcomb and Henry M. Morris, *The Genesis Flood: The Biblical Record and its Scientific Implications* (Grand Rapids: Baker Book House, 1981 [1961]) xx. They also quote approvingly the Warfield passage cited above.

24. Hodge, *Systematic Theology*, 1:18.

25. Reuben Torrey, *What the Bible Teaches*, 17th ed. (New York: Fleming H. Revell, 1933 [1898]) 1.

26. Charles C. Ryrie, "The Bible and Evolution," *Bibliotheca Sacra* 124 (1967) 66 and 67.

27. Cf. George M. Marsden, *Fundamentalism and American Culture: The Shaping of Twentieth-Century Evangelism, 1870–1925* (New York: Oxford University Press, 1980) especially pp. 15–16, 55–62, 215–221.

28. Quoted in William G. McLoughlin, Jr., *Modern Revivalism* (New York: Ronald Press, 1959) 372. Original source not clear, from 1906. Cf. William B. Riley, "The Faith of the Fundamentalists," *Current History* 26 (June 1927) 434–36, reprinted in Willard B. Gatewood, Jr., ed., *Controversy in the Twenties: Fundamentalism, Modernism, and Evolution* (Nashville: Vanderbilt University Press, 1969), who says, "Fundamentalism insists upon the plain intent of scripture-speech. . . ." This "scientific" approach he contrasts with the liberal "weasel method" of interpretation (pp. 75 and 76).

29. This phrase is suggested to me by Michael A. Cavanaugh, "Science, True Science, Pseudoscience: The One-eyed Religious Movement for Scientific Creationism," draft of unpublished manuscript, 13 September 1982, p. 17. Cavanaugh's completed work is "A Sociological Account of Scientific Creationism: Science, True Science, Pseudoscience" (Ph.D. dissertation, University of Pittsburgh, 1983).

30. Dorthy Nelkin, *The Creation Controversy: Science or Scripture in the Schools* (New York: W. W. Norton, 1982) 70–90.

31. Morris, *That You Might Believe*, p. 4.

32. Cf. the arguments of Duane T. Gish, "It is Either 'In the Beginning, God' —or '. . . Hydrogen,'" *Christianity Today* 26 (8 October 1982) 28–33.

33. R. L. Wysong, *Creation—The Evolution Controversy: Toward a Rational Solution* (Midland, MI: Inquiry Press, 1976) 17 and 29.

34. Cf. Marsden, *Fundamentalism*, pp. 55–62, 215–21.

35. Cavanaugh, "Science, True Science . . . ," draft of 21 February 1983, passim. Another felicitous phrase from Cavanaugh is "the epistemic priesthood of all believers," draft of 13 September 1982, p. 21.

36. Christian Heritage College, where patriotic evangelist Tim LaHaye is a leading figure, has close links with the Institute for Creation Research. Creation-

science is promoted by the Moral Majority (in which LaHaye is also active). Missouri Synod Lutherans perhaps are an exception, showing less concern for the Christian American ideal.

37. Cf. George M. Marsden, "Fundamentalism as an American Phenomenon, A Comparison with English Evangelicalism," *Church History* 36:2 (June 1977) 215–32. Eileen Barker, "In the Beginning," in Wallis, ed., *On the Margins of Science*, pp. 179–200, seems to confirm that, although creation-science in England is similar to that in the United States, it has much less support and influence.

38. Michael Cavanaugh, "Science, True Science, Pseudoscience," draft of 13 September 1982, p. 32, shows that the actual creation-science movement is not especially strong in the states of Arkansas and Louisiana where creation-science legislation has been adopted. He suggests that the reason for this is that the movement is redundant in those states.

39. Recent polls have confirmed these generalizations. Cf. Corwin Smidt, "'Born Again' Politics: The Political Attitudes and Behavior of Evangelical Christians in the South" (Unpublished paper, March 1982).

40. A comparison of southern white and black attitudes on the subject might be illuminating.

41. *Texas Presbyterian*, 19 September 1884, quoted in Ernest Trice Thompson, *Presbyterians in the South*, Vol. 2: *1861–1890* (Richmond: John Knox Press, 1973) 466. Cf. p. 477 on the unusually positive reception to anti-revolutionary statements in the Southern Presbyterian religious press.

42. Thompson, *Presbyterians*, 2:454.

43. Clement Eaton, "Professor James Woodrow and the Freedom of Teaching in the South," *Journal of Southern History* 28:1 (February 1962) 10.

44. Quoted in Thompson, *Presbyterians*, 2:481.

45. Woodrow, clearly, was personally respected. He also did remain in good standing as a minister in the denomination, an indication that even his opponents recognized that he did not follow his doctrines to their allegedly heretical conclusions. The most complete account of the incident is in Thompson, *Presbyterians*, 2:457–90.

46. Quoted in Thompson, *Presbyterians*, 2:447.

47. Charles Reagan Wilson, *Baptized in Blood: The Religion of the Lost Cause* (Athens: University of Georgia Press, 1980).

48. Quoted in Thompson, *Presbyterians*, 2:448.

49. Cf. E. Brooks Holifield, *The Gentlemen Theologians: American Theology in Southern Culture, 1795–1860* (Durham, NC: Duke University Press, 1978).

50. Anti-evolution does not typically appear in the various lists of "fundamentals" drawn up by fundamentalists in the years immediately after World War I.

51. This account is based on Marsden, *Fundamentalism and American Culture*, pp. 141–228.

52. Two recent accounts that are helpful on the role of Bryan are Willard H. Smith, *The Social and Religious Thought of William Jennings Bryan* (Lawrence, KS: Coronado Press, 1975); and Ferenc Morton Szasz, *The Divided Mind of*

Protestant America, 1880–1930 (University, AL: University of Alabama Press, 1982). Szasz argues particularly well for the crucial influence of Bryan.

53. James R. Moore, *The Post-Darwinian Controversies*, p. 73.

54. *The World's Most Famous Court Trial: State of Tennessee v. John Thomas Scopes: Complete Stenographic Report* (New York, 1971; Cincinnati, 1925) 302. Bryan admits that he thinks the "days" of Genesis 1 are long periods and observes, "I think it would be just as easy for the kind of God we believe in to make the earth in six days or six years or in 6,000,000 years or in 600,000,000 years."

55. Cf. *A Debate: Resolved That the Creative Days in Genesis Were Aeons, Not Solar Days*, William B. Riley for the affirmative, Harry Rimmer for the negative (Duluth: Research Science Bureau, n.d., c. 1920s). Riley was president of the World's Christian Fundamentals Association.

56. Numbers, "Creationism," *Science*, 5 November 1982, p. 540.

57. Bryan, "Darwinism in Public Schools," *The Commoner*, January 1923, pp. 1 and 2.

58. Numbers, "Creationism," p. 540.

59. Moore, *Post-Darwinian Controversies*, pp. 19–49.

60. Richard Hofstadter, *Anti-Intellectualism in American Life* (New York: Vintage Books, 1962) 135. Act 590 of 1981, State of Arkansas, 73rd General Assembly Regular Session, 1981, section 4. Creationists indicate that "relatively recent inception" means from 6,000 to 20,000 years ago. Judge William R. Overton, in the United States District Court, Eastern District of Arkansas Western Division Judgment, Rev. Bill McLean, et al., vs. The Arkansas Board of Education, et al., 5 January 1982, p. 24.

61. Szasz, *Divided Mind*, pp. 122–23.

62. Carl Sagan, *Cosmos* (New York: Random House, 1980), 4. Cf. R. C. Lewontin, "Darwin's Revolution," *New York Review of Books* 30:10 (16 June 1983) 22, who insists that "Science cannot coexist" with "an all-powerful God who at any moment can disrupt natural relations."

63. David N. Livingstone, "Evolution as Myth and Metaphor," *Christian Scholar's Review* 12:2 (1983) 111–25, quotation from p. 119.

8

Catholic Contentiousness: The Public Consequences of Denominational Disputes

DAVID J. O'BRIEN

M y reflections here are not on disputes among religious groups but rather those within one large community of faith. I do so with no illusions that "interreligious hostility" has been left behind. Indeed, having observed local disputes over a full pregnancy clinic, sponsored by planned parenthood and located on Main Street across from city hall in Worcester, and having participated as a panelist in a public debate between antiabortion activist Mildred Jefferson and a local Unitarian minister representing planned parenthood and the ACLU, I am more than aware of the persistence of fairly deep divisions in our community that more or less reflect latent religious hostility. That comment is made not simply as an observer; at one early public hearing on this matter, I had not listened very long to alternating testimony from working-class Catholic activists and Junior League matrons before I felt the old, and I thought forgotten, tribal juices rise within me and the return of some of that old combative solidarity I thought I had left behind when I graduated from Notre Dame so many years ago. I admit it; I was hostile. Perhaps for our purposes it is significant, however, that I have become equally hostile toward certain Catholic right-to-lifers during recent political campaigns. That hostility bordered on rage when the Rev. Robert Drinan was driven from office, I suspect, by right-to-life agitation. I suspect that it also says something about the state of liberal Catholicism, that all but extinct hybrid of Catholic faith and civil religion, that this twin hostility has as its companion a feeling of political homelessness.

Needless to say, while my anti-Reaganism is more than sufficient to sustain my loyalty, yes, perhaps tribal, to the Democratic party, the knee-jerk identification of women's rights and abortion by that party's candidates makes that homelessness more than a feeling.

I am particularly interested in the relationship between internal Catholic controversy and what is known as public religion. I will not attempt to define that term, but simply refer to the collection of images, extending from de Tocqueville to Robert Bellah, which suggest that there is a public moral consensus of a more-or-less religious character that provides a perhaps necessary backdrop for public action. I would address this problem of public religion from the perspective of a person who is an American, concerned about our nation's public life, and a Catholic, concerned with the integrity of the church and committed to its mission. I wish to be these things both and at once, neither an ambassador from the church to the public world, with my true loyalties either in Rome or a disembodied Kingdom of God making me a stranger in my land, nor a Trojan horse within the church, dividing the house of faith and distorting the church's energies with inappropriate secular concerns. Yet I admit that integrity in these twin commitments is difficult to achieve and, if forced to a choice, I cannot be certain ahead of time which way I would go. Posing the possible need for such choice and expressing uncertainty about it perhaps already says something of the state of American Catholicism and the condition of the public religion.

I have argued for many years that the present state of American Catholicism can only be understood when the changes associated with Vatican II are seen in the context both of the changing social composition and location of American Catholics *and* the shocks to American self-consciousness that came simultaneously in the 1960's.[1] I want to qualify and refine, but am still in fundamental agreement with, Norman Mailer's insight in *St. George and the Godfather*: "In America, the country was the religion. And all the religions of the land were fed by that first religion which was the country itself, and if the other religions were now full of mutation and staggering across deserts of faith, it was because the country had been false and ill and corrupt for years . . . corrupt to the point of terminal disease, like a great religion foundering."[2] Mailer's record of the travails of his ego from *The Armies of the Night* to *St. George* both described and illustrated the crisis that the great Sydney Ahlstrom argued marked a major turning point in American religion, the end of that long era when the nation was seen as the primary agent of God's purpose in history.[3] For even longer Robert Bellah has been writing of this crisis of civil religion, first in terms of the presence of common symbols embodying American experience and the need for their renewal to turn

Americans outward to a vision of global responsibility, more recently in terms of an absence of an ethic of citizenship marked by love of the Republic and care for its good.[4] Striking close to home, Bellah told the Catholic Theological Society of America two years ago that the decline among Catholics of a vital sense of the church as the Body of Christ was depriving the nation of yet another symbol and religious belief that might structure such an ethic of mutual care and responsibility, one capable of sustaining our nation.[5]

Lutheran pastor Richard Neuhaus is another who has perceived the crisis of public religion and has attempted to persuade both Catholics and evangelicals to fill the vacuum of public language left by what he regards as the collapse of mainline Protestantism's claim to civil leadership.[6] Catholic Michael Novak has followed a very different route to a similar end. Like Neuhaus an activist, Novak shares with him an understanding of public culture as a kind of battleground where groups contend for control of the symbols, images, analytical categories, and modes of interpretation through which individuals and groups understand and evaluate experience and reach decisions about action.[7] Whatever one may think of Novak's arguments about democratic capitalism, there can be no doubt that he and a growing number of Catholic allies are engaged in a very serious effort to checkmate the liberal initiatives of the American hierarchy and, if possible, capture the machinery that shapes the substance and image of Catholic participation in public debate.

The Roman Catholic bishops have apparently shared something of this perception. In little-noticed statements extending from their negative judgment of the morality of the Vietnam War in 1971 through an evaluation of the economy in 1975 to statements on political responsibility in several presidential elections, the hierarchy has demonstrated a surprisingly active understanding of their responsibilities in shaping the public moral consensus. Most dramatic, of course, was their pastoral letter on nuclear weapons published in 1983. There they pursued two purposes: to help Catholics form their consciences and to help shape the public debate on nuclear-arms policy. They thus self-consciously addressed two audiences, church members and the general public, and did so in what they called "two complementary but distinct styles of teaching." The distinction manifested their understanding of the civic dialogue and the role of the church within it:

> The religious community shares a specific perspective of faith and can be called to live out its implications. The wider civil community, although it does not share the same vision of faith, is equally bound by certain key moral principles. For all men and women find in the depths

of their consciences a law written on the human heart by God. From this law reason draws moral norms. These norms do not exhaust the gospel vision, but they speak to critical questions affecting the welfare of the human community, the role of states in international relations, and the limits of acceptable action by individuals and nations on issues of war and peace.[8]

In applying these norms, the bishops reached some very controversial conclusions about the use of nuclear weapons, the strategy of deterrence, and on some specific issues of weapons policy. More generally, they clearly wished to help shape a critical, and responsible, public; they expressed their desire to help form public opinion "with a clear determination to resist resort to nuclear war as an instrument of national policy," to "build a barrier against the concept of nuclear war as a viable strategy of defense," and to "encourage a public attitude which sets stringent limits on the kind of action our own government and other governments will take on nuclear policy."

While by no means resolving internal problems, the hierarchy clearly wishes to draw Catholics into civil life in an effort less to influence policy directly than to help define a set of principles that will structure public debate and policy. Since publication of the pastoral the bishops' conference has resisted pressure to testify on specific weapons proposals; Bryan Hehir, the bishops' chief staff person, recently told an activist group that the church makes its most important political contribution when it helps "define the issues." Since the pastoral, Cardinal Joseph Bernardin has clarified this position by insisting on a consistent, prolife philosophy, a "seamless garment," encompassing the church's positions on armaments, abortion, and the death penalty. Prolife activists are furious at this seeming surrender to the liberals, allowing abortion to be swallowed up in a range of issues incapable together of mobilizing any considerable "clout."[9]

It should be noted that this struggle to shape a public dialogue aimed at building a national and indeed international consensus on the value of the human person runs directly counter to the position of many philosophers and social critics who contend that pluralism in the context of modern industrial and bureaucratic society has all but eliminated the possibility of developing a common language, much less a public ethic. Churches at best can become what the bishops call communities of conscience, bearing witness to their distinctive beliefs and thereby challenging the practices of the larger society of which they are a part, but they do not in themselves possess the resources to participate in a common life whose language and symbols necessarily exclude specific religious considerations. In the words of Stanley Hauerwas:

It is the duty of the church to be a society which through the way its members deal with one another demonstrates to the world what love means in social relations. So understood, the church fulfills its social responsibility by being an example, a witness, a creative minority formed by its obedience to nonresistant love.[10]

This position, which enjoys growing support within the church and even, as we shall see, attracts the support of a growing number of bishops, stands in sharp contrast to the position of Vatican II, upheld by Archbishop Bernardin and central to the pastoral letter, that the church "has a positive responsibility to participate in the process of building a more just and peaceful human society."[11] While obviously deriving from the church's long tradition of natural law, the persistence of this tradition, and with it the persistence of just-war teaching, arises less from the presumptions of that tradition about human reason than from the concrete circumstances of the church in contemporary American life.

Historical Background

I have argued elsewhere that the mainline of Roman Catholic reflection on church and state in the United States has emphasized three major themes.[12] First was a sharp distinction between spiritual and temporal matters, between religion and politics, a distinction upheld by American Catholics even after European Catholicism had moved in another direction in the ultramontane movement which climaxed at Vatican I. It was this distinction that enabled John Carroll and his successors to combine the spiritual supremacy of the Holy See with wholehearted acceptance of the first amendment. Upholding their own spiritual authority, the bishops refrained from partisan political activity; some even refused to vote. Indeed, they shared with many other national leaders a profound suspicion of political parties or "factions," regularly warning against the machinations of selfish and unscrupulous politicians. This contempt was wonderfully illustrated when Cardinal William O'Connell responded to a question about the colorful James Michael Curley: "It seems I have heard of the man."

At the same time the bishops argued that by confining themselves to religious matters, bringing people into an organized relationship with the church, instructing them in the doctrines of their faith, providing them with moral guidance, and encouraging them to associate with one another for mutual assistance, they were making a valuable contribution to American life. Good Catholics made good citizens, for they understood the demands of the moral life, their dependence on God, the subordination of worldly ambition to eternal salvation, and the requirements placed on all Christians to conduct themselves with restraint, decency, and a regard for the concerns of others. Far from jeopardizing community consensus, Catholicism actively contributed to it by imposing on its members, with the authority of Christ himself, the very values and attitudes required for the success of the American experiment in self-government in a setting of religious and cultural pluralism.

Second, the church fought strenuously for recognition of its right to be the church. Perceiving anti-Catholic movements as upholding a theory of national religious uniformity, Catholics demanded their full rights as citizens, including access to public institutions, a fair share of educational funds, and freedom from anti-Catholic texts in public schools. Few went as far as John Hughes, who sponsored his own slate of candidates in the 1841 New York State Assembly elections; rather they spoke out on issues seen as vital to the church's freedom, they lobbied legislatures and used what influence they could muster to protect the church's interests and defend its rights, all in the name of church-state separation and religious liberty. Sometimes such efforts had unexpected benefits; by sharpening intergroup tensions, they drew together the diverse and often contentious groups that comprised the church. But such efforts could also backfire, fueling nativist and anti-Catholic sentiment, and forcing the state toward more neutral and necessarily secular policies. What is important, however, is that these efforts were always justified in terms of the First Amendment and never led Catholics to any serious criticism of American constitutional arrangements.

Finally, the church combined nonpartisanship and defense of the church's rights with public spiritedness. At moments of crisis, the bishops rallied Catholics to the national cause, even putting aside private doubts about the wisdom or morality of national policy. Of course such decisions reflected the self-interest of a minority church, but more frequently they expressed the widely held conviction that as moral leaders the bishops had a responsibility to modify legitimate diversity and help shape the public consensus required by a free society. In a nation with no established church or dominant religious group, the leaders of every church had a responsibility to provide moral leadership, including mobilizing the conscience of the nation to accept the sacrifices required when its existence or ideals were at stake.

Within the framework of this basic policy there were differences of emphasis. The liberal tradition in American Catholicism generally emphasized a preference for the third element of the strategy. At times its advocates seemed generally convinced that it was necessary to uphold the first principle, the distinction between spiritual and temporal authority, less against the American government than against the Holy See. They almost always saw the second objective of securing the church's place in America as achieved and they went on to demand a fuller effort to take on a significant public role. Carroll and Bishop John England, for example, were Americanizers who favored the rapid assimilation of immigrants and the emergence of an authentically American Catholic Church whose members would be accepted as full participants in society and would bear those responsibilities with a disinterested concern for the common good. Orestes Brownson regularly criticized the selfish, group-centered approach to public issues of the Irish American leaders of the church; he and Isaac Hecker yearned for the conversion of America to Catholicism, not in the spirit of Catholic triumphalism but in the conviction that Catholicism's truth, unity, and universality could alone in the long run make Americans one people and insure the survival of those ideals of liberty, justice, and progress that gave meaning to American democracy. John Lancaster Spalding and other liberals of the late nineteenth century, inspired in part by Hecker, assumed the relative autonomy of the secular order and called upon American Catholics to enter fully into American life, not in order to win respect for the church and rewards for its people, but to make the American experiment work. Defeated by a combination of Roman intervention and Catholic exclusiveness, the liberal tradition survived in the twentieth century as a voice for reason, moderation, and public spiritedness in a Catholic community dominated by intense minority consciousness legitimated by an ideology that placed the church at the center of human history. Liberals of the interwar period, therefore, fought a two-front war against what they perceived to be creeping secularism without and narrow-minded self-interest within, hoping to move beyond ethnic politics to a serious Catholic dedication to American public purpose.

This was reflected in the arguments Catholics made in support of social reform. Drawing upon the Catholic tradition of natural law, supported by selected passages from the social encyclicals of Pope Leo XIII and Pius XI, they argued that each person, made in God's image, possessed basic rights, including the right to life and the means to maintain life in dignity. On this basis, they argued to the demand for a living wage, for a just distribution of the benefits and rewards of economic activity, and to a defense of private property. They also argued for the right of labor to organize and bargain collectively and for the responsibility of government to meet the needs of those unable to work and to exercise a general supervision of the economy to insure that rights were respected and justice was insured. "Social justice" meant the responsibility of each person and institution to pursue the common good of the whole community, a good which included recognition of personal and group rights but placed these in a framework of overall societal well-being.

This positive understanding of the role of government and of the importance of social rights was balanced by an insistence on personal liberty, including religious freedom and private property. By means of the principle of subsidiarity, Catholics argued that the provision of social goods should always take place at the level closest to the people concerned. This meant less an emphasis on local government than on unions, trade associations, and other such bodies that should engage in self-determination, subject only to general governmental supervision, an American version of Catholic corporatism which John A. Ryan baptized "economic democracy." Thus Catholic progressivism balanced individual rights with social obligations; the church recognized the need not only to defend rights, such as the right to a living wage, but to address the question how such rights could be met in the concrete conditions of American life. The virtue of social justice included both the defense of rights and the promotion of the common good or the general welfare. Catholic teaching, then, was not explicitly confessional or religious; rather it professed to offer arguments not only compatible with American democracy but arising from the very values of liberty and justice on which that democracy rested. It was an approach, and a set of proposals, that Catholics regarded as moral, practical, and capable of implementation within the setting of American institutions, including religious pluralism.

In the years following World War II theologian John Courtney Murray put a theoretical framework on the Catholic experience in the United States. On the one hand he argued that church-state separation and religious liberty as practiced in the United States were civil and temporal, not religious arrangements; they implied a political theory; they grounded a constitutional structure; they did not constitute a theological position and did not threaten the right of the church to be the church. Like his American Catholic predecessors, Murray distinguished sharply between spiritual and temporal affairs, and he argued that, far from making Catholics bad citizens, Catholicism taught as true those doctrines of human dignity, justice, and freedom that were central to the American experiment. The Catholic, drawing not directly from scripture and not unduly dependent on the teaching authority of his church, entered civil society with the heritage of a long wisdom of political and social thought that affirmed human reason and provided a basis for pluralism, civic order, and harmony. In the future as in the past, the church could and should defend its right to be the church. It should contribute to civic well-being by upholding the American consensus, and its people should share in public life with others on the basis not of distinctive Catholic tenets of political morality but on the basis of commonly shared values and principles that for Catholics were solidly grounded in faith. Catholics spontaneously and honestly supported the "American proposition" of equality and inalienable rights, and the constitutional system based on them, because that proposition was true.

Murray's argument was given authority by the Second Vatican Council in its *Declaration on Religious Liberty* and in *The Pastoral Constitution on the Church and the Modern World*. While the church has no political agenda of its own, the Council Fathers taught, it has a responsibility to share in public life and in particular to defend and promote human rights. On this basis the American bishops have continued their long practice of collectively addressing public issues. Public-policy decisions necessarily involve moral judgments, the bishops argue, so that the church has a clear responsibility to share in the development of a public moral consensus on the basis of which such decisions must be made. Citizens have a responsibility to consider the moral dimensions of issues when deciding among parties and candidates. The moral principles to be considered include the catalogue of human rights developed in church teaching since John XXIII's *Pacem in Terris* of 1963, including both political and civil rights like free speech, freedom of the press, freedom of religion, the rights and duty of political participation, and the social and economic rights flowing from the right to life and to those things necessary for living in dignity. Clearly the bishops continue to believe, as Murray did, that Catholics share with other Americans a commitment to these rights, so that moral judgments based on such criteria constitute no unconstitutional intrusion into politics and no violation of church-state separation. Rather the church, by addressing such problems on the basis of human rights, fulfills a long-standing requirement of American political culture: the church must help shape a moral consensus and form a people, which alone will allow the American experiment in free government and freedom of religion to work.

Thus the three-part strategy of the past holds firm. Distinguishing between spiritual and temporal matters, the bishops insist on the duty of Catholics to be good citizens, to participate in public life with a concern for human rights and for the common good. The church thus contributes to the vitality of democracy and the stability of American institutions both by instructing its own members in their moral obligations and by sharing in the wider public dialogue. Second, with no violation of that distinction, the church has the right and responsibility within the pluralistic framework of American religion to defend its own freedom, its right to be the church, to worship, to govern itself, to educate, and to comment freely on public affairs. And finally the church has the responsibility to share with others in upholding the institutions of American society, rallying to their support when they are in danger, calling for their reform when that is needed, working with others to insure that they correspond to the requirements of the common life and the values which inform that life, always in a way that affirms and strengthens the community and the nation.

Historically this tradition has had to contend against the group-centered consciousness of most Catholic leaders, clerical and lay.[13] Until recently, church self-interest, material and psychological, ordinarily overwhelmed pretensions to public spiritedness, giving rise to charges of dishonesty and hypocrisy. In a very real sense, the liberal tradition took for granted the unity of the church and its secure position in American society. In the 1960's the American Catholic subculture, out of which this position developed, entered into a period of such profound change that the very existence of the American church became problematic.

Contemporary Catholic experience is shaped by the collapse of the American Catholic subculture that seemed so strong a generation ago and still dominates the Catholic imagination. This collapse, or "disintegration," as Philip Gleason has called it, resulted from the convergence of three major streams of change.[14] First, the social composition and location of Catholics changed. Once an immigrant, working-class people in a church that saw itself as a minority in American society, Catholics have become a highly Americanized church whose income and class distribution mirrors that of the society at large. No longer do we see ourselves as outsiders, an excluded minority, but as full participants in American life. So, if nothing else had happened, there would have been enormous changes in American Catholic life and culture. But the Council did happen, replacing our image of the church as an institution that, through its sacraments, provided the ordinary means of salvation, with a variety of more open and fluid images, among them the communitarian image of the people of God, placed at the center of the church's self-denomination. Along with affirmation of religious liberty and emphasis on the worldly vocation of the church, the Council disturbed settled notions of success and failure and initiated a process of renewal that disrupted the already disturbed Catholic subculture. Add to that the turmoil in American society during the decade of the sixties, an eruption of energy that all but ended the historic American innocence and called into question long-accepted images of America as a uniquely endowed nation and Americans as specially graced people, and the very foundations of American Catholic self-understanding were exploded. In Mary Gordon's novel *Fi-*

nal Payments the heroine exclaims in the rush of freedom that follows the death of her father: "I would have to invent an existence for myself."[15] So do we all.

One result has been the emergence of the word "ministry," unknown among Catholics a few years ago. Standing in some tension with hierarchical, clerical church organization, ministry brings with it themes of community, mutuality, equality, participatory democracy, if you will. It makes marriage, the baptism of children, and confirmation moments of adult decision about the content of faith and the degree of participation in community life; it finds its premiere expression in the Rite of Christian Initiation of Adults. Studies of successful parishes by Andrew Greeley and by the Parish Renewal Project provide evidence of the widespread influence of ministerial styles, and with it a growing problem not simply of priestly numbers but priestly identity.[16] The American historian might speak of the same phenomena in terms of the evangelical style long dominant among Protestants: an emphasis on individual decisions of faith, on the scriptures rather than sacraments, dogmatic formulas, or denominational confessions, on fellowship and congregational autonomy, and on benevolence and good will as expressions of Christian faith in action.[17]

For our purposes several things need to be emphasized. First, freedom has taken on new meaning. Religious liberty now means the right not only to select a church for oneself but to define the terms of one's membership. As Karl Rahner predicted a generation ago, faith has become "a matter of personal decision constantly renewed amid perilous surroundings," that faith tested less by canons of orthodoxy than by reference to scripture and human experience.[18] What is true of doctrine is even more true of ethics: the faithful Catholic will consider the teachings of the magisterium and will listen more or less attentively to the advice of a respected pastor, but in the end people will make up their own minds. Whatever one may think of this in theory, there is no doubt that it is a reality in practice, shaping all the work of evangelization and religious education. As historian Sidney Mead noted years ago, in a free society persuasion necessarily replaces coercion as the means by which the church is built and exerts its influence on its own members and the larger community.[19]

Secondly, as freedom becomes more and more a matter of internal experience, religion tends inexorably to accommodate to the culture in which it finds itself. In advanced industrial societies like our own, that tendency is one which confines religion largely to the private sphere of life, to relationships, family, friendship, recreational and social activity. Modern culture excludes overt religious considerations from public life, increasingly dominated by large institutions, megastructures, professedly organized on the basis of rational systems of evaluation and control. Bureaucracy, specialization, professionalism, expertise are characteristic of political, economic, and even cultural life. These are experienced in another sphere from the personal, affective, emotional, and diffuse experiences of community, whether they take place in family, ethnic group, neighborhood, voluntary association, or church. The intensity of that search for community results from the breakdown of those places where community once flourished. Thus freedom is one thing when seen in terms of private life, now marked by a radical voluntarism, and another when spoken of in terms of public life, now marked by massive systems over which none of us professes to have much control.

Thirdly, and finally, this freedom that Catholics experience as voluntarism, is confined largely to the private side of life and locates the church even more fully as one specialized institution among many. It is that institution which deals with religion, and it is left to its own resources to define what religion might mean. Any particular church is dependent upon its members for support and vitality; it presents itself to those members or potential members as something that fills a need they might have. Other institutions provide work, education, social services, access to political power, protection against emergencies; many other groups make better provision of opportunities for cultural and recreational activity. Necessarily, the church drifts toward a preoccupation with those matters that are defined as private and personal, rather than public or political, and it tends to do so in ways that accentuate the difference. Clues to what I mean can be found again in the history of American Protestantism. On the frontier the churches provided continuity, order, and stability where these were absent and upheld those values against a lawless world outside. In the cities they emphasized sobriety, sexual restraint, thrift, and stewardship against an urban world defined in terms of intemperance, hedonism, materialism, and the headlong pursuit of wealth. Catholic immigrants built their churches as centers of traditional values of particular immigrant groups, with frequent reminders of the dangers to those values present in the society beyond the church. Occasionally this ideological statement of difference and implied superiority burst forth in reform movements; more often the church's preachments against the world were confined to a language that limited the difference in order to erect no barriers to its members' success; naturally enough Christians preferred to have their cake of economic success and political participation while not eating it as religious indifference or one or another form of worldliness.

Karl Marx contended that man makes his own history, but not in conditions of his own making. In Mary Gordon's terms, one invents an existence for oneself, but with little control over the conditions in which the invention takes place. Freedom to invent is confined to the private side of life, for we cannot, unfortunately, reinvent the world. Personal questions of meaning, identity, faith, and purpose give rise to a yearning for community; the absence of these things is experienced as a freedom that the scholars call alienation, the sense that the world outside the self is indeed outside, indifferent if not positively hostile to people's needs and aspirations. Having nowhere else to turn, people reach out to one another. They come to measure the church in terms of its ability to answer their need for meaning, to provide support and affirmation, to be an island of assurance in a difficult and dangerous world. And the church, in turn, reflects that sense of estrangement from the world in a language and style that serves its own interests by confirming that experience. The church is a small group, deliberately set off against the world, if not in opposition to it. In the words of the bishops' pastoral letter on nuclear weapons:

> It is clear today, perhaps more than in previous generations, that convinced Christians are a minority in nearly every country of the world —including nominally Christian and Catholic nations. . . . As believers we can identify rather easily with the early church as a company of witnesses engaged in a difficult mission. . . . To obey the call of Jesus means separating ourselves from all attachment and affiliation that could prevent us from hearing and following our authentic vocation. To set out on the road of discipleship is to dispose oneself for a share in the cross. To be a Christian, according to the New Testament, is not simply to believe with one's mind, but also to become a doer of the word, a wayfarer and witness to Jesus. This means, of course, that we must regard as normal even the path of persecution and the possibility of martyrdom. We readily recognize that we live in a world that is becoming increasingly estranged from Christian values. In order to remain a Christian, one must take a resolute stand against many commonly accepted axioms of the world. To become true disciples, we must undergo a demanding course of induction into the adult Christian community. We must continually equip ourselves to profess the full faith of the church in an increasingly secularized society.[20]

It is understandable, then, that many people in the church regard the pastoral as an interim document, produced by a church on the way from just war to pacifism. Even many bishops regard the just-war teaching and the carefully nuanced treatment of deterrence as somehow involving a compromise of Christian faith. The Hauerwas position, which would short-circuit the public dialogue in favor of a sectarian, confessional community, seems more and more the sole means by which the church can salvage its integrity. Conscientious objection, tax resistance, refusal of defense work become the standards of acceptable Christian peacemaking. If this reading of the pastoral is correct, then the predictions of many students of the church are also correct. Avery Dulles, for example, predicts that the church of the future will be a smaller, more committed church composed of persons who have made personal decisions of faith over against a culture that is becoming increasingly pagan.[21] Morris West and Walker Percy sketch similar scenarios, envisioning a beleaguered church in a God-forsaken world.[22]

As one might suspect, many Catholics are distinctly uncomfortable with this movement which is especially strong among the church's professional elites, theologians, scripture scholars, religious orders of men and women, and a segment of the hierarchy. At the other extreme from such moralism, and developing in almost dialectical relationship to it, is a neorealism that claims the legacy of John Courtney Murray and Reinhold Niebuhr. Founded in the experience of success of many lay Catholics, and reflecting what Andrew Greeley calls the "communal Catholic," at home in the world and identifying as Catholic without any vigorous participation in church affairs, this position reflects as well the widespread public tendency to limit moral responsibility to the boundaries of the present situation. On the issue of nuclear war, for example, lay leaders like Michael Novak and James Finn refuse either to join their fellow Catholics in moralistic resistance or follow the lead of moderates like Hehir and Bernardin in seeking to transform the "sinful situation" of international anarchy in the direction of international organization and a more rational world order. To escape from a morality of lesser evils by professing "the full faith of the church" is to court martyrdom and inflict greater evils on the world. To avoid totalitarian slavery, one must prepare for nuclear war; to avoid nuclear war, one must prepare to wage it; to make modest arms reductions possible, one must increase conventional arms; to resist totalitarianism, one must accommodate and arm authoritarian and quite murderous governments. There is no way to go beyond the "peace of a sort" achieved through deterrence or the "justice of a sort" achieved through the admitted anarchy of the international system. With their idealistic enemies of the "what would Jesus do?" school, such pseudorealists share a belief that history is beyond human control and therefore beyond human responsibility. To take significant action leads to greater evils; to refuse to act at all brings the same result.[23]

In this situation, we have a new variety of contentious Catholics. Novak and those associated with the American Catholic Committee and such journals as *Catholicism and Crisis* argue for a church whose leadership confines its teaching to specifically religious matters and offers at best very general principles for the guidance of public or secular life. More or less convinced that present American institutions and policies are the best attainable, they would summon the church to affirm the relative goodness of the nation and provide spiritual energy for the hard tasks of defending freedom and affirming economic liberty. Their difference with the bishops is more political than theological; they admit the distinction between the community of faith and the larger community of the nation; they resist the application of theological categories to secular affairs and uphold the autonomy of the secular order and a strictly personal integration of faith and politics. Some among them, reflecting the older traditions of the Catholic subculture, are ardently committed to a specifically Catholic agenda of abortion, tuition tax credits, and "pro-family" social policies, but are at one with their more political associates in denying that the church has anything of value to say on matters of peace, social justice, or public policy. They draw upon notions of toleration to marginalize the witness of radicals like the Berrigans and the culture of expertise to delegitimate Christian language and trivialize religious demands. At the pastoral level the evangelical left makes inroads by arousing conscience, but its prophetic prescriptions limit its impact, leaving in its wake a pious mysticism of peace and justice with at best a charitable and prayerful outcome. The right has no pastoral strategy to speak of, save to confirm the privatization of religion and accommodation to the status quo, but among the middle class that may be enough. Politically the conservatives ask only that people form their consciences without any direct reference to the Gospel or the living church. For Novak it is simply intolerable that the bishops would divide the church over political matters at a time when it is difficult enough to sustain orthodox faith and faithful practice. On the Catholic campuses, where the evangelical style inhibits efforts to enlist academic resources for political and social action, neorealism appeals to the armies of Catholic intellectuals who have accommodated easily to the bureaucratic contours of the modern knowledge industry. On the other hand, the conservatives know they have lost, at least temporarily, most of the church's middle management and many of the bishops, so they must go through public channels to reach the Catholic middle class; there their language, style, and sophistication give them fair prospects. They also anticipate, and seem to be getting, some help from Rome, which has its own agenda.

The bishops are thus caught in a classic bind. If they ground themselves exclusively in the scriptural imperative of Christian love and withdraw from the effort to influence the public consensus and public policy, they may indeed mobilize considerable support for a critical, prophetic witness, even if it costs the church many members and opens the community to charges of public irresponsibility. At the other extreme, they may stand too closely to the prevailing framework of responsibility, looking at issues through the lens of decision-makers, become sympathetic to their dilemmas, and accept only the limited alternatives that seem to be presently available. If they move one way they seem utopian, unrealistic, and irresponsible. If they move the other way they appear to have lost their integrity as Christian leaders by acquiescing in situations they themselves have defined as unjust and immoral.

The debate over the pastoral letter on nuclear weapons reflects this dilemma quite clearly. So far, while individual bishops have adopted one or another of these conflicting positions, the hierarchy as a whole has continued to insist that they can be both responsible participants in the public debate and faithful custodians of the Gospel. In this they reflect the experience of many Catholics, who also are torn between the apparent demands of Christian love and their responsibilities in daily life. The process has highlighted the fact that a perfectionism based on exclusive Christian standards and a realism that all but exempts the policy process from Christian moral evaluation are equally dangerous for the church, the nation, and the world. The bishops have placed themselves on the edge, at the boundaries between faith and politics, where they have always tried to be, but now at a time and on an issue when faith and politics seem to be moving from tension to contradiction.

The ambivalence of the pastoral letter on armaments and the conflicts occasioned by early drafts of the upcoming pastoral on the economy suggest that contentiousness among Catholics will continue. At the moment the traditional balancing position of liberal Catholicism enjoys little popular support outside the hierarchy. Yet with the help of the Reagan administration's liaison officer with Catholics, with a host of new publications, and with the Vatican's effort to crack down on venturesome experimentation, the right now enjoys a new prominence and may well begin to win a following among lay people and many priests. The left wing, in contrast, lacks the organizational capability significantly to influence church policy or to exert much leverage in national affairs. Yet at the grass roots their practice is impressive.

Inspired by the new social gospel, grass-roots activism is stronger than ever. Community organizing, parish outreach, care for and advocacy on behalf of the poor and homeless, pastoral progress among Hispanics, burgeoning justice and peace centers organizing around Central America—all these are striking signs of the strength of social concern and the vitality of distinctively American Catholic forms of social action. Catholic Worker houses are more numerous than ever before, while Catholic schools and colleges have small but influential cadres of peace and justice activists. Even more important are renewal programs centered on scripture and community formation which are revitalizing parishes and feeding movements and programs for spiritual enrichment, marriage and family life, and benevolent social service, all making more real the notion of a fundamental option for the poor and an orientation toward peace as central elements of contemporary Christian faith. Long on dedication and increasingly skilled in tactics, however, these groups and movements are short on theory. Like Thomas Merton, they know the need for public action and the dangers of privatization, but they are proudly innocent of social theory, weak on economics, conscience-stricken when confronted with the ambiguities of politics within or without the church, and appalled by the suggestion that they need to take up the cause of their nation by enlisting in the public dialogue on public terms.

To connect all this work to the Bernardin effort to renew public life will require a more strategic theology appropriate to American realities. Neither evangelical radicalism nor amoral realism reflect that experience, for Catholics and their church do not stand on the margins of society in the United States. Among poor, oppressed, or alienated people anywhere in the world, the Gospel message invariably seems to say: "God loves you. Jesus is your brother. You don't deserve to be treated this way. Those who are oppressing you must change, and the society that rejects or exploits you must be transformed." Christian community in this context is necessarily radical, countercultural, sectarian, or revolutionary. Most American Catholics, and certainly most bishops, priests, religious, and theologians, while perhaps "concerned" about one or another aspect of American society, are quite at home in it. They do not live in monasteries, they are not poor, they are not and do not want to be members of an isolated sect or a revolutionary front. Quite the contrary, they are generally grateful for their income, their education, their respectable status, and most of all for the freedom they enjoy. At their best they recognize that for them, unlike their poor or alienated brothers and sisters, no question of social morality or public policy is a matter of Catholic outsiders and non-Catholic insiders, us and them. On every issue, from family life and morality in media to economic justice and nuclear strategy, Catholics and Catholicism are involved on both sides, as persons, as an institution, even as an ideology. In short, Catholics share responsibility for what is, however different they might like it to be. Even if they enter the monastery or join a Catholic Worker community, they remain irreversibly American, like it or not. Those who live more ordinary lives may or may not recognize their responsibilities as citizens and as participants in this society and culture, but they delude themselves if they think that nuclear war or any other moral issue is somebody else's problem.

It is this reality of an increasingly evangelical church among an increasingly Americanized people that accounts for the complexity and apparent contradictions of contemporary American Catholicism. A group of bishops meeting in an expensive hotel issues a statement denouncing consumerism. A North Carolina prayer group pledges itself to the prolife movement though most of its members earn their living from cigarettes. An independent Catholic social-action group testifies before a state legislative committee on housing conditions in the heavily Hispanic center of the city. Most of the members of the committee, most of the Hispanics, and most of the landlords and realtors are Catholics. Like Pogo of another generation, "We have met the enemy and it is us."

This is the web, the fabric of life from which the pastoral springs. As Catholic Christians, the bishops cannot escape, and to their credit they do not want to escape, the clear peace imperatives of the Gospel. They cannot deny, and no longer wish to deny, the power and authenticity of Christian nonviolence for to do so would be to deny a part of themselves. Yet to denounce the government and the military, to ignore the realities of power and the ambiguities of politics, would be to deny another part of themselves. They have met too many citizens, politicians, bureaucrats, generals, and admirals to write them off as killers. Part of the church, so part of each bishop, has been to the mountaintop with Martin Luther King and in the streets with Daniel Berrigan; part of the church, so part of each bishop, has been to the brink with John Kennedy and in the corridors of power with Joseph Califano and Alexander Haig.

The bishops would like to follow Jesus and refuse cooperation with the state, even at the risk that, in our absence, evil might temporarily triumph. They, like most of us, would also like to defend freedom, bring about greater justice, and make war a bit less likely or a bit less destructive, even at the risk of compromising our faith. The bishops wish to encourage their people to be more true to the Gospel, to be apostles of peace and witnesses to its possibility. They explicitly seek to win a conversion of heart from the ways of war to the ways of peace. Most clearly, they wish to say an unequivocal "No!" to nuclear war. But they also wish to influence public policy, to shape public opinion, to encourage the hard-headed political work of negotiating disarmament and building a more rational, just, and peaceful world order. They want Catholics as Christians to be more political, to translate their commitment to Christ's peace into ideas, programs, strategies, action; they want Catholics as citizens to be more Christian, more believing, more committed, more risk-taking, more hopeful. As shepherds, they want to keep the flock together, discussing their differences, learning from each other, seeking common ground. As witnesses to the faith of their church they wish to speak on its behalf, articulating that shared faith in ways that will be heard by those not of the faith.

Unfortunately, the bishops do not fully grasp the nature of this church-and-society relationship. Instead of grounding their approach to the issue of nuclear war in the concrete situation of American Catholicism, they draw upon an abstract notion of a minority church in a pluralist society, requiring two "styles" of teaching, one for Catholics and another for the wider society that cannot be expected to respond to a message framed in explicitly Catholic or Christian terms. Unfortunately, they import along with these "styles" a dualism of morality and politics and a separation of church and world that have little relevance to the actual experience of Catholics or of most ordinary Americans. At times it leads them to slip into the very things they want to avoid, a religious renunciation of worldly responsibility or a worldly trivialization of moral demands.

How different the discussion becomes when we anchor the two styles not in a mythical abstract church located as one minority among others in an abstract marketplace kind of world, but in a living Christian community that is fully alive in the United States. This world is already in us, shaping and informing even our supposedly religious symbols and language, while the church and all of us are simultaneously in the world, a world which we, with others, have made. The two styles of discourse are not one that is Catholic and ours, and one that is public and largely theirs, but two expressions, ways of embodying our living experience as American Catholics. We reject a sectarian, nonpolitical Christianity not as Catholics or Americans, but as both, for it does not adequately express our experience or our responsibility as people who are church members and citizens all at once. We similarly reject an amoral realism on both Christian and American grounds. As decent human beings we recognize the justice of granting exemptions to persons of eccentric belief, but our dissent is not like that, satisfied by provision in a manual, alternative service, or refusal of work. We claim that our position is the proper American position and it cannot be marginalized by toleration. If we remain in the midst of life and do not join the monastery or revolution, it is not because we have made a second-best choice but because we have been called there and believe it is right for us to be there. We want no exemption, but policies, goals, strategies to which we can give our wholehearted support, to which we can devote our lives.

The point is that we need more and not less politics, and we need churches to say yes to political action. "Situations of sin," described without reference to the decisions that created those situations, easily become "mystification" and devalue politics as much as the neoconservative exemption of politics from morality or the radical exemption of morality from politics with a small "p." This country has had more than enough of moralistic denunciations which end up defining things so broadly that only a fool would try to do anything about them. And it has also had more than enough denunciation of mythical radicalism, as if the slaughter in Vietnam or the destructiveness of nuclear weapons were products of Philip Berrigan's imagination. Nuclear war is in the end not a problem of weapons or technology or ideology; it is a problem of power. (Who cares if weapons exist as long as no one can use them? Who cares if people are Communists or Capitalists as long as they don't have the power to kill others in the name of their beliefs?)

Social ministry without pastoral ministry, a public church unattentive to personal and community needs, will never have the resources of faith, hope, love, and courage that the community of God's people alone can generate. Where will the people come from to bear the burdens of social change if not from families and churches and voluntary associations in which they experience a taste of their own dignity and catch a glimpse of what human life can be like? Both are necessary because both are not only a part of the world in which we live, they are also a part of us. All of us live in both worlds each day, the world of community and the world of society. In the world of marriage and family, friends and neighbors, churches and bars and clubs, we find affirmation and support, we share values and experiences, we speak in a language outsiders may find hard to understand, we need not finish each other's sentences and communicate through looks and movements as well as words. Yet each day we live as well in that other world, also a part of us. We ride on the bus and go to the bank and shop at the store and go to our school or our work. There we are judged by rational standards and resent being judged by the standard of other private worlds; we expect fairness and equity, not affection and personal involvement. We may introduce standard accounting procedures into our church in order to make its work more effective, but we judge the church by qualities other than its efficiency. At work we try to be personable and we form friendships, but we do not expect to be judged by how nice a person we are, but by how well we contribute to the tasks at hand. We practice two psychological repertoires everyday and are shocked when they are confused, when the pastor ignores the low-income parishoner or when our boss makes a decision based on sentiment rather than calculation. We expect our schools to help mediate between these two worlds. At home we may teach our children the values of love and compassion and the giving of self to others, but we know that there are other things to be learned and we send them to school to learn the ways of getting on in the world. If the school ignores the values of our private world, we are angry; but we are also angry if it ignores the requirements of the public world and substitutes good will and kindness for good instruction and solid learning. Like our parents and grandparents we wish our children to be loyal Catholics and good citizens, committed Christians and effective men and women of the world, and we teach them two ways of thinking and acting, related at best, but different.

Thus it is simply wrong to think that we can build the church without reference to the world; that is why we have poor homilies and dull liturgies. It is equally wrong to think we can change the world without community, for worldly men and women who never experience community are normless, anxious, driven people with no solid values, no ground on which to stand; they confront the world with fear and not with hope. A church that tries to change the world without renewing community life will soon find it has no ideas worth listening to, no witness worth giving, no people to carry out the changes, much less make things work after the changes are made.

However, in our society, one marked by pluralism and freedom, the danger is more grave on the private, not the public, side. For the enduring temptation of the church in such a society is to measure its success or failure by its own standards. Recognizing the intimate relationship between private life and religion, and told by others that religion has no role in public life, churches are apt to regard their only task as personal and communal, to measure vitality and strength by numbers and activities, by the purity of doctrine, the integrity of moral life, the strength of organization. Liberals and conservatives alike measure society by the standards of the church; moral majorities and social actionists alike find the world wrong and attempt to change it in accord with the values of their private worlds. In the process the church becomes a tribe, or an interest group, or a contestant in various public contests; public life is reduced to a colosseum where representatives of private worlds contend for power and recognition. And then, in reflective moments, all wonder what happened to the public interest, why common values are not translated into public policy, why power alone seems to matter and nice people do horrible things. The Mafia chieftain who loves his family, prays to the Virgin, and funds the parish building drive, the machine boss who never misses Mass, the executive who serves on the local United Way Board but closes his plant because wages are lower in Taiwan, the loving Christian who plots nuclear strategy are products of the same culture that produces the radical Christian who confuses prophecy with disengagement from a corrupt society, the spiritual director who directs souls deeper into themselves and never turns them back toward the world in which they live, the bishop or pastor who thinks things will be all right as soon as everyone has had a conversion experience.

To be sure, both theological self-understanding and sociological imperatives require close attention to the construction of forms of associational life that will provide the experience of community. There is no escaping that. But radicals and conservatives often seem at one in focusing exclusive attention on the private dimension; the one regards the public as all but lost, the other as beyond the appropriate reach of the church. Yet, what the church committed to justice and a world badly in need of it both require are new types of persons who integrate community and society, men and women of faith, deeply committed to their community, and at one and the same time men and women of their age, competent in their professions and disciplines, engaged in other organizations, intelligently active in public affairs. To be sure, we need the church, and it is a self-conscious project so we need ministers. But they are ministers to the ministers, servants of those who do God's work in the world, in family, community, profession, politics, culture. For all the strength of our renewal since Vatican II, we have yet to learn that lesson.

Social change begins with social consciousness, but that is consciousness not only of how bad or good things are as measured by the Gospel, but consciousness of how we already are participants in this culture, this world, and not another, awareness of how deeply and inescapably American we already are. Like it or not, there are no mountaintops to which we can withdraw to be Christian, not American. The missionary in Africa, the black writer on the Left Bank, the ambitious Bostonian in the papal court all discover, in the end, that they are Americans. Some days we would like to be wholly Catholic or wholly Christian, uncontaminated by time and place and culture. But history isn't like that. When we loved America too much, sending our sons to die for it and comparing their sacrifice to Christ's, when we hated America too much, calling it murderous and welcoming its anger, we were equally its children. We are not the first generation to experience exile, internal or external, to be spiritual refugees in the heart of our country, and to mistake our exile community for the saving remnant of the Lord. Most of us will eventually feel called home again.

Our Americanness is the concrete, fleshy human context of our call to be Catholic Christians. Like all contexts, it is internal as well as external, shaping not just the conditions of our public life but our very feelings about God and one another. Authentic prophecy takes place within and on behalf of a specific people; authentic church is in and for the world, not the abstract world of humankind or "the poor" or "women," but the real world around us, open to all, speaking on behalf of all, inviting all to the full realization of their humanity, sacramentalizing the rich human experience around us, liberating all persons from the slavery of poverty and tyranny, sin and death. We desperately need an American standpoint, sufficiently Christian to understand and illuminate human experi-

ence in this our land, yet not so super- or pseudo-Christian as to claim to
be judge and contradiction of all that America means.

Perhaps all this seems distressingly intramural. The fight between
Catholic radicals and conservatives may be interesting, and the bishops'
clumsy, sometimes pathetic, effort to enlist them in dialogue in order to
build a more responsible public witness may make amusing material for
cartoons or nice reading for people caught up in a new fascination with
bishops. But leave aside theology for a moment and ask two questions:
(1) What other national institution connects people of all classes and
races around a set of ideas about the meaning of history, the value of people, and the possibility of justice and peace? (2) What other national institution connects significant numbers of Americans through missions,
societies, religious orders, regional and national organizations, scholarly
exchanges with people in all other parts of the globe? If the notions of a
"common good" at home and a single human family abroad seem to
have something to do with human survival and the future of our nation,
then this church is important. Left to itself, American Catholicism will go
the way of American Protestantism, bonds of solidarity will loosen and
structures of unity will become more and more marginal to people's lives.
Good will be done, to be sure, but it may not be public good. If you think
that the drift of history will somehow work out, that may be fine. If, with
John Paul II, you think that human survival has become a matter of "conscious choice and deliberate policy," or if you think simply that this century of holocausts should be turned around, the prospect of a frag-
menting of Catholicism may be depressing. In our times history has
become a self-conscious human project. Catholics around the world are
struggling to assist one another and their brothers and sisters to create a
human future. For better or for worse, all the works of the church have
social content and political implications; neither spiritual directors nor
marriage counselors nor religious educators nor social activists can claim
to be at the center or on the frontier; there are centers and frontiers everywhere the Gospel is being preached, community is being formed, faith is
being celebrated, people are growing in their care for one another and for
God, and men and women are seeking justice not only through discrete
actions but also through lives oriented toward transforming the world so
that justice is both valued and made possible. We will never again be a
taken-for-granted church as we once might have been; neither should we
think that we must inevitably become a tiny remnant holding forth the
banner of truth as the world follows its headlong path toward disaster.
The strength of our Catholicity will be found in our ability to embrace a
seemingly bewildering variety of communities and movements, to enlist
them in conversation with one another and with the seemingly more con-

ventional, and to direct all toward that larger world of men and women like ourselves, announcing the good news that history has meaning and life has purpose, that there are promises still to be realized, alive even now in communities of people like ourselves, our neighbors and friends, promises that will in God's time bring all of us to a Kingdom that will be His because it will be ours.

Notes

1. See in particular *The Renewal of American Catholicism* (New York: Oxford University Press, 1972); "Some Reflections on the Catholic Experience in the United States," in Irene Woodward, ed., *The Catholic Church: The United States Experience* (New York: Paulist Press, 1979) 5–42; and "The Roman Catholic Experience in the United States," *Review and Expositor* 79 (Spring 1982) 199–216.

2. Norman Mailer, *St. George and the Godfather* (New York: New American Library, 1972) 87.

3. Sydney Ahlstrom, *A Religious History of the American People* (New Haven: Yale University Press, 1972), chapter 63.

4. Robert Bellah, *The Broken Covenant* (New York: Seabury Press, 1976); idem, "The Role of Preaching in a Corrupt Republic," *Christianity and Crisis*, 25 December 1978, pp. 317–22.

5. Robert Bellah, "Religion and Power in America Today," *Commonweal* 109 (3 December 1982) 650–55.

6. Richard Neuhaus, *Time Toward Home* (New York: Seabury Press, 1975); idem, Unpublished paper prepared for the U.S. Catholic bishops' meeting in Collegeville, Minnesota, June 1982.

7. Michael Novak, *The American Vision* (Washington, DC: American Enterprise Institute, 1978); idem, *The Spirit of Democratic Capitalism* (New York: Simon and Schuster, 1982).

8. *The Challenge of Peace: God's Promise and Our Response* (Washington, DC: United States Catholic Conference, 1983), paragraph 17.

9. Some good reflection on these matters is contained in the collections of essays on the pastoral letter edited by Philip J. Murnion, *Catholics and Nuclear War: A Commentary on The Challenge of Peace* (New York: Crossroad, 1983).

10. Quoted in J. Bryan Hehir, "The Just War Ethic and Catholic Theology: Dynamics of Change and Continuity," in Thomas Shannon, ed., *War or Peace?* (Maryknoll, NY: Orbis Books, 1982) 33.

11. Hehir, "Just War Ethic," 33.

12. David J. O'Brien, "American Catholics and American Society," in Murion, ed., *Catholics and Nuclear War*, 16–29. Sections of the following are taken from that essay.

13. See Mary Hanna, *Catholics and American Politics* (Cambridge: Harvard University Press, 1976).

14. Philip Gleason, "In Search of Unity: American Catholic Thought 1920–1960," *Catholic Historical Review* 65 (April 1979) 192.

15. Mary Gordon, *Final Payments* (New York: Random House, 1978) 3.

16. John Coleman, "The Future of Ministry," *America,* 28 March 1981, pp. 243–50; Andrew Greeley, *Parish, Priests and People* (Chicago: Thomas More Press, 1981).

17. See my "Literacy, Faith and Church: An American Religious Perspective," in John V. Apczynski, ed., *Foundations of Religious Literacy: Proceedings of the College Theology Society, 1982* (Chico, CA: Scholars Press, 1983) 3–30.

18. Karl Rahner, "The Present Situation of Christians," in *The Christian Commitment: Essays in Pastoral Theology* (New York: Sheed and Ward, 1963) 3–37.

19. Sidney Mead, *The Lively Experiment* (New York: Harper & Row, 1962), chapter 2.

20. *The Challenge of Peace,* part IV.

21. Avery Dulles. *A Church to Believe In: Discipleship and the Dynamics of Freedom* (New York: Crossroad, 1982) 1–18.

22. Morris West, *The Clowns of God* (New York: William Morrow and Co., 1981); Walker Percy, *Love in the Ruins* (New York: Farrar, Straus & Giroux, 1971).

23. James Finn, "Nuclear Terror: Moral Paradox," *America,* 19 February 1983, and the subsequent exchange of correspondence between Peter Steinfels and myself.

IV

Established Versus Emerging Groups

Although the United States has long seen itself as a haven for victims of religious persecution, religious tolerance has not been as universal as is often supposed. The first amendment was intended to restrict only the Federal government, leaving individual states free, until the fourteenth amendment was ratified in 1868, to support official religions.[1] To this day, however, there exists a kind of "approved" orthodoxy which, although not a specific denomination, makes certain religious groups more acceptable than others.[2] Nonetheless, the extreme hostility some small groups encounter from much older, larger, and more secure denominations is surprising. Such splinter groups can hardly constitute a real threat to the survival of mainline denominations, which have in fact often shown themselves perfectly capable of tolerating religious diversity. This kind of hostility must therefore result from something other than an accurate appraisal of the likely success of these groups.

Relations between established groups and newer religions, of which America has always had a profusion, are complicated by the inevitable tendency of new groups to threaten the social consensus, espousing positions outside the accepted norm. The fact that they often see themselves as persecuted no doubt affects their behavior as well, creating a self-fulfilling prophecy that drives them to react defensively to the unjust treatment they believe they have received.

American denominationalism demands toleration. This deeply ingrained expectation works its will on new, radical groups, which must conform to be accepted. Despite their sense of separateness, accompanied by ideological rigidity and social defensiveness, there often follows a process of cultural absorption, as such groups find their niche in the landscape of American religious life. Through such compromises, even the most "radical" of sects may eventually become a welcome denomination.

Notes

1. In fact, Massachusetts had already become the last state to eliminate its established church in 1833 (see Anson Phelps Stokes, *Church and State in the United States* [New York: Harper & Brothers, 1950] I:426–28). The New Hampshire legislature, however, which is required to grant equal protection of the law to "every denomination of Christians," is still empowered to authorize local bodies to provide support for "public Protestant teachers," apparently in order to ensure the existence of "morality and piety, rightly grounded on evangelical principles" (article 6 of the New Hampshire Bill of Rights, *Constitutions of the United States, National and State* [Dobbs Ferry, NY: Oceana Publications, 1962]). On the other hand, the Maryland constitution requires only "a declaration of belief in the existence of God" for those who would hold office or be granted religious freedom (Declaration of Rights, articles 36–37; ibid.)

2. So W. Herberg, *Protestant–Catholic–Jew: An Essay in American Religious Sociology* (Garden City, NY: Anchor Books, 1960).

9

Cults in Conflict:
New Religious Movements and the
Mainstream Religious Tradition
in America

LAWRENCE FOSTER

F ew conflicts in human history have been more devastating than religiously inspired wars, persecution, and strife. Even the twentieth-
century world, which likes to think of itself as "enlightened" and "secular," has repeatedly fallen victim to deadly religious and ethnic conflicts.
During World War I, more than one million Christian Armenians were
systematically slaughtered by the Ottoman Turks. As part of Hitler's
preparations for his "thousand-year Reich," at least six million Jews, as
well as other religious and ethnic minorities such as Jehovah's Witnesses
and Gypsies, were brutalized and sent to their death in his "final solution" during World War II. When India was partitioned after World War
II, a communal bloodbath ensued that took the lives of more than one
million people and caused approximately seven and one-half million
Muslims to flee from India to Pakistan and about ten million Hindus to
flee from Pakistan to India. During the 1960s and 1970s, long-
smouldering hostilities between Catholics and Protestants in Northern
Ireland burst into the flames of repeated terrorism and counterterrorism,
costing more than a thousand lives. And in the Middle East, religious and
ethnic divisions have resulted in intergroup violence that is baffling in its
complexity. As only one of many examples, in September 1982, Christian phalangist forces carried out the grisly massacre of more than eight
hundred men, women, and children in the Palestinian refugee camps of
Sabra and Shatila near Beirut, Lebanon. Unfortunately, these episodes

constitute only a small part of the brutality and hatred that have been unleashed by religious and ethnic conflicts in the twentieth century alone.[1]

By contrast with such destructive interreligious conflicts world-wide, the United States in the twentieth century and throughout its history has been largely free from interreligious strife that has assumed life-and-death intensity. In fact, so hospitable has the United States been to religious diversity that, by J. Gordon Melton's latest count, at least fourteen hundred distinct religious groups can currently be identified in this country, eight hundred of them with Christian roots and six hundred of them with non-Christian roots.[2] Like the great Roman Empire of antiquity, which tolerated a wide range of religious and ethnic groups within its boundaries, the United States has been characterized by a high degree of religious pluralism.[3] Tensions and hostilities have repeatedly surfaced here, of course, but seldom have they approached the level found elsewhere in the world. Baptists may feel superior to Catholics and vice versa, Jews may resent exclusion from White Anglo-Saxon Protestant social clubs, and Mormons may chafe at still being characterized as a "cult," but no major group would seriously consider advocating the forcible destruction or blatant repression of other religious groups in America today. Even the deprogrammer Ted Patrick, who refers to Billy Graham as a dangerous cultist and finds as bland a movement as Transcendental Meditation a threat to the Republic, has not advocated killing or maiming members of far more unpopular religious movements such as the Hare Krishnas, Moonies, or Children of God, against whom his primary efforts are directed.[4]

Although the United States has shown greater tolerance for religious diversity than much of the rest of the world, relations between competing groups have often been far from harmonious. For example, tensions have repeatedly developed between relatively established or "mainstream" religious groups and new or unorthodox groups, frequently labeled pejoratively as "cults." I shall here explore some of the reasons for these tensions as well as ways in which they have eventually been overcome. After developing a working definition for new, unorthodox, or cultic groups in America, I shall analyze why such groups have been less persecuted in America than elsewhere in the world. Nineteenth-century Mormons will then serve as an example of the complexity of American reactions to new religions, illustrating both how intense hostility toward such groups could develop and how such hostility could eventually be overcome. In conclusion, I shall reflect briefly on the broader significance of American religious pluralism and its lessons for dealing constructively with religious and ethnic conflicts world-wide.

I

The problem of developing a working definition for religious movements in American that are considered new, unorthodox, or "cultic" is a knotty one. American religion has never fit neatly into the classic typologies based on European models. For example, Troeltsch's distinction between "church" and "sect," appropriate for an environment in which a dominant Roman Catholic Church (and eventually some Protestant state churches) could be contrasted with dissident Protestant groups, is not satisfactory to describe the situation that developed in the United States. In America, rather paradoxically, many groups that were viewed as "sects" in Europe eventually came to comprise an informal Protestant establishment, and cooperation between leading Protestant groups led to the creation of the "denominational" system in the nineteenth century. Faced by such Protestant dominance, Roman Catholicism would for a time acquire many of the characteristics of an unpopular and persecuted "sect," until it also began to gain grudging acceptance. And by the twentieth century, not only Protestants and Catholics but also Jews would increasingly constitute a religious triumvirate, working together as an elite to uphold broader American values.[5]

Difficulties of analysis increase still further if one moves beyond the "mainstream" to groups that are viewed as new, cultic, or otherwise outside the Judeo-Christian tradition. Following the November 1978 tragedy at Jonestown, Guyana, when over nine hundred people committed mass suicide at the behest of their leader, there arose an upwelling of concern over the dangers of the so-called cults.[6] Flo Conway and Jim Siegelman, for example, wrote flamboyantly about what they called "snapping," "America's epidemic of sudden personality change." Failing to realize that conversionistic and ecstatic phenomena have been widespread in many cultures throughout history, Conway and Siegelman, among many others, argued that such practices represented a new and unprecedented use of hitherto unknown and dangerous mind-control tactics or "brainwashing." Cries for legislation to control the possible excesses of new religious movements were heard, and the media became interested in what has been called "deprogramming"—a practice that might more accurately be called "reverse brainwashing."[7]

When the dust finally began to settle, several things had become apparent. First, there is no analytical substance to the popular definition of a cult as a dangerous group with bizarre religious beliefs that follows a deranged or cynically opportunistic leader. One person's "cult" is another person's "true faith." I remember my amusement, for example, listening to a militant rabbi from the Hassidic movement (which some might characterize as a Jewish fringe or cultic group) harangue a respectable middle-aged Jewish audience about the dread dangers of the "cults." His primary concern was not with the Moonies or Hare Krishnas, but mainstream Protestant groups that he felt were attracting Jewish converts. Similarly, I was somewhat taken aback in talking with an East Asian student who expressed his repugnance at the "cultic" character of Christianity, especially its periodic "ritual cannibalism" of its founder. For a moment, I failed to realize that he was referring to the Eucharist or Lord's Supper. Beliefs or rituals that appear similarly bizarre to an outsider can be found in all the major world religions—Judaism, Christianity, Islam, Hinduism, and Buddhism alike. In effect, the only popular meaning of the word "cult" is, "a religious group that someone else doesn't like." Such definitions are less than useful as analytical tools.

The popular stereotype of cult is in part derived from the traditional social-scientific definition that can also be less than useful analytically. Social scientists have generally described cults as groups that deviate widely from the dominant faith of the society in which they live, follow a charismatic leader, have a transient membership, and usually die out after the original leader's death.[8] Recent research has cast doubt on much of this definition. As only one example, many of the cult groups that have arisen in the United States during the past one hundred fifty years are still alive and even thriving today. Of Hoekema's "four major cults"—Christian Science, Jehovah's Witnesses, Mormonism, and Seventh-Day Adventism—three are today among the fastest growing groups in the United States.[9] From the perspective of world history, it is apparent that many groups that were initially viewed as cults—Christianity, Islam, and Buddhism, among others—have subsequently become among the largest and most influential religious movements in the world.[10]

As J. Gordon Melton and Robert L. Moore have pointed out, cults are best understood as a form of first-generation religion, with both the strengths and weaknesses of newness. In this initial phase, "new religions tend to be built around a single person, who starts or creates the new faith because he or she has had a new insight, a strong religious experience, a vision, a revelation, or a strong sense of mission. . . . During the first generation, members are most radical in their behavior, strongest in their attachment to the faith (there is no stronger member of any group than a recent convert), and most changeable, as feedback from the culture and group processes are routinized."[11] In a classic article, anthropologist Anthony F. C. Wallace has argued that such "revitalization movements" are indeed the basis upon which many of the great religious traditions of the world have been established.[12]

Groups that are commonly labeled "cults" in the United States really represent two separate, but closely related phenomena: (1) new religions that have developed out of older, more established groups in America and (2) alternative religious traditions that originated in other parts of the world such as India or the Far East and are only "new" as imports into the United States. Since "cult" is essentially a pejorative term without analytical precision, I shall henceforth refer to such groups as "new religious movements" or "new religions."

II

Identifying the reasons that new religious movements have frequently encountered less hostility in America than elsewhere in the world presents a complex problem. Let us look, in turn, at the world-wide and the American situations. Throughout the world, new religions are typically criticized for religious, political, and social deviation from the norm.[13] Religiously, such new groups challenge the validity of existing beliefs, either by demanding that new beliefs be substituted for old ones or by insisting that a traditional faith actually live up to the standards it professes but does not practice. Such challenges are anything but popular with the authorities. For example, many Hebrew prophets, who denounced the failings and complacency of the religious establishment of their day, were killed. Jesus of Nazareth, who called for a new order and preached repentance from sin, was crucified. Mohammed, who criticized the merchant society's idolatry and corruption, was forced to flee Mecca. And on several occasions, Martin Luther, who called for salvation by faith and denounced the selling of indulgences and other corruptions of the late medieval Roman Catholic Church, barely escaped with his life.

Criticism of the dominant system of religious belief is not the sole or even the primary basis for persecuting new religions world-wide. Intimately associated with disagreement over beliefs is an implicit or explicit challenge to the established political order. This is particularly true in the case of aggressively expansive new religions, fervently committed to the idea that they have a unique understanding of truth which everyone else must eventually adopt. Such fervor can make new religions at best an annoyance and at worst an apparent threat to all political order, especially in societies with a single established religious tradition associated with and supported by the government. After the English Reformation, for example, the monarch officially served both as head of state and as "supreme governor" of the Church of England. To criticize the established religion, even on matters of seemingly minor religious ritual, was thus implicitly to criticize the government itself.[14]

In addition to religious and political deviance from the norm, new religions throughout the world often advocate social practices that may provoke conflict. As a means of distinguishing themselves from what they take to be an evil or corrupt world, new religions often isolate themselves, adopting distinctive styles of dress, behavior, or speech which, while perhaps innocuous, create concern about their deviance from the norm. Sometimes such divergent social practices arise naturally from the group's beliefs. At other times, new practices may be deliberately fostered as a form of "boundary maintenance," to set the group apart from the world. Whatever the reasons and however slight the divergences, such visible differences tend to invite hostility, especially during times of social uncertainty and unrest. If the group is small and relatively unobtrusive, persecution may be minimal. But if it is expanding aggressively and if its social practices are seen not simply as different but also as "wrong," intense persecution may result.[15]

In America, an immigrant society with substantial and ever-increasing ethnic diversity, many of the characteristic religious, political, and social causes for persecuting new religions became less salient.[16] Virtually all the initial colonists were Protestants of English extraction. At the very least, they were united by hostility toward Roman Catholicism and by belief in the authority of the Bible as the basis for religious truth. Although Protestant biblicism encouraged religious divergence, splintering, and a "fierce war of words," as differing individuals and groups found different messages in the same biblical passages or emphasized different parts of scripture, such disputes constituted more of a disagreement within the family than a life-and-death struggle between strangers. Even groups emphasizing free thought often shared common moral and intellectual attitudes with the more evangelically oriented, and hence were not viewed as totally beyond the pale. Catholic and Jewish immigrant groups would create more of a problem of adjustment, but by the time they began arriving in large numbers, patterns of religious toleration were sufficiently well established both legally and in practice that tendencies toward more extreme forms of persecution could usually be contained.

Politically, new religions also seemed less threatening in America than in England or continental Europe. The diversity of religious groups in the original Colonies made it impossible for any one religion to become the established religion for all the Colonies. This social reality was recognized nationally in the first amendment to the Constitution, which stipulates that "Congress shall make no law respecting an establishment of religion, or prohibiting the free exercise thereof." Although a dwindling number of states, notably Massachusetts and Connecticut, continued to retain *state* religious establishments into the nineteenth century, the guarantee of freedom of religion at the national level had profound long-term consequences, making national persecution of controversial groups both unnecessary and unconstitutional. New religious groups in America would have to diverge very far indeed before they would be seen as a serious threat to the government.[17]

Socially, as well, the diversity of American ethnic groups inhibited religious conflict of the intensity that had been seen in Europe. There was substantial prejudice and harrassment of new or unorthodox groups from time to time but, especially in urban areas, tolerance for diversity of practice as well as belief increasingly became the norm. The legal support for religious freedom and the sense that one must allow others freedom in order to retain it for oneself kept religious persecution to a minimum. For example, the right of groups such as the Amish to maintain their own schools has been upheld, and members of the historic peace churches have been allowed to claim conscientious-objector status. Only when religious practice poses a threat to personal safety, as in the case of Appalachian snake-handling groups, have restrictions on religious practice long stood the test of legal challenge.[18]

The religious pluralism that generally kept hostility toward new or unorthodox groups from becoming too intense has developed gradually over the past 400 years. Each new immigrant group has faced difficulties adjusting to its new environment and each, in turn, has contributed to the development of greater religious diversity. During the colonial period, settlers representing various Protestant groups, many of them dissenters against the Church of England, attempted to establish religious uniformity in a majority of the Colonies. They eventually found, however, that they would have to respect the rights of others in order to preserve their own. The development of revivalistic proselytizing techniques between the American Revolution and the Civil War contributed to the expansion of new Protestant groups such as the Baptists and Methodists, who competed with older groups for members while increasingly cooperating on issues of larger concern. When unprecedented numbers of non-English–speaking immigrants, many of them Catholic or Jewish, began to arrive, they faced initial hostility from Protestant groups before finally reaching an accommodation. Since World War II, as the United States has assumed a more prominent role in the world, non-Western religious traditions from India and the Far East have become more visible and controversial, further adding to America's religious diversity.[19]

Faced with such ever-increasing religious pluralism and the lack of a single state church, Americans have found unity in their "civil religion," to use the concept popularized by Robert Bellah.[20] Patriotism, a sense of higher loyalty to "America," has often functioned as an overarching religious ethos, reducing the tendency toward internal conflicts between the various tribal faiths. The pattern of religious accommodation has been the same across time: each new group has initially aroused suspicion and hostility, but eventually become at least tolerated as part of the American religious scene. Quakers and Baptists were viewed as dangerous or absurd in colonial days; Mormons and Adventists in the early national period; and Catholics and Jews at the turn of the century. If long-standing trends in American development are any indication, even such controversial present-day groups as the Moonies and Hare Krishnas may eventually find a niche in the pluralistic American context.[21]

III

Although the United States has been remarkably successful in accommodating itself to religious diversity, tensions and conflicts between more established groups and new religious movements have been a recurrent problem. A useful test of the limits of nineteenth-century religious tolerance was provided by the Church of Jesus Christ of Latter-day Saints, or Mormons as they are popularly known. This faith appears quintessentially American in some respects, yet it suffered extreme persecution until the end of the nineteenth century when it began to give up its most controversial practice, polygamous marriage. Today the Mormon church is rapidly expanding, with over five million members world-wide, and has achieved substantial acceptance and respectability in the United States. By its very extremes, the Latter-day Saints' experience highlights both the reasons for hostility toward new religions and the ways in which initially unpopular groups eventually can be integrated into the American religious scene.[22]

Nineteenth-century persecution of the Latter-day Saints appears anomalous in the context of American tolerance for religious diversity. Hostility was expressed not simply by verbal and social pressure, but also through violence, military action, and extraordinary legal assaults. For example, after a Mormon leader made inflammatory statements in 1838, the governor of Missouri publicly declared that the group must be "exterminated or driven from the state." Eventually thousands of Mormons fled, many lives were lost, and property whose value the Mormons estimated at more than $2 million was confiscated without compensation.

Another confrontation occurred in 1857, when President Buchanan dispatched 2,500 federal troops to Utah to put down supposed Mormon "disloyalty." Fortunately, direct clashes between the troops and Mormon settlers were averted and the troops were withdrawn after the start of the Civil War. By the late 1880s, the attack on Mormon polygamy in Utah had become a national crusade. Federal marshals roamed Utah, arresting polygamists; supporters of polygamy were disenfranchised and hundreds of Mormon leaders were thrown in jail. After an antipolygamy law, which also dissolved the Church of Jesus Christ of Latter-day Saints as a legal corporation, was upheld by the United States Supreme Court in 1890, the Mormon church promised to submit to the antipolygamy laws and not sanction any further plural marriages in the United States.[23]

What caused hostility toward the Mormons to reach such intensity during the nineteenth century? More than any other religious movement of the period, with the partial exception of the Roman Catholic Church, the Mormons posed a fundamental challenge to the American religious, political, and social consensus. Religiously, the group sharply challenged American pluralism. The young Mormon prophet Joseph Smith claimed that all existing religions were wrong and that he had been uniquely commissioned by God to prepare the way for the "dispensation of the fullness of time" which would be associated with the coming of the millennium. God had not ceased to speak directly to man in apostolic days; rather, He was continuing to provide new revelation to the world through Smith, to whom had been restored the keys of St. Peter, with power to bind and to loose on earth and in heaven. Smith also dictated and published the Book of Mormon, purportedly a continuation of Old and New Testament history in the New World. He set up an extremely hierarchical church structure and militantly began to seek converts to the new faith. Mainstream Protestants saw Smith not only as a religious con man and heretic, but also as successful and dangerous. Partly as a result, the Mormons were forced to move from New York to Ohio, to Missouri, to Illinois, and eventually to Utah in an effort to free themselves to establish the all-encompassing faith in which they believed.[24]

Hostility toward the Mormons was exacerbated by their political exclusivity. Partly as a defense against religiously motivated persecution and partly out of their millenarian belief in reintegrating all life into a unified whole, the Mormons increasingly sought to establish an essentially theocratic state in which religious, political, and social life would be inseparable. They viewed themselves as a literal "new Israel" and developed an almost tribal sense of kinship and group loyalty. In northern Missouri, the persecuted Mormons established a secret vigilante organization, nicknamed the Danites, which engaged in various excesses. Five years after being driven out of Missouri, the Mormons created in Nauvoo the second largest city in Illinois, secured a city charter that allowed them to become virtually autonomous from the state, set up a 2,000-person militia, and voted as a political bloc that was perceived as holding the balance of political power in the state. Privately, Joseph Smith set up his secret Council of Fifty and talked of a Mormon empire that would eventually encompass all of North and South America.

Following Joseph Smith's assassination in 1844 and the heroic migration to Utah and adjacent areas of the Great Basin region, isolation from the surrounding society and the demands of survival in an arid and inhospitable environment further encouraged Mormon theocratic tendencies. For example, Brigham Young served as both president of the Mormon church and governor of Utah for a time. Direct Mormon political control over Utah would not be effectively challenged until the end of the century. Many Americans feared that such centralized control posed a threat to American democratic values and believed that unless checked such tendencies might eventually lead to the destruction of the American political system.[25]

The greatest overt hostility toward the Mormons, however, came to be focused on their divergence from American social norms, specifically their introduction of a form of polygamy in the 1840s and 1850s. The 1852 announcement that the Saints considered polygamy an integral part of their religious and social life provoked outrage from the non-Mormon public. Many Americans felt it was one thing for "lesser breeds without the law" in Asia or Africa to engage in such "backward" and "primitive" customs, but it was something very different and far more reprehensible for white Anglo-Saxons of Protestant extraction to do so. The Mormons declared that God not only approved of the practice, but had also commanded them to start it. By the 1880s, more than one hundred thousand Latter-day Saints in the American West were ideologically committed to plural marriage as the highest form of marriage, and approximately one-quarter of all Mormon families in Utah were polygamous. Such deviance seemed to pose a severe threat to the monogamous Victorian American ideal and indeed to the whole social order itself.

As early as 1856, both the Democrats and the Republicans denounced Mormon polygamy in their national platforms as a "relic of barbarism." In 1890, when more than a decade of intense federal pressure on polygamy left the Mormons with a choice of seeing their church legally dissolved, emigrating to another country, or giving up polygamy, church leaders moved to begin eliminating the practice of polygamy, which had become the major basis for hostility toward the group.[26]

How could a group that had become the focus of such intense hostility during the nineteenth century become an accepted, even respected, participant in the American religious scene a century later? As suggested above, nineteenth-century Mormons encountered hostility primarily because they pushed far beyond the acceptable limits of American religious, political, and social pluralism. In their millenarian fervor, they believed that they were a "chosen people" with a unique handle on truth. They were a literal "new Israel," a "peculiar people" called by God to establish Zion, in effect their own national homeland, in the wilderness of the American West. Mormons were uncompromising in their critique of the larger American society; that society, in turn, eventually gave the group an ultimatum: begin to accommodate to American patterns or face continuing persecution and possible destruction as an organization. Faced with such a choice, the Mormons, like other successful "revitalization movements" about which Anthony F. C. Wallace has written, began the slow process of accommodation to the larger society.

The process by which this accommodation was achieved is a fascinating story that has only recently begun to receive serious scholarly attention.[27] Just as new immigrant groups faced initial misunderstandings and hostility prior to becoming acculturated to America, so successful new religious groups have eventually restrained tendencies toward extremes of peculiarity and have backed away from frontal challenges to the values of the larger society. The Mormons provide a classic example of such religious acculturation or "Americanization," as one Mormon scholar described the process.

As old leaders were dying or being replaced some fifty years after the start of the movement, internal and external pressures for change were mounting. Ironically, Mormon success in establishing a dynamic society in the American West helped undercut their religious exclusivity, as had happened with the Massachusetts Puritans in the seventeenth century. Many Mormons were simply not prepared to risk losing all they had struggled so hard to build in order to continue an increasingly fruitless effort to maintain extraordinary autonomy from the larger society.

During the 1890s, the Mormon church responded to such pressures by beginning the painful process of giving up the polygamous practice to which it had been so adamantly committed and ending its direct theocratic control over Utah politics. The old values upon which such earlier practices had been based were not so much given up as transformed into new and more acceptable forms. For example, instead of having close-knit polygamous families with extended kinship ties, the Mormons encouraged close-knit monogamous families with strong kinship relationships. Similarly, while formal political control was given up, social control was maintained by instituting a variety of new social programs and by emphasizing new behavioral standards such as not smoking, not drinking alcohol, tea, or coffee, and paying a regular tithe to the church.

By the close of World War II, Mormonism had reinterpreted or transformed many of its most controversial earlier beliefs and practices. The movement was thus freed to begin dramatic expansion. From approximately one million members at the close of World War II, the church had grown to more than five million members in 1985. Although the group still espouses an exclusivistic theology and engages in social practices that set it apart from the larger society, Mormons today are de-emphasizing elements of their faith that might give offense to nonmembers. Particularly in the American West, they constitute a distinctive ethnic subculture but are no longer viewed as archetypical heretics, except by those fundamentalist Christian groups from whom they increasingly convert their members. The degree of present-day Mormon acceptance was dramatized by a nationally televised Billy Graham revival in Seattle. During the closing appeal, the names of the big three religious groups in America were flashed on the screen: Protestant, Catholic, and Jewish, and then a fourth—the Mormons. In many ways, their story is that of all new religious movements in America. Theological peculiarities, however great they may be, can eventually become acceptable so long as the group itself lives within the limits of American pluralism.[28]

What conclusions can we draw from this brief overview of the reactions to new religious movements in America? Two points stand out. Internally, the United States' response to religious diversity appears to represent a remarkable success story. New religious movements have, of course, suffered hostility and pressure due to a complex set of religious, political, and social factors. Yet severe persecution has generally occurred only when a group diverges too radically from the accepted norms and refuses to respect its competitors' rights also to function freely within America's broad pluralistic consensus. When deviation has been too great, both the larger society and thoughtful members within the new group have acted to bring it more nearly into compliance with acceptable social standards. Because of most Americans' higher loyalty to their country, to "Americanism," to the "civil religion," religious divergence has been tolerated to a far greater extent in the United States than in many other countries. Leaders have consistently sought to find elements that unite rather than those that divide, de-emphasizing ideological and theological differences as a potential source of conflict.

Externally, however, the United States' reaction has been far more problematic. While the American civil religion of "freedom," "democracy," and "Americanism" has allowed for considerable tolerance of diversity *within* the United States, overseas it has been increasingly associated with intolerance for those who do not accept American standards and guidance. Of course, the United States has not been alone in turning its nationalism into a destructive force in the world. The greatest worldwide conflicts in the twentieth century have come not so much between religious movements as between nationalistic and economic ideologies—"capitalism," "democracy," "fascism," and the like. The devastating and self-destructive conflicts of World War I and World War II caused the Western European nations, which stood at an unprecedented peak of success in 1914, to weaken and largely destroy their power, causing untold millions to experience death, suffering, and disease. Whether the United States and the Soviet Union, the two dominant powers after World War II, can learn to coexist peacefully with each other, or whether civilization as we know it may eventually be destroyed in yet a third world conflict, may ultimately depend, in part, on whether the United States can realize in its foreign as well as its domestic affairs a genuine sense of pluralism and respect for religious and cultural diversity.[29]

Notes

1. Among the studies that have especially influenced this article are: Roland H. Bainton, *The Travail of Religious Liberty* (New York: Harper, 1951); Kai Erikson, *Wayward Puritans: A Study in the Sociology of Deviance* (New York: John Wiley, 1966); and Sidney E. Mead, *The Lively Experiment: The Shaping of Christianity in America* (New York: Harper, 1963). On the Armenian massacres that culminated in 1915, see Christopher J. Walker, *Armenia: The Survival of a Nation* (London: Croom Helm, 1980) 197–240. An introduction to the enormous literature on Hitler's "final solution" is provided in Nora Levin, *The Holocaust: The Destruction of European Jewry* (New York: Schocken, 1973); and Lucy S. Dawidowicz, *The War Against the Jews, 1933–1945* (New York: Bantam, 1976). Estimates on the disruption that followed the partition of India are from William H. Harris and Judith S. Levey, eds., *The New Columbia Encyclopedia* (New York: Columbia University Press, 1975) 1331, although no fully reliable figures on the casualties are available. On the turmoil in Northern Ireland, see John Darby, *Conflict in Northern Ireland: The Development of a Polarised Community* (New York: Barnes & Noble, 1976). For the massacres at Sabra and Shatila, see reports in *Time* and *Newsweek* in September 1982 and after.

2. J. Gordon Melton and Robert L. Moore, *The Cult Experience: Responding to the New Religious Pluralism* (New York: Pilgrim, 1982) 18. More detailed information on these groups is found in J. Gordon Melton, *The Encyclopedia of American Religions*, 2 vols. (Wilmington, NC: McGrath, 1978); and in the earlier classic: Elmer T. Clark, *The Small Sects in America*, rev. ed. (New York: Abingdon-Cokesbury, 1949). Other studies with extensive coverage of new and

unorthodox religious groups in America include: Charles S. Braden, *These Also Believe: A Study of Modern American Cults and Minority Religious Movements* (New York: Macmillan, 1949); J. Stillson Judah, *The History and Philosophy of the Metaphysical Movements in America* (Philadelphia: Westminster, 1967); Irving I. Zaretsky and Mark P. Leone, eds., *Religious Movements in Contemporary America* (Princeton: Princeton University Press, 1974); Charles Y. Glock and Robert N. Bellah, eds., *The New Religious Consciousness* (Berkeley: University of California Press, 1976); and Howard Kerr and Charles L. Crow, *The Occult in America: New Historical Perspectives* (Urbana: University of Illinois Press, 1983).

3. The comparison is by no means exact. The United States is a true immigrant society, without national homelands, whereas the Roman Empire was basically a multinational empire, held together by its military and political superstructure. In both societies, however, considerable freedom and diversity in religion was allowed, so long as ultimate allegiance was given to the larger state: J. M. Roberts, *The Pelican History of the World* (New York: Penguin, 1983) 244–71; and George A. Rothrock, *Europe: A Brief History* (Chicago: Rand McNally, 1971) 12–23.

4. Ted Patrick, with Tom Dulack, *Let Our Children Go!* (New York: E. P. Dutton, 1976); and Ted Patrick's interview in *Playboy*, March 1979, pp. 53ff.

5. For a classic assessment of the tripartite American religious consensus in the 1950s, see Will Herberg, *Protestant-Catholic-Jew: An Essay in American Religious Sociology* (Garden City, NY: Doubleday, 1956). The primary distinction between the "church" and "sect" as ideal types is that the "church" embraces or aspires to embrace the whole of a culture, while the "sect" is a voluntary association that a person must enter by an act of his or her own (typically, by the experience of conversion). See Ernst Troeltsch, *The Social Teachings of the Christian Churches*, trans. Olive Wyon, 2 vols. (New York: Macmillan, 1931) I:331–49; *From Max Weber: Essays in Sociology*, ed. and trans. H. H. Gerth and C. Wright Mills (New York: Oxford University Press, 1946) 59–60, 323–26; Reinhard Bendix, *Max Weber: An Intellectual Portrait* (New York: Doubleday, 1960) 280–86. H. Richard Niebuhr, *The Social Sources of Denominationalism* (New York: Henry Holt, 1929) 10, has argued that the "sect" can exist in a pure form for about a generation, and thereafter must adopt some of the institutions of the "church." If a "sect" is seen as a group that partially withdraws from a society in order to try to purify established doctrine, then "cults," it is said, emerge when groups completely withdraw from prevailing religious practices and members commit themselves wholly to the leadership of charismatic and highly authoritarian figures. At best, such typologies can be only suggestive when dealing with the complexities of existing groups. In "From Movement to Sect," in *The Social Development of English Quakerism, 1655–1755* (Cambridge: Harvard University Press, 1969) 197–208, Richard T. Vann convincingly argues that the term "movement" best characterizes the early formative stages of new religious groups such as the early Quakers.

6. On Jonestown, Judith Mary Weightman's *Making Sense of the Jonestown*

Suicides: A Sociological History of People's Temple (New York: Edwin Mellen, 1983) is an excellent analysis that includes an up-to-date bibliography, pp. 213–20. The best, and possibly the definitive, biography of Jones himself is Tim Reiterman, with John Jacobs, *Raven: The Untold Story of the Rev. Jim Jones and His People* (New York: E. P. Dutton, 1982). Perhaps the most incisive article on the topic is John R. Hall, "The Apocalypse at Jonestown," in Ken Levi, ed., *Violence and Religious Commitment: Implications of Jim Jones's People's Temple Movement* (University Park: Pennsylvania State University Press, 1982) 35–54.

7. Flo Conway and Jim Siegelman's book, *Snapping: America's Epidemic of Sudden Personality Change* (New York: J.B. Lippincott, 1978), was published just prior to the Jonestown suicides and subsequently was hailed as prescient in predicting the dangers of cults. Although the book displays considerable knowledge of the relevant psychological literature on the topic, the anlaysis shows no awareness of the rich anthropological and historical literature that could have been used to place the phenomena into a larger context. More balanced and reliable treatments of the phenomena of "brainwashing" and "deprogramming" are presented in Melton and Moore, *Cult Experience*, pp. 36–92; Carroll Stoner and Jo Anne Parke, *All God's Children: The Cult Experience—Salvation or Slavery?* (New York: Penguin, 1979) 236–69, 307–457; David G. Bromley and Anson D. Shupe, Jr., *Strange Gods: The Great American Cult Scare* (Boston: Beacon, 1981) 92–127; 177–204; and William Sargant, *Battle for the Mind: A Physiology of Conversion and Brainwashing* (Garden City, NY: Doubleday, 1957).

Among the vast literature of anthropological and historical studies overlooked by Conway and Siegelman are: I. M. Lewis, *Ecstatic Religion: An Anthropological Study of Spirit Possession and Shamanism* (Baltimore: Penguin, 1971); Anthony F. C. Wallace, "Revitalization Movements," *American Anthropologist* 38 (April 1956) 264–81; Kenelm Burridge, *New Heaven, New Earth: A Study of Millenarian Activities* (New York: Schocken, 1969); Victor W. Turner, *The Ritual Process: Structure and Anti-Structure* (Chicago: Aldine, 1969); Mircea Eliade, *Shamanism: Archaic Techniques of Ecstasy* (New York: Pantheon, 1970); Erica Bourguignon, ed., *Religion, Altered States of Consciousness, and Social Change* (Columbus: Ohio State University Press, 1973); Vittorio Lanternari, *Religions of the Oppressed: A Study of Modern Messianic Cults*, trans. Lisa Sergio (New York: New American Library, 1965); and Norman R. Cohn, *The Pursuit of the Millennium: Revolutionary Millenarians and Mystical Anarchists of the Middle Ages*, rev. enl. ed. (New York: Oxford University Press, 1970). Sylvia L. Thrupp, ed., *Millennial Dreams in Action: Studies of Revolutionary Religious Movements* (New York: Schocken, 1970) is an excellent collection of essays on the topic. For a bibliography of studies of groups that typically employ such techniques, see Weston La Barre, "Materials for a History of Studies of Crisis Cults: A Bibliographic Essay," *Current Anthropology* 12 (February 1971) 3–44.

8. Useful recent analyses are Rodney Stark and William Sims Bainbridge, "Churches, Sects, and Cults," *Journal for the Scientific Study of Religion* 18 (June 1979) 117–31; Rodney Stark, William Sims Bainbridge, and Daniel P.

Doyle, "Cults of America: A Reconaissance in Space and Time," *Sociological Analysis* 40 (1979) 347–59; and Geoffrey K. Nelson, *Spiritualism and Society* (New York: Schocken, 1969) 217–37.

9. Anthony A. Hoekema, *The Four Major Cults: Christian Science–Jehovah's Witnesses–Mormonism–Seventh-Day Adventism* (Grand Rapids, MI: Wm B. Eerdmans, 1963). Of the four groups, only Christian Science appears to be in decline.

10. For a persuasive and sympathetic analysis of early Christianity as a millenarian movement, see John G. Gager, *Kingdom and Community: The Social World of Early Christianity* (Englewood Cliffs, NJ: Prentice-Hall, 1975).

11. Melton and Moore, *Cult Experience*, p. 17.

12. Wallace, "Revitalization Movements," p. 264. An ambitious but not fully convincing attempt to use Wallace's "revitalization" model to explain American religious history is found in William G. McLoughlin, *Revivals, Awakenings, and Reform* (Chicago: University of Chicago Press, 1978).

13. Other factors in persecution, such as economic ones, also could be suggested, but I believe that religious, political, and social differences usually are the most salient concerns. Economic factors, for example, can often be subsumed under political and social considerations.

14. Analyses that set the religious situation of Tudor–Stuart England into its political and social context include: S. T. Bindhoff, *Tudor England* (Middlesex, England: Penguin, 1979); and J. P. Kenyon, *Stuart England* (Middlesex, England: Penguin, 1978).

15. An introduction to the role of social deviance and "boundary maintenance" as a cause of religious persecution is found in Erikson, *Wayward Puritans*, pp. 3–29.

16. Among the most suggestive overall interpretations of the development of American religious history are Mead, *Lively Experiment*; Winthrop S. Hudson, *Religion in America* (New York: Charles Scribner's Sons, 1965); Martin E. Marty, *Righteous Empire: The Protestant Experience in America* (New York: Dial, 1970); Sydney E. Ahlstrom, *A Religious History of the American People* (New Haven, CT: Yale University Press, 1972); Catherine L. Albanese, *America: Religions and Religion* (Belmont, CA: Wadsworth, 1981)., and Edwin S. Gaustad, *Historical Atlas of Religion in America* (New York: Harper, 1962).

17. Mead, *Lively Experiment*, emphasizes the importance of the establishment of religious freedom at the national level.

18. Informal pressures continue to be applied in the effort to limit deviance, and the struggle to maintain a distinctive life style is an ongoing one, but without the full weight of legal sanction and public opinion such pressures tend only to restrict but not to eliminate social differences.

19. This summary is influenced especially by the analysis in Hudson, *Religion in America*, and by Melton and Moore, *Cult Experience*, pp. 22–28.

20. For an introduction to Robert Bellah's important work on American "civil religion," see his influential article: "Civil Religion in America," *Daedalus*, Winter 1967, and his *Varieties of Civil Religion* (New York: Harper, 1980). Another

overview of the concept in historical perspective is found in Sydney E. Ahlstrom, "Civil Religion," in Mark A. Noll et al., eds., *Eerdmans' Handbook to Christianity in America* (Grand Rapids, MI: Wm. B. Eerdmans, 1983) 434–35.

21. Melton and Moore, *Cult Experience*, p. 28.

22. The interpretation presented in this section is based on Lawrence Foster, *Religion and Sexuality: Three American Communal Experiments of the Nineteenth Century* (New York: Oxford University Press, 1981) 123–225, reprinted in a paperbound edition, with identical pagination, as *Religion and Sexuality: The Shakers, the Mormons, and the Oneida Community* (Urbana: University of Illinois Press, 1984). This book includes the first study of the origin and development of Mormon polygamy by a non-Mormon who had full access to the relevant Latter-day Saint archival records in Salt Lake City, Utah. For the best overall introductions to the history and spirit of nineteenth-century Mormonism, see two pathbreaking analyses: Thomas F. O'Dea, *The Mormons* (Chicago: University of Chicago Press, 1957); and Leonard J. Arrington, *Great Basin Kingdom: An Economic History of the Latter-day Saints, 1830–1900* (Cambridge, MA: Harvard University Press, 1958). An authoritative narrative history, based on full knowledge of recent scholarship, is James B. Allen and Glen M. Leonard, *The Story of the Latter-day Saints* (Salt Lake City: Deseret Book Company, 1976). It includes a comprehensive bibliography of scholarly sources on major topics in Mormon history, pp. 638–700. Also useful is the thematic analysis in Leonard J. Arrington and Davis Bitton, *The Mormon Experience: A History of the Latter-day Saints* (New York: Alfred A. Knopf, 1979). Always interesting, but sometimes highly speculative, is Klaus J. Hansen, *Mormonism and the American Experience* (Chicago: University of Chicago Press, 1981). An important recent interpretation is Jan Shipps, *Mormonism: The Story of a New Religious Tradition* (Urbana: University of Illinois Press, 1985). Some of the most significant scholarly essays in Mormon history are collected in Marvin S. Hill and James B. Allen, eds., *Mormonism and American Culture* (New York: Harper, 1972).

23. For a balanced overall assessment of the factors causing hostility between Mormons and non-Mormons during the nineteenth century, see Allen and Leonard, *Story of the Latter-day Saints*. Also see the treatments in O'Dea, *The Mormons*, and Arrington and Bitton, *The Mormon Experience*. Possibly the most important analysis of changing patterns of hostility toward the Mormons is Jan Shipps, "From Satyr to Saint: American Attitudes toward the Mormons, 1860–1960" (Paper presented at the 1973 annual meeting of the Organization of American Historians in Chicago, Illinois). Also revealing is Gary L. Bunker and Davis Bitton, *The Mormon Graphic Image, 1834–1914: Cartoons, Caricatures, and Illustrations* (Salt Lake City: University of Utah Press, 1983).

24. On early Mormon religious beliefs and the hostility they sometimes aroused, see the treatments in Foster, *Religion and Sexuality*; O'Dea, *The Mormons*; Mario S. De Pillis, "The Quest for Religious Authority and the Rise of Mormonism," *Dialogue: A Journal of Mormon Thought* 1 (March 1966) 68–88; Marvin S. Hill, "The Shaping of the Mormon Mind in New England and New York," *Brigham Young University Studies* 9 (Spring 1969) 351–72; and

Jan Shipps, "The Prophet Puzzle: Suggestions Leading toward a More Comprehensive Interpretation of Joseph Smith," *Journal of Mormon History* 1 (1974) 4–20. In a class by itself, both as a pathbreaking analysis and as a critical assessment, is Fawn Brodie's controversial biography, first published in 1945: *No Man Knows My History: The Life of Joseph Smith, the Mormon Prophet,* 2d ed. rev. (New York: Alfred A. Knopf, 1971). Brodie's interpretation has been qualified by the more balanced, but less incisive, biography by Donna Hill: *Joseph Smith: The First Mormon* (Garden City, NY: Doubleday, 1977). Altogether excellent, both in its scholarship and writing style, is Linda King Newell and Valeen Tippetts Avery, *Mormon Enigma: Emma Hale Smith—Prophet's Wife, "Elect Lady," Polygamy's Foe* (Garden City, NY: Doubleday, 1984). This definitive biography of Emma Smith also includes the first fully believable portrayal of her husband, Joseph Smith, as a human being. Also see Marvin S. Hill, "Religion in Nauvoo," *Utah Historical Quarterly* 44 (1976) 170–80. For the conventional critical account of Mormon history, see William J. Whalen, *The Latter-day Saints in the Modern Day World* (Notre Dame, IN: University of Notre Dame Press, 1964). Lawrence Foster, "Career Apostates: Reflections on the Works of Jerald and Sandra Tanner," *Dialogue: A Journal of Mormon Thought* 17 (Summer 1984) 35–60, analyzes the career of a contemporary anti-Mormon couple who oppose Mormonism primarily on religious grounds.

25. On the political basis for persecution of the Mormons in the nineteenth century, see O'Dea, *The Mormons;* Allen and Leonard, *Story of the Latter-day Saints;* Arrington and Bitton, *The Mormon Experience;* Klaus J. Hansen, *Quest for Empire: The Political Kingdom of God and the Council of Fifty in Mormon History* (East Lansing: Michigan State University Press, 1967); Robert B. Flanders, *Nauvoo: Kingdom on the Mississippi* (Urbana: University of Illinois Press, 1965); Dallin H. Oaks and Marvin S. Hill, *Carthage Conspiracy: The Trial of the Alleged Assassins of Joseph Smith* (Urbana: University of Illinois Press, 1975); and Norman F. Furniss, *The Mormon Conflict, 1850–1859* (New Haven, CT: Yale University Press, 1960).

Other specialized treatments include: Max H. Parkin, "The Nature and Cause of Internal and External Conflict of the Mormons in Ohio Between 1830 and 1838" (M.A. thesis, Brigham Young University, 1966); Leland H. Gentry, "A History of the Latter-day Saints in Northern Missouri from 1836 to 1839" (Ph.D. dissertation, Brigham Young University, 1965); Warren Jennings, "Zion Is Fled: The Expulsion of the Mormons from Jackson County, Missouri" (Ph.D. dissertation, University of Florida, 1962); and Kenneth W. Godfrey, "Causes of Mormon–Non-Mormon Conflict in Hancock County, Illinois, 1839–1846" (Ph.D. dissertation, Brigham Young University, 1967).

For Mormon economic autonomy, which often was a factor in their persecution, see Arrington, *Great Basin Kingdom;* Arrington, "Early Mormon Communitarianism: The Law of Consecration and Stewardship," *Western Humanities Review* 7 (Autumn 1953) 341–69; Mario S. De Pillis, "The Development of Mormon Communitarianism, 1826–1846" (Ph.D. dissertation, Yale University, 1960); and Leonard J. Arrington, Feramorz Y. Fox, and Dean L. May, *Building the City of God: Community and Cooperation among the Mormons* (Salt Lake City: Deseret Book Company, 1976).

26. The most thorough analysis of the problems and conflicts associated with the introduction and practice of Mormon polygamy is found in Foster, *Religion and Sexuality*, pp. 123–225. Recent scholarly studies of Mormon polygamy are analyzed in Davis Bitton, "Mormon Polygamy: A Review Article," *Journal of Mormon History* 4 (1977) 101–18. A valuable book-length treatment from a sociological perspective is Kimball Young, *Isn't One Wife Enough? The Story of Mormon Polygamy* (New York: Henry Holt, 1954). The basis for hostility toward Mormon polygamy when it was being introduced in Illinois during the early 1840s is evident in Charles A. Shook's documentary analysis: *The True Origin of Mormon Polygamy* (Cincinnati: Standard Publishing Co., 1914). Also useful on the early hostility toward Mormon polygamy is Danel W. Bachman, "A Study of the Mormon Practice of Plural Marriage Before the Death of Joseph Smith" (M.A. thesis, Purdue University, 1975).

Literary critiques of polygamy are analyzed in Leonard J. Arrington and Jon Haupt, "Intolerable Zion: The Image of Mormonism in Nineteenth-Century American Literature," *Western Humanities Review* 22 (Summer 1968) 243–60; David Brion Davis, "Some Themes of Counter-Subversion: An Analysis of Anti-Masonic, Anti-Catholic, and Anti-Mormon Literature," *Mississippi Valley Historical Review* 47 (September 1960) 205–24; Charles A. Cannon, "The Awesome Power of Sex: The Polemical Campaign against Mormon Polygamy," *Pacific Historical Review* 43 (February 1974) 61–82; and Gail Farr Casterline, "'In the Toils' or 'Onward for Zion': Images of the Mormon Woman, 1852–1890" (M.A. thesis, Utah State University, 1974).

For a bibliographic introduction to the extensive literature on the political campaign against Mormon polygamy, see Allen and Leonard, *Story of the Latter-day Saints*, pp. 681–87. The most useful book-length study is Gustive O. Larson, *The "Americanization" of Utah for Statehood* (San Marino, CA: Huntington Library, 1971). Also valuable are Kimball Young, *Isn't One Wife Enough?*; Richard D. Poll, "The Twin Relic: A Study of Mormon Polygamy and the Campaign by the Government of the United States for its Abolition, 1852–1890" (M.A. thesis, Texas Christian University, 1939) and "The Mormon Question Enters National Politics, 1850–1856," *Utah Historical Quarterly* 25 (1957) 117–31; Ray Jay Davis, "The Polygamous Prelude," *American Journal of Legal History* 6 (January 1962) 1–27; Orma Linford, "The Mormons and the Law: The Polygamy Cases," *Utah Law Review* 9 (Winter 1964–Summer 1965) 308–70, 543–91; and Henry J. Wolfinger, "A Reexamination of the Woodruff Manifesto in the Light of Utah Constitutional History," *Utah Historical Quarterly* 39 (Fall 1971) 328–49.

27. The most important treatments of the transformation of Mormonism that began in the late nineteenth century are Allen and Leonard, *Story of the Latter-day Saints*, pp. 377–638; Arrington and Bitton, *The Mormon Experience*, pp. 243–335; O'Dea, *The Mormons*, pp. 97–263; and James B. Allen and Richard O. Cowan, *Mormonism in the Twentieth Century*, 2d ed. (Provo: Brigham

Young University Press, 1967). On the transformation of the role of women in Mormonism during this period, see Lawrence Foster, "From Frontier Activism to Neo-Victorian Domesticity: Mormon Women in the Nineteenth and Twentieth Centuries," *Journal of Mormon History* 6 (1979) 3–21. Sharply critical treatments of the current status of Mormon women are Marilyn Warenski, *Patriarchs and Politics: The Plight of the Mormon Woman* (New York: McGraw-Hill, 1978); and Sonia Johnson, *From Housewife to Heretic* (Garden City, NY: Doubleday, 1981).

28. An extraordinarily incisive critical analysis of the strengths and weaknesses of Mormonism in the 1980s is Robert Gottlieb and Peter Wiley, *America's Saints: The Rise of Mormon Power* (New York: G. P. Putnam's Sons, 1984). Other useful treatments are Robert R. Mullen, *The Latter-day Saints: The Mormons Yesterday and Today* (Garden City, NY: Doubleday, 1966); and Wallace Turner, *The Mormon Establishment* (Boston: Houghton Mifflin, 1966).

29. Americans who may have difficulty seeing themselves as others see them would do well to read Stephen E. Ambrose's trenchant study, *Rise to Globalism: American Foreign Policy, 1938–1976*, rev. ed. (New York: Penguin, 1976). Whether the pluralistic experience of American immigrant society can be utilized effectively in the polarized international world of ethnic and national divisions remains to be seen. The consequences of a failure to reach some sort of global accommodation, however, appear grim indeed. On this issue, perhaps the most compelling analysis is Thomas Powers, *Thinking about the Next War* (New York: New American Library, 1983).

10

Constructing Evil as a Social Process: The Unification Church and the Media

ANSON SHUPE

E vil is conventionally thought of as a theological or moral problem. The existence of evil presupposes a model of good, which is
ultimately a value judgment and therefore presumably removed from the
concern of any secular science. For that reason—or because of that
reasoning—sociology, which has just about the most secular post-Enlightenment reputation among the social sciences, rarely speaks of evil
per se. When individual sociologists deal with phenomena that others
might consider evil or wicked, they use euphemisms that sound evalu-
atively neutral, such as sociopathology, social disorganization, social
problems, dysfunction, deviance, maladjustment, and value conflict.[1] As
Lyman has observed:

> Evil is a term that is rarely found in a modern sociology text. The "sci-
> ence of society" seems to go about its task without the gnawing encum-
> brance of ethics. . . . Evil seems to be too great, too impersonal, and too
> absurd to be a serious topic for sociological concern.[2]

Yet there is simultaneously a strong sociological foundation, shared
with philosophy, for understanding evil. In part it can be traced back to
Emile Durkheim's classic distinction between the *sacred* and *profane* elements of every society. Work by scholars of comparative religion special-
izing in myths, rituals, and symbolism, such as Mircea Eliade and Roger
Caillois (among many others), has shown that Durkheim's dichotomy
did not go quite far enough. The very concept of the *sacred* includes its

polar opposite—what Roger Caillois termed the "sacred of transgression"[3]—so that alongside the mundanely profane taken-as-they-are aspects of any culture there must be an additional supramundane category of deeds and symbols. This "antisacred" type (unlike the *asacred profane* type) has the potential power to negate or defile the sacred, thereby partaking of the same awe and instilling (on occasion) the same fear. Thus, in the presence of the *evil* polar type within the sacred category, as sociologist Richard Stivers describes it, "The power of the holy is transferred to that which desecrates it."[4]

In part also a recent strain of theorizing in the sociology of deviant (i.e., nonconforming) behavior coincides closely with phenomenology and cultural hermeneutics in philosophy. Grounded in what sociologists refer to as symbolic interactionist theory (and informed by a healthy dose of cultural relativism from anthropology), the *labeling* approach looks less at any inherent characteristics of a rule offender or of a specific act and more at the political process of establishing and enforcing rules. In other words, *who* decides what is deviant and anathema? In criminology this means studying the politics of lobbying, interest-group strategies, and the values of law-creators.[5] In the study of social movement conflict, which has preoccupied me since the mid-1970s, this reduces to studying the war of conflicting labels, i.e., how opposing groups seek to have their labels of "evil" applied to their enemies. Antisocial or deviant "evil" behavior, in this view, is understood as a construct, negotiated by persons with more or less amounts of power in society.

New Religions and the Evil of Heresy

I propose looking briefly at a recent (indeed, ongoing) example of the social construction of evil. It is the so-called contemporary "cult" controversy that began during the 1960s and 1970s. This surge of religious innovations, some home-grown and some imported, stimulated strong resistance in our society. Part of this resistance was the resurrection of a concept that had fallen into disuse for many Americans in twentieth-century secular, ecumenical mainline society: that of *heresy*.

Sociologists have long recognized heresy in analytic terms as a particularly insidious form of evil. As the German sociologist Georg Simmel pointed out,

> At times the reaction of the group against the heretic is even more hostile than against the apostate. Whereas the latter deserts the group in order to go over to the enemy, the heretic presents a more insidious dan-

ger: by upholding the group's central values and goals, he threatens to split it into factions that will differ as to the means for implementing its goals.[6]

The heretic claims to be orthodox, the representative of pure tradition, even as he threatens and subverts this very tradition. In the first three centuries of the Christian Era many religious heretics were Gnostics. Over a century ago in this country they were the Mormons, then the Christian Scientists, then Jehovah's Witnesses. In our age they are Sun Myung Moon's Unification Church, Witness Lee's Local Church, the Hare Krishna movement, and the Church of Scientology, among others.

Sociologically speaking, however, heresy cannot be limited to the religious sphere any more than evil can be thought of in a strictly theological sense. If evil is defined more broadly as the contradiction or violation of any sacred value, then heresy is in service to evil. Heresy misleads away from sacred values that orthodoxy tries to protect. These values may just as easily be political, economic, or social as religious.

The Unification Church is a classic example of how evil is socially constructed and how heresy is used to impute evil. The Unification Church, among all other new religious movements or "cults," has always been the *bête noire* of the modern anticult movement in America.[7] It offers a veritable archetype of the dimensions that offend, infuriate, and threaten conventional society, thereby calling down accusations of heresy and setting in motion the ritual process of assigning the label "evil." For this reason, as well as because of my own research into that organization's corporate development in this country, I have selected the Unification Church for illustration. Here I will emphasize how it has been inconsistently treated by the public and the information media, for in the labeling perspective it is they who frequently decide how evil any group may be. Public awareness of Sun Myung Moon's theocratic movement in the United States has passed through five stages, each corresponding to a different perception of the evil purportedly existing in his efforts:

1. Latent, Preconstruction
2. Benign Construction
3. Skeptical Construction
4. Accepted Malicious Construction
5. Postmalicious Construction

At each state, too, Moon's heresy has been part of an evolution from incipient (but unnoticed) deviance to fully matured and condemned unorthodoxy to, finally, a kind of "mellowed" state of quasi-détente with status-quo society.

Latent, Preconstruction

Ironically, the Unification Church, which has aroused so many fears and prompted such enormous outrage in the United States, arrived here in 1959 as a tiny outpost of an unpromising, fragile Korean charismatic Christian sect. Though a number of Unificationist scholars—graduates of the church's Barrytown, New York, seminary now pursuing accredited doctoral degrees at prestigious divinity schools across the country —have begun writing theses on its earliest mission here, the definitive account (descriptive and analytical) of this initial period is John Lofland's *Doomsday Cult*.[8] Lofland began this research as a sociology graduate student in the early 1960s, initially published a book and journal article from it, and then eventually put the whole project aside. The ineptly organized Moonies, he concluded, showed little prospect of dynamic growth or even survival. They were perceived as simply one among a myriad of competing millennial/esoteric/New Age groups in the countercultural milieu of the San Francisco Bay area. Lofland's analysis, employing pseudonyms, focused mainly on the phenomenon of conversion. At the time the Unification Church received no direct publicity from his study (and its portrayal of them was far from flattering). By the mid-1960s the group showed every sign of languishing from public indifference, poor recruiting strategies, and organizational inertia. Certainly the media at the time did not find the Unification Church newsworthy and would not have noticed its demise.

Benign Construction

When my colleague David Bromley and I first surveyed the early 1970s media handling of the Unification Church, we were struck by the overall positive tone of coverage. The church deliberately masked its postmillennial aspirations and did its best, with lavish funding, patriotic bombast, and energetic public-relations legwork to woo the local "luminaries" of cities and towns across the nation. It was frequently successful in "passing" as a positive, if slightly eccentric, Christian revival crusade. The result was an initially favorable press reaction. Journalists equated freshly scrubbed, conservatively dressed, continuously smiling young Moonies with the "Up With People" singers.[9] Contrasted with the polar stereotype of antiwar, unshaven, drug-using hippies then shocking many Americans, the Moonies of 1971-73 looked downright wholesome and constructive. Moon (whose press pictures always showed a youthful, smiling face full of beneficence) was portrayed as a kind of Oriental Billy Graham, certainly nothing to worry about when faced with the likes of Jerry Rubin, Timothy Leary, Eldridge Cleaver, and Jane Fonda.

The Korean evangelist was also a frequent visitor on Capitol Hill, not only to Congressmen's offices but also at prayer breakfasts. His members tirelessly lobbied on behalf of all legislation that benefited South Korea. Moon repeatedly (and successfully) sought to have his picture taken with national figures such as Hubert Humphrey and Richard Nixon. Mayors of cities proclaimed special "Days of Unity" in Moon's honor, and Moon received a string of honorary positions in state militias and governments. As diverse a group of officials as President Richard Nixon, Alabama and Georgia Governors George Wallace and Jimmy Carter, and Los Angeles Mayor Tom Bradley thanked Moon in public documents for the evangelist's work among their constituencies. Media coverage at this time, while usually favorable, was still sporadic despite the fact the Moon's people were continually trying to thrust him into the limelight. The Unification Church was not yet defined as a "cult" by the media, not dangerous, not sensational, not worth following closely or investigating.

Skeptical Construction

The precipitating event that reshaped the church's image in the United States occurred during the fall of 1974 in the context of the Watergate investigation. In November, Moon claimed to have received a vision in which God revealed to him that President Richard Nixon was a divinely appointed "archangel" working in God's providence to establish the Kingdom of God on earth. Thus, Moon proclaimed, Nixon had the heavenly mandate to dissolve both houses of Congress if need be to preserve a strong, united America. God had chosen Richard Nixon for this special task at this critical moment in history, and only God could remove him. Nixon welcomed cheering Moonie demonstrators at the occasion of the lighting of the White House Christmas tree that year, but suddenly Moon stopped being invited to Washington prayer breakfasts, and media reporters began taking a second, more critical look at this Korean evangelist and his message.

During the same time as Moon's unsuccessful attempt to popularize a "divine right of kings" defense of Nixon, the Koreagate scandal of influence buying and bribery in Washington began to unfold. Moon was linked to this investigation as well, adding to critical media treatment.[10]

There were other factors at work that by the mid-1970s had begun to find expression and exposure. Families of young adults who followed a variety of unconventional religious groups—not just the Unification Church, but also the Hare Krishnas, the Children of God, the Church of Scientology, and a host of lesser publicized gurus, cults, covens, and crusades—had been struggling to raise public awareness about what they considered to be a clear and present danger in these groups. These families saw a number of offenses in such groups.[11] Parents in particular resented their offspring, in the prime of promising young adulthood and at a critical career stage when educational preparation was paramount, fairly abruptly rejecting conventional careers and domestic trajectories (for which the parent had often saved and sacrificed long to subsidize) in favor of millennial crusades. Likewise, the unquestioning loyalty and obedience these youthful adults seemingly gave to mysterious foreign gurus disturbed their former friends and relatives. It was the practice, for example, of "Moonies" to sign their letters and memos to one another ITN—"in Their [Mr. and Mrs. Moon, the True Spiritual Parents of Mankind] Names"—which served as a virtual slap in the face to many biological parents.

These families founded voluntary-interest groups, many of which later obtained tax-exempt status as educational foundations, to "spread the word" about the Unification Church. They also found a ready-made construction to explain their family members' attraction to such culturally bizarre groups: that of the Korean war "brainwashing/thought control" literature.[12] These writings, simplistic or ethnocentric as they seemed to many professionals many years after the Korean war, offered a plausible explanation with the veneer of scientific respectability. The "brainwashing" construction also excused the youthful adults and their families from any responsibility for what could variously be youthful adventurism and irresponsibility, gullibility, and even poor childrearing.

Churches also began to take notice of the Unification Church and express misgivings. In the early 1970s certain evangelical groups had followed Moon during his series of rallies and public appearances to protest him as the "anti-Christ" and false messiah, but these were localized and few in number. Moon, however, through his aggressive public-relations efforts, found himself under inspection by major Jewish and Christian groups. While Jews generally resented the church's doctrinal insensitivity to Jewish concerns (e.g., Moon's claims that the Nazi Holocaust was God's punishment on the Jews for rejecting Christ), the Christians found Moon applying for legitimate status in their ecumenical organizations, such as the National Council of Churches of Christ and the New York Council of Churches (both groups rejected the application just as Jewish groups published denunciations of Moon's *Divine Principle* as anti-Semitic). In short, the Unification Church had desired publicity and worked hard to generate it. Soon, however, it had more than it wanted, and the messages given the public were out of its control.

Accepted Malicious Construction

Most Americans have no memory of the first three stages in the construction of a public meaning of the Unification Church. Few, however, have not been exposed to this fourth stage of accepted maliciousness. By 1975 press and television coverage of the movement was overwhelmingly negative and cynical. Moon was portrayed as a flamboyant, high-rolling demagogue and his followers either as exploited dupes or zombies. A succession of ex-members became short-lived celebrities when they turned apostate and told widely publicized "atrocity tales" about their regimented, deprived lives within the organization. Their credibility was uncritically assumed by sympathetic reporters who disseminated their stories over the wire services to every town and suburb in America, creating a virtual folklore about Unification Church recruiting techniques and social-control strategies. These notions ranged from the highly plausible (e.g., that church leaders discouraged open questioning and criticism among rank-and-file members) to the absurd (e.g., that males who joined the Unification Church soon after began to lose their secondary sex characteristics, such as facial hair). A small number of psychiatrists,[13] clinical psychologists,[14] and sociologists[15] reinforced the worst fears of these families and added to the anticult folklore. The anticult offensive was complete when Jewish and Christian groups alike began publishing special anti-Unification Church tracts, study guides, articles, and books warning of the "cult menace."[16]

The most extreme extension of conceiving the Unification Church as evil came in the practice of deprogramming. This was literally a secular form of ritual exorcism, premised on the same metaphor of invasion and capture of a person's individuality and free will by a sinister antisocial force. The confrontation between the deprogrammer/priest with the young cultist/possessed allegedly enables the Moonie (or Krishna or "premie" or whoever) to shake off the effects of mind control and to begin thinking on his or her own again. If resistance or even struggle occurred after the young family member was forcibly abducted from the "cult," then this too was interpreted as confirming evidence that deprogramming was indeed necessary. The media's fascination with deprogrammed ex-cult members and its willingness to report unchallenged virtually any accusation against the given group helped spread the folklore of evil.

In most cases attempts to define just what "cults" were came down basically to a transparent caricature of the Unification Church and Sun Myung Moon. The fact that many other "fringe" religious groups lumped into the "cult" category departed considerably from the leadership style, life-style requirements, and theology of the Unification Church was generally ignored. Moon was repeatedly portrayed as a heretic (evangelical publications openly referred to him as satanic) and Unificationism as heresy, not just with regard to Christianity or Judeo-Christian traditions but to the very American Way of Life.

There is other evidence that Moon's movement became regarded as the archetypal essence of sinister "cultism." In February, 1976, a coalition of regional family-based anticult groups petitioned and successfully secured from Kansas Senator Robert Dole an "unofficial" public hearing in Washington, D.C., concerning the "cult" problem. The two-hour format arranged by the groups permitted participants to come before a variety of Federal officials and list their grievances about "cults." While many groups were represented by parents, friends, and angry ex-"cult" members, it was decided by the hearing organizers that the Unification Church would be concentrated upon as the target, not only to give the hearings some focus but also because Moon's groups were believed to offer the best precedent for attack. If the Unification Church could be "gotten," so went the logic, then virtually any other "cult" could be as well.[17]

These "unofficial" hearings set the general pattern for the anticult offensive. The Unification Church became equated with the generic "cult." In presenting the Unification Church to the public the media followed a standard formula, as I and several colleagues discovered when we analyzed a geographically diverse sample of North American newspaper articles about the church.[18] Not only was the typical set of charges brought against it a predictable litany of "horrors" (articles frequently borrowing wholesale from other articles without any attempt at original background research), but also the "functions" or consequences of the articles became obvious: they outraged and mobilized sentiments for punishment of groups like the Unification Church as well as authorized or legitimated such actions. Such testimonies of ex-members given to reporters also became a form of expiation for both themselves and their families, a channel of reconciliation within the family group and between the errant apostate and the community of traditional values.

Thus, in the fourth stage, the evil of the Unification Church was set and accepted by the larger public. The definitions of it as dangerous, its members' faith a "programmed" cant, its leader a charlatan, and its purpose genuinely subversive were assumptions rarely questioned by most Americans not directly involved in researching the group. There were the occasional exceptions that attempted to prick the bubble of Moonish hysteria,[19] but they simply made less interesting reading.

Postmalicious Construction

It may be too early to claim that a fifth stage, one beyond the acceptance of a simple definition of the Unification Church as malicious and evil, has been entered, but I think I can support the contention that we are at least close to entering it. The People's Temple massacre in Jonestown, Guyana, in late 1978 temporarily rekindled the anticultists' worst fears and led a number of the countermovement's spokespersons to predict a wave of similar mass-suicide/murders in the near future across this country.[20] Jonestown occurred years ago, however, and we have yet to see anything resembling repetition of that event. Moreover, once Richard Nixon left office, Koreagate involved so many high Washington officials that little if any prosecutions were forthcoming. The Moonies were obviously not about to take over the youth of the country; hence the media began to lose interest in them. Most popular magazines had run their "cult" articles and looked elsewhere for fresh topics. Perhaps the clearest sign that the apogee of regarding Unificationism as threatening evil was passed came when Moon and his movement became the butt of humor. In the late 1970s *Mad Magazine, National Lampoon*, the "Doonesbury" comic strip and television's "Saturday Night Live" all did parodies of the Unification Church. Moonies became laughable. Perhaps they had always been ludicrous in the public mind, with only anticultists and the social scientists who studied them intent on maintaining seriousness.

The Unification Church had also begun to accommodate. Moon sent increasing numbers of his seminary's graduates on to accredited universities; he married large waves of members who often began to bear children and live reasonably conventional lives; the movement poured staggering amounts of money into good-will and academic conferences to sponsor genuine scholarly dialogue about value concerns of the movement; and some degree of sympathy for the Unification Church as underdog in a situation of overreaction began to grow. When Moon was convicted of tax evasion in the early 1980s, his appeal gained the support of a wide variety of conventional religious groups beyond just liberal civil libertarians, including the National Council of Churches and even the Church of Jesus Christ of Latter-day Saints.[21]

In short, the accusations of the 1970s—that Unification Church leaders possessed mysterious but effective brainwashing abilities, that the church was swelling in numbers at an alarming rate, or that Moon was still trying to take over an entire generation of America's college-age youth—began to wear thin. Moon's movement's membership rolls, in fact, peaked in the mid-1970s at only several thousand persons. The

Ayatollah Khomeini soon overshadowed Sun Myung Moon as America's number-one nemesis as concern about Unificationists leveled off (allowing for lag time), coinciding with the movement's own retreat from the limelight.

The Persistence of Evil in Industrial Societies

The targeting of the Unification Church as archetypal "cult" and heretic by a number of institutional representatives illustrates a fundamental sociological reality. Evil survives in industrial societies not only because some members consciously wish to believe in it in theological terms, but also because it is a fundamental way of reacting to threatening aspects of social life per se. Just as things important to a society, such as its heroes, traditions, and institutional values become considered sacred, so things perceived inimical to these are consciously considered evil (if theological worldviews dominate) or unconsciously treated thus (if more rationalistic paradigms prevail).

The sacred, including its polar "evil" subtype, is as inseparable a part of any social order as the profane. So-called secularization has not eradicated concern for sacred things or this fundamentally social, human response to things that threaten social order. As Richard Stivers observes, our modern technological society is only secularized (or *desacralized*) in terms of things *previously considered sacred*. That is, the sacred is not consigned to the past but is continually being recreated and rejuvenated. Less technologically sophisticated peoples had an intuitive or diffuse sense of what things had sacred significance. Our modern perception is to possess a more specific historical sense of the sacred and imagine it is a thing for ideational museums. Our temporocentrism leads us to imagine that we are beyond the sacred or have outgrown it, that issues such as "cultism" can be strictly and cleanly dealt with in rationalistic, post-Enlightenment psychiatric/legalistic terms. Modern rationalism has lent a superficial impression that the sacred is receding as a factor in industrial societies, while in fact it has merely taken on new forms. Says Stivers:

> Modern man is in awe of technology exactly the way primitive man was in awe of nature. It is both security and threat. . . . We are often told that science takes away a sense of mystery because it lays bare reality. [However] at the level of application and operation, science actually induces a sense of the mysterious and even the occult.[22]

The same argument has been made in other studies. For example, Winston Davis argued that, *contra* Weber, magic could easily survive in a highly technological society simply because the ambiguities and uncertainties of life that magic addresses are not resolved by sheer technology.[23] Davis studied an eclectic right-wing exorcism cult in modern Japan and came to the conclusion that a faith in the most traditional type of religion (folk healing, shamanism, and spirit possession) could function well alongside a sophisticated *Gemeinschaft* life-style. In essence, technology and science do not eliminate the theodicies and injustices of life. Evil, explicitly conceived theologically or implicitly realized, certainly does not lack for new forms to assume.

In a previous study David Bromley and I detailed some of the regularities in this construction of evil.[24] We examined parallels between America's pre-Revolutionary War witch craze and the current anticult movement. We found that in situations where evil is believed to exist without effective control a pressure emerges to designate at least some persons able to identify and contain the evil. In England at one time these people were "witch-prickers" (such as Matthew Hopkins), on the Continent some centuries earlier they were the Dominicans, and in America of the late twentieth century they were the "deprogrammers."

When evil is believed to spread contagiously (and for most of the current "cult" controversy a biological/medical model of viral disease, rather than learning, has predominated), the natural response is to develop a typology of visible, unmistakable traits that identify the dangerous type of person. In medieval times these were called "witches' marks." In the 1980s, North American scientists sympathetic to the anticult movement sometimes developed their own lists of "stigmata" that purportedly separate "cult members" from more "normal" persons. The modern American tradition of religious liberty has made many officials reluctant to act against many religious groups for fear of being accused of "repression." This in turn has actually promoted a "folklore" of evil about them and their purposed abilities as well as a process (i.e., deprogramming) for exorcizing the evil. This last response has magical properties attributed to it by believers; however, it is dressed up in scientistic veneer. This should not surprise us, since as Guy Swanson noted in his classic *The Birth of the Gods*, magic flourishes best in communities where other forms of social control are weak.[25]

I see this process as sociologically normal. "Evil" is a regular part of every society, just as are its fundamental values. Societies formulate theories of who will violate these values, why and how to recognize such persons. The reaction is anticipated in the violation. That a group such as the Unification Church should have emerged as the archetypal "cult" during a period of religious innovation is also not surprising. Too many values and interests were being violated. Some group, corresponding more or less to an ideal type grounded in the vested interests of persons and institutions that were threatened, would have been singled out as the Unification Church was and attacked. This admittedly deterministic view is the clue to the heresy and evil of the Unification Church as society perceived it over a decade's time. In the long run, the mythology of Moonism says more about the society that reacted to the Unification Church than about the objective features of the group. The same could be said about the nineteenth-century nativists' views of Roman Catholics and for other persecuted religious groups in American history. This conclusion provides a plausible link between social deviance, threat, the social construction of evil, and repression. The process is fundamental to every society. It does not fade with the onset of high technology or industrialization but rather works in the same way with new subjects and symbols. What is called evil may be new and unprecedented. Why there is evil is not.

Notes

1. There is a sparse literature in social science that directly addresses the problem of evil as something generic in societies. Leonard Doob (*Panorama of Evil: Insights From the Behavioral Sciences* [Westport, CT: Greenwood Press, 1978]) brought a psychological perspective to bear on the subject, fleshing out a series of social roles in the defining/judging/reacting processes by which evil is recognized and handled. Sociologist Sanford Lyman (*The Seven Deadly Sins—Society and Evil* [New York: St. Martin's Press, 1978]) approached evil much as I do in this paper, but all his examples dealt with traditional vices (avarice, sloth, gluttony, lust, and so forth), somewhat removed from the religious controversy in this paper. Richard Stivers (*Evil in Modern Myth and Ritual* [Athens, GA: University of Georgia Press, 1982]) offers a perspective much closer to my own and is discussed in the body of this paper. Likewise, Nevitt Sanford and Craig Comstock (*Sanctions for Evil* [Boston: Beacon Press, 1971]) analyzed the process by which the label "evil" is applied so as to rationalize and justify violent and deadly action. Finally, there are anthropological phenomena, such as the plethora of "trickster" tales and myths in cultures world-wide (see, for example, William J. Hynes, "Mystic Tricksters: Profane Imps of Metaplay" [Unpublished manuscript, Denver, CO: Regis College]), which are certainly relevant to conceptualizing evil nontheologically, though that is a literature of considerable size that I will not incorporate here.

2. *The Seven Deadly Sins*, p. 1.

3. *Man and the Sacred*, trans. Meyer Barash (New York: Free Press, 1959).

4. *Evil in Modern Myth and Ritual*, p. 33.

5. See, for example, Edwin M. Schur, *The Politics of Deviance* (Englewood

Cliffs, NJ: Prentice-Hall, 1980), and *Labeling Deviant Behavior* (New York: Harper & Row, 1971).

6. See Lewis A. Coser, *The Functions of Social Conflict* (New York: Free Press, 1956) 70.

7. Length limitations make it impossible to give even a brief summary of this major twentieth-century countermovement. It is not the first such movement in American history, and its complex development since the early 1970s shows a number of parallels with the groups it opposes. For a history and organizational analysis see Anson D. Shupe, Jr., David Bromley, and Donna L. Oliver, *The Anti-Cult Movement in America: A Bibliography and Historical Survey* (New York: Garland Publishing Company, 1984); and Anson D. Shupe, Jr., and David Bromley, "Witches, Moonies, and Accusations of Evil," in *In Gods We Trust: New Patterns of American Pluralism*, ed. Thomas Robbins and Dick Anthony (New Brunswick, NJ: Transaction Press, 1980).

8. New York: Irvington, 1977; enlarged edition.

9. David G. Bromley and Anson D. Shupe, Jr., *"Moonies" in America: Cult, Church and Crusade* (Beverly Hills, CA: Sage Publications, 1979) 149–67.

10. For a thorough but biased account, see Robert Boettcher and Gordon L. Freeman, *Gifts of Deceit* (New York: Holt, Rinehart and Winston, 1980).

11. Cf. Anson D. Shupe, Jr., and David G. Bromley, "The Archetypal Cult: Conflict and the Social Construction of Deviance," in *the Family and the Unification Church*, ed. Gene G. James (New York: Rose of Sharon Press, 1983) 1–22; *Strange Gods: The Great American Cult Scare* (Boston: Beacon Press, 1982); "Apostates and Atrocity Stories: Some Parameters in the Dynamics of Deprogramming," in *The Social Impact of New Religious Movements*, ed. Bryan Wilson (New York: Rose of Sharon Press, 1981) 179–215; *The New Vigilantes: Anti-Cultists, Deprogrammers and the New Religions* (Beverly Hills, CA: Sage Publications, 1980); and, with Roger Spielmann and Sam Stigall, "Cults of Anti-Cultism," *Society* 17 (March/April 1980) 43–46.

12. E.g., Edward Hunter, *Brainwashing in China: The Calculated Destruction of Men's Morals* (New York: Vanguard, 1953); and Robert J. Lifton, *Thought Reform and the Psychology of Totalism* (New York: W. W. Norton, 1963).

13. E.g., John C. Clark, Jr., Michael D. Langone, Robert E. Schecter, and Roger C.B. Daly, *Destructive Cult Conversion: Theory, Research, and Treatment* (Boston: American Family Foundation, Center on Destructive Cultism, 1981).

14. E.g., Marvin E. Galper, "The Cult Indoctrinee: A New Clinical Syndrome" (Paper presented to the Tampa–St. Petersburg Psychiatric Society, Tampa–St. Petersburg, FL, 1976).

15. E.g., Ronald M. Enroth, *The Lure of the Cults* (Chappaqua, NY: Christian Herald Books, 1979).

16. For a detailed, annotated bibliography dealing with religious and behavioral-science sources on modern "cultism," see Shupe, Bromley, and Oliver, *The Anti-Cult Movement in America*, pp. 51–80 and 81–112.

17. Shupe and Bromley, *The New Vigilantes*, pp. 96–97.

18. David G. Bromley, Anson D. Shupe, Jr., and J. C. Ventimiglia, "Atrocity

Tales, the Unification Church and the Social Construction of Evil," *Journal of Communication* 29 (Summer 1979) 42–53.

19. E.g., Chris Welles, "The Eclipse of Sun Myung Moon," *New York Magazine*, 27 September 1976, pp. 33–38.

20. Shupe and Bromley, *The New Vigilantes*, pp. 207–32.

21. As I worked on the manuscript for this paper, the *Fort Worth Star Telegram* published an essay by columnist William Raspberry under the title, "Did Leader of the Moonies Get a Fair Trial?" 20 April 1984; originally printed in the *Washington Post* on 18 April 1984, p. A27, as "A Fair Trial For Rev. Moon."

22. Stivers, *Evil in Modern Myth and Ritual*, pp. 21–22.

23. Winston Davis, *DOJO: Magic and Exorcism in Modern Japan* (Stanford, CA: Stanford University Press), 1980.

24. "Witches, Moonies, and Accusations of Evil."

25. Ann Arbor, MI: University of Michigan Press, 1968.

Conclusion:
Competing Visions of the Role of
Religion in American Society

ROBERT N. BELLAH

It may seem obvious that in order for me to know who I am I
need to know who I am not. I am not you; that is the beginning of the
definition of me. It is the same with groups. In order to know what my
group is, I need to know what it is not—I need to know its boundaries.
Thus inclusion and exclusion are basic to the very idea of identity. Every
society, every religious community and, indeed, every person is defined
by a dialectic of inclusion and exclusion. Societies, religious communities, and persons, in order to have an identity, require an idea of boundary that defines them in relation to others.

Prejudice, discrimination, and hostility to others arise from this inevitable fact of human personal and social life. It is not that prejudice, discrimination, and hostility are inevitable. They are not. But the forming of
identities and the drawing of boundaries *are* inevitable, and they do always require a definition of who I am or my group is and a discrimination relative to what I or my group are not.

When I am uncertain about myself or there are conflicts within my
group, it will be tempting to project those uncertainties onto outsiders.
When the boundaries of personal or group consciousness have become
uncertain, they can be strengthened by imagining that the internal problems are outside the person or group. This is a very primitive mechanism
for maintaining personal or group identity, but one hard even for the
most mature of us to avoid altogether. And since religion is often such a
central aspect of personal or group identity, it is terribly easy to shore up

one's religious identity by looking down on or even feeling hostility toward those of another religion. That is why the problem discussed in this volume is so serious and so perennial.

In view of the ubiquity of religious prejudice, discrimination, and hostility, some people have argued that it might be best to get rid of religion altogether, since it seems to have caused nothing but trouble. A moment's reflection shows why this is not a real solution: It is merely another example of the inveterate human tendency to draw boundaries and then look down on those on the other side. For those who would get rid of religion are saying in effect, "Here are we good secular people who don't draw boundaries, while over there are the bad religious people who do."

As an illustration of our human tendency to draw boundaries, consider for a moment the boundary between man and beast. What could be clearer? We are humans, and they are animals. But this is a boundary across which we are apt to express quite a bit of prejudice and hostility. If we really don't like someone, we say he is an animal or a beast. Mary Midgley has shown that our characterization of animals in such a comparison is stereotyped and unfair.[1] Wolves, for example, have a very bad reputation. But ethologists tell us wolves are unusually nice animals, well socialized, even caring of one another. They attack humans only under dire necessity. Yet we say *homo homini lupus est* (man is a wolf to man), projecting our own wolfishness onto the wolves. The *homo* is more of a *lupus* than the *lupus*.

The answer to the general problem is already apparent in this simple example of the relation between humans and animals. We do not need to choose between drawing an absolute boundary and dissolving the boundary altogether—particularly since, in another sense, humans are animals. (It is possible that the religious opponents of the theory of evolution fear that evolution destroys the boundary altogether and that only "creationism" will maintain the boundary between humans and animals.) We can see that we are not the same as animals while recognizing that we are related. If we don't have to project all our human evil on them, maybe we will treat them better, remembering that there is a sense in which "us and them" are a "we."

But to return to our problem, why is religion so often involved in intergroup hostility? Just because religion is one of the most important ways of defining our identity and thus making personal and collective boundaries. In modern times religious identity is only rivaled (and sometimes surpassed) by national identity as a source of group belongingness and therefore as a source of intergroup hostility and conflict. Given their strength, it is not surprising that these two powerful forms of group identity frequently clash. Indeed all modern nations have had to deal with the potential conflicts between them.

In the history of the relation of nation and religion in America we can discern two polar visions that can set the terms for our discussion. One of these is the notion of the establishment of religion: one people, one faith. The other is the dissolution of religious organization: one individual, one faith. We are familiar with the idea of establishment, since it existed in some of the Colonies before the founding of our Republic. We may be less familiar with the second idea, though there is much in our social life today that presses toward that conclusion. The great majority of religious organizations in America almost certainly favor neither of these solutions, though there may be some Americans who favor one or the other.

Through much of our history most people concerned with the issue feared the establishment possibility. The ACLU is still fighting that war. But I believe the more dangerous threat today comes from the second alternative—the complete privatization of religion, so that religion becomes entirely personal with no collective expression at all. Indeed, in a significant sector of our population (which is not necessarily "secularized") that has already happened.

Richard M. Merelman has spoken of the decline of group belongingness and the rise of individualization in terms of a culture of "tight-boundedness" being replaced by a culture of "loose-boundedness." He writes:

> The contemporary weakness of [group belongingness in America] has released large numbers of Americans from firm cultural moorings. The liberated individual, not the social group, must therefore become the basic unit. Although many people continue to be members of and identify with groups, they believe their group identities to be matters of individual choice, which can be changed without stigma. Group membership thus becomes voluntary, contingent, and fluid, not "given," fixed, and rigid.[2]

Merelman points out that in a culture of loose-boundedness group membership does not do very much to tell people who they are or to define others for them. Thus individuals must "personalize" their relationships and seek to relate to others through "friendship" when more stable communal markers have been weakened. But, he points out, "Paradoxically enough, friendship becomes most desirable in a society when loose boundaries between individuals place so heavy a burden of insecurity on all relationships as to make real friendship most elusive. We therefore crave most what we find increasingly difficult to obtain."[3] Another consequence of loosely bounded culture is that, as Merelman points out, "real controversy is always a danger and never an opportunity."[4] Loosely bounded culture lacks the mediating cultural and institutional structures that would allow a genuine argument to take place. Instead, loosely bounded individuals "communicate" empathetically so as to try to reach an emotional "understanding." Since this understanding cannot be normatively specified, it has to be renegotiated in every situation, an endless, exhausting, and finally impossible task. Though the strong of heart and the self-confident may enjoy the openness and flexibility of loose-boundedness, others are disoriented and confused and try to reassert the tightly bounded structures that have been so weakened in our society. Thus many of the conflicts in our society at the moment are not between members of traditional communities, religious or otherwise, nor even between liberals and conservatives as those terms have classically been defined, but rather between proponents of loose-boundedness and defenders of tight-boundedness. Indeed, it is this distinction that the terms liberal and conservative in our society really signify.

Liberal-Conservative Tensions

George Marsden's discussion of the evolution controversy is a case in point. His argument could be rephrased to say that "creationism" is a doctrine intended to define the identity of a tightly bounded religious community. Since it is a boundary-maintaining mechanism, it tends precisely to exclude the middle. In a talk at a public university several years ago, I pointed out that the Declaration of Independence derives our most fundamental rights not from the state or from the people but from God when it says "that all men are *created* equal; that they are endowed by their *creator* with certain inalienable rights." By stressing the words "created" and "creator," I was arguing that Jefferson and his colleagues believed in a biblical God who had created heaven and earth and from whom our personhood is derived. But I was then astounded during the question period when a woman in the audience commented how pleased she was that a professor at the University of California believes in creation science. That I could believe in the doctrine of creation without believing in "creation science" was clearly beyond her ken. I decided that was not the moment to try to explain the difference.

Evolution, as I have already suggested, raises the boundary issue in especially acute form, for it seems to deny the crucial distinction between humans and animals. Because of this, fundamentalists regard belief in evolution as emblematic of false modernity in contrast to true religion. They are not mistaken in seeing ideological modernism as consistently relativizing and historicizing all their most cherished beliefs. What they do not see is that there is another possibility beyond fundamentalism's identity rigidity and modernism's identity diffusion. That alternative is the effort to maintain clear boundaries that tell us who we are without excluding relationships across the boundaries.

George Marsden's paper is devoted largely to a group that has opted for tight-boundedness. The very notion of "fundamentalism" is an exquisite expression of a tightly bounded culture. David O'Brien, however, is dealing with Catholic Christians, our largest American religious community, among whom the tension between tight-boundedness and loose-boundedness gives rise to considerable contentiousness. The tendency that O'Brien singles out which seems to be a good example of tight-boundedness is found in a group composed largely of clergy, but not without lay support, that views Christians today as a minority in a neopagan world, whose first duty is to preserve the purity of Christian life regardless of consequences. On the other hand, O'Brien also discerns a tendency among much of the Catholic laity, and more than a few priests, toward a loss of firm Catholic identity. What takes its place is a privatized American evangelical piety in which the church almost becomes dissolved into its constituent individuals. The American Catholic Church was probably never so monolithic as it appeared, but today much of it seems to have suffered the same pressure toward loose-boundedness that has long affected Protestantism.

O'Brien's own position in the face of some of his fellow Catholics' tendency to erect new barriers against the world and the tendency of others to dissolve the barriers altogether is to opt for what he calls the "radical middle" (perhaps not unrelated to Marsden's "excluded middle"). O'Brien's notion of a Catholic radical middle is one that would assert a clear Catholic identity and a clear sense of boundary but also a deep and continuing relationship with what lies across the boundary. O'Brien's quote from the heroine of Mary Gordon's *Final Payments* upon the collapse of her old sense of a closed Catholic world, "I would have to invent an existence for myself,"[5] suggests the paradigmatic quality of that fine novel. Gordon vividly portrays her heroine moving from a tightly bounded world to one that she indeed tries to invent for herself with no boundaries at all, but ending with a middle ground where she accepts the fundamental givenness of her identity without being trapped in it. That the end of the novel is still tentative suggests that none of us knows exactly what the radical middle that we seek is really like.

Samuel Heilman's description fits with almost uncomfortable neatness into my schema, as is evident from his title, "Orthodox Jews: An Open or a Closed Group?" Orthodox Jews, particularly those Heilman calls "traditionalist," have feared that unless tight boundaries are maintained assimilation will result. This fear does not seem to lack foundation: secularized, so-called "enlightened" Jews have indeed had a difficult time transmitting an effective Jewish identity. The Orthodox "modernists" that Heilman discusses seem to be another example of our "middle" in that they hope to maintain Jewish identity while relaxing to some extent the rigid boundaries of traditionalist practice. What is interesting in Heilman's description is that unlike the Catholic case, but somewhat like the fundamentalists, the middle seems to be weakening rather than growing stronger. A resurgent Orthodoxy seems to be tightening the boundaries rather than loosening them. Whether this is a long-term trend or not remains to be seen.

Mainline Attitudes toward Emerging Religious Groups

The usefulness of the boundary concept in clarifying religious conflicts is demonstrated also in the papers on cults. Indeed, Lawrence Foster analyzes conflict between the religious establishment and new religions as having the function of "boundary-maintenance" for both the establishment and the new group. The establishment persecutes new groups whose practices threaten to break the existing consensus, while new groups use persecution to convince themselves that the "world" is evil and impure and so loyalty to the group should grow even stronger.

While recognizing religious conflict in America and analyzing the case of Mormonism in some detail, Foster points out how minimal religious conflict has been here compared to many other societies. He is undoubtedly right on this point, and his discussion of some of the reasons for American religious tolerance is suggestive; but before congratulating ourselves too soon, we should consider that one of the reasons for our religious tolerance might be the existence of racism. Americans have been so preoccupied with drawing boundaries between the races that religious boundaries have seemed less important. If the treatment of religious minorities has been, on the whole, exemplary, the same can hardly be said for the treatment of racial minorities, at least until relatively recently.

The Mormon case is interesting because the degree of conflict was unusually high, even though the period of intense conflict is now far in the past. If Foster is correct, its intensity was due to the degree to which the early Mormons violated widely shared social norms, such as monogamy, that in part define the majority identity. One might even ask whether the intensity of the conflict does not increase if the disapproved practices are at the same time attractive. Not only was Mormon polyg-amy probably appealing to the fantasies of many men in the majority population, but also Mormon collectivism undoubtedly had conscious or unconscious appeal to members of a society that so relentlessly empha-sized individual self-reliance. When the forbidden is attractive, it must be fought all the more vigorously.

Anson Shupe places his analysis of changing views of the Unification Church in the context of a general sociological theory that sees the exis-tence of heresy and evil as a natural corollary of processes of group main-tenance and the control of dominant groups. Just as a group must have "fundamental values," so it must have a theory about people who violate those values. Again, group identity and boundary-maintenance seem to be the key to religious conflict.

One might suggest that one of the "values" that new religious groups such as the Moonies were violating was the very value of loose-bound-edness itself, to return to Merelman's terminology. Indeed, one might see the hysteria about cults in the 1970s as the response of a loosely bounded culture to the threat of tightly bounded cults. That children of ambitious, upwardly mobile, middle-class Americans would be attracted to tightly bounded cults indeed suggests that all was not well in loosely bounded culture. The extreme atomistic individualism of our culture set up wishes for authority and closure that were above all missing in the dominant mi-lieu. By the end of the 1970s major sectors of our culture seemed to be moving toward tight-boundedness (one thinks of the new Christian right and political conservatism generally), although whether this was some-thing more than superficial—a form of symbolic nostalgia—is not yet clear. In any case, in such an atmosphere the tight-boundedness of cults is less of a threat. It is interesting that Shupe's dispassionate analysis breaks down at the point where he discusses deprogramming. The deprogram-mers are repugnant because they seem even more tightly bounded than the cultists themselves.

Catholic-Protestant Tensions

In a sense, the tensions between Protestants and Catholics and between Christians and Jews exhibit similar issues to those discussed concerning cults, although for the most part the conflicts have been less intense. Bar-bara Welter suggests that Protestant hostility to Roman Catholics from the mid-nineteenth to the mid-twentieth centuries was not sheer irra-tional bigotry but arose from real anxieties that Protestants had about as-pects of Catholic belief and practice. In one form or another Protestant anxieties focused on blind obedience to papal or priestly authority, an obedience that was thought incompatible not only with republican citizenship but with genuine religious freedom. That some Protestant converts to Catholicism found in their new faith an authority that was sadly missing in the uncertainty and aimlessness of the culture in which they were raised only suggests that here, too, what was feared was at another level deeply attractive.

Jay Dolan shows that during the period described by Welter Catholicism was indeed moving in directions calculated to enhance Protestant fears. After a period of relative accommodation to the environing culture in the early Republic, the Catholic Church in the later decades of the nineteenth century moved toward a tighter drawing of boundaries and a firmer assertion of the superior truths entrusted to Catholics alone. As a minority group, Catholics were less prone to violence against the Protestant majority than was occasionally the case with Protestants in their hostility to Catholics. Yet Catholics were tempted to treat Protestants with disdain or to ignore them altogether as they created an ever more inclusive network of Catholic institutions within which one did not need to know that others existed.

Most of the tensions described by Welter and Dolan have either disappeared or markedly decreased in recent years. Mark Noll documents the dramatic change in Protestant-Catholic relations since Vatican II. To some extent this is only the culmination of long-term tendencies toward greater religious tolerance relative to which the work of Paul Blanshard was only a late and brief regression. The rise of loose-boundedness in American culture through much of the twentieth century makes it hard to maintain religious boundaries as much as any others, and consequently the temptations of out-group hostility and in-group withdrawal decline. But Vatican II surely had to some degree an independent role. The very process of Vatican II belied the Protestant stereotype of Catholic authoritarianism. As the church removed barriers to Catholic participation in a variety of spheres, the experience of a separate Catholic world began to fade. It is too soon to assess the massive changes that have occurred in the relationship of American Catholics and Protestants, but some things are obvious. Religiously the two communities are influencing each other at an increasing tempo. Catholics are becoming more evangelical; Protestants more liturgical.

Yet, as Noll points out, new lines of cleavage are occurring—this time not so much between the great communions as within them. Noll speaks of the emergence of Old Catholics and New Catholics, of Old Protestants and New Protestants. To translate Noll's argument into the terms of this essay, we could say that the new versions of both faiths represent loose-boundedness and the old ones a revival of tight-boundedness. A close examination of the documents of Vatican II would suggest that the Council intended to change the definition of the boundaries of the Catholic community but certainly not to dissolve them. O'Brien's centrism would seem to be a faithful reflection of the spirit of Vatican II. But when boundaries that have been rigidly maintained for a long time are redefined, there is always a temptation to abandon them altogether. Ironically, what happened is in part the very thing against which the upholders of the older notion of the boundaries feared, namely indifferentism. Yet it is still possible to discern somewhere between Noll's Old and New Protestants and Catholics a religious center that affirms the separate traditions but tries to form a conception of Christian religious identity in which oneness of faith takes priority over separateness of communion. Such a position would not surrender to loose-boundedness, for it is not indifferent to issues of religious identity. But, as we have seen, the "radical middle" position is not easy to maintain in America today where the pull of polarization is strong.

Jewish-Christian Tensions

It is difficult for two groups who share in part a common past but understand it differently to define themselves and maintain their boundaries without offending each other. This is true between Catholics and Protestants. The very self-definition as "catholic" means "universal" and so inevitably implies that Protestants are a mere heretical fringe. On the other hand, the self-definition as "protestant" implies that Catholics must be protested against. These terminological implications are only superficial indications of how deeply Protestantism defined itself over against Catholicism from the beginning and how deeply post-Tridentine Catholicism defined itself over against Protestantism. But if these differences between Catholics and Protestants have begun to be mitigated, the differences of this sort between Jews and Christians would still seem to be considerable.

For example, Jonathan Sarna is offended, and surely many Jews are, by the reading of Christianity into the Hebrew scriptures. But this is not a recent prejudice. Christianity is rooted in and unthinkable without a Christian reading of the Jewish scriptures, which are also canonical for Christians. The reading of the Christian message as the fulfillment of Jewish prophecy begins in the New Testament itself and in the words of Jesus himself as the community has handed them down. Jesus quotes from the opening line of the 22nd Psalm as he hangs from the cross.

What else would we expect? Jesus and Peter and John and Paul were all believing Jews who saw themselves linked to the Jewish past and the Jewish promise.

Further, however reprehensible many efforts of Christians to convert Jews have been, Christians believe they have a commission to bear witness to their faith to all nations. This can be done respectfully and noncoercively, though it often has not been. But to renounce the obligation to witness would be to renounce Christian identity.

Conversely, it is part of Jewish identity and the maintenance of the boundaries of the Jewish community to deny that Jesus is the Christ, the Messiah. This is to claim, however tacitly, that Christianity is a false religion.

Thus, since Christianity began as a Jewish sect (or cult, if you will) the very identities of the two communities involve beliefs that are offensive to each other. To assert that this is simply unfortunate, that we are all human beings and it doesn't matter what traditions we come from, is to opt for an indifferentism that would dissolve both Judaism and Christianity. Without doing that, we can nonetheless try to understand the nature of the boundaries that divide us and to mitigate the offensiveness so far as possible. More deeply, we can, as in the case of Catholics and Protestants, try to understand better that which we share, above all the Hebrew Bible. This does not mean arguing for some easy notion of the "Judaeo-Christian tradition" in which Jews are inevitably subordinated to Christian understandings. But it does mean moving toward a conception of a community of communities that includes us both, even though the boundaries that divide us are not dissolved.

John Cuddihy raises the interesting issue of feelings of superiority that Jews have toward Christians, though one would also want to look at the feelings of superiority that Christians have toward Jews (or Catholics toward Protestants and vice versa). To draw on an ideology that Cuddihy finds expressive of the Jewish Enlightenment, namely psychoanalysis, one might see that such feelings of superiority are often covers for feelings of inferiority. Indeed, one might wonder whether one who was unduly offended by Jewish feelings of superiority might not himself feel that Jews really are superior, really are chosen, really are more moral. Conversely, if one thinks of some of the examples of Jews with a strong sense of superiority that Cuddihy cites, particularly Philip Roth and Woody Allen, one finds not only a feeling of superiority but also quite a bit of self-hate and a feeling that Christians are really right about Jews. Certainly some of the scenes in *Portnoy's Complaint* would suggest as much. And alongside the caricature of Italian-Americans, the film *Broadway Danny Rose* includes a scene depicting Jews in the Borscht Belt that is so grotesque that it could only be interpreted as a form of Allen's self-hate. Superiority and inferiority feelings, love and hate for self and others are part of the mechanisms of boundary maintenance. They can be lessened by understanding better who we are, what the boundaries are, and who the people on the other side are.[6]

Conclusion

The papers gathered here thus support Richard Merelman's argument that the key tension in our culture at the moment is that between tight- and loose-boundedness. The important competing visions of the role of religion in American society today are not based primarily on differences between Catholics, Protestants, and Jews but to a certain extent are differences within each of the great communions and to some extent between secularists and all the religions. There is an important sense in which the radical individualism of American culture is against all "structural religion," a term of opprobrium we heard more than once in the interviews for *Habits of the Heart*.[6] In the research for that book, we met a young woman named Sheila Larson who had named her own religion ("my own little faith") Sheila-ism, after herself.[7] That suggests the possibility of over 220 million American religions, one for each of us. On the basis of our interviews we were not surprised at the finding of a 1978 Gallup poll that 80 percent of Americans agreed with the statement that "an individual should arrive at his or her own religious beliefs independent of any churches or synagogues."[8] These individualist ideas turn the religious community into simply a club for the like-minded. In our society it is difficult even to understand the idea of the religious community as the people of God or the Body of Christ.

In spite of the erosion of a deep sense of religious community in much of American society, the churches and synagogues continue to be among the most important of the voluntary associations to which such large numbers of Americans belong, whether measured in terms of amount of monetary contributions or of time donated. Indeed, religious groups and societies derived from them are among the most important of the intermediate associations that exist between individual Americans and the state. If they become severely fragmented and increasingly privatized, the result will be not only the loss of a coherent religious tradition but the weakening of a democratic form of life. Should loose-boundedness triumph completely, the ground will be prepared for administrative despotism, since only the state will be left to control the atomized individuals.

The reasons for the rise of loose-boundedness in America are complex and largely beyond the scope of this essay to consider. But modern social science, an increasingly influential cultural form, has certainly contributed to that rise. It has done so by relativizing religious and moral beliefs and explaining them in terms of social or psychological factors, depriving them of the objectivity that would make them effective in defining group identity. Anson Shupe, in relativizing good and evil as functions of group self-maintenance or the dominance of particular strata within groups, is a good example. In the discussion of his paper, Shupe argued that social science can say nothing about objective good and evil, and in so doing he undoubtedly expresses the majority view. Yet it is not the only possible view.

If one viewed social science as a form of social self-understanding in which the aim was to put one's own society in some larger perspective and to understand so far as possible its meaning in terms of the larger experience of mankind, then judgments of good and evil would be appropriate. Indeed, sociology arose as an effort to understand modern society and the process of modernization partly to see whether they were pathological and certainly to see whether their grave defects could be ameliorated.

Emile Durkheim, the quintessential sociologist, was quite willing to talk about right and wrong. He argued that the whole history of social development moves in the direction of respect for the sanctity of the human person. When he threw himself into the defense of Dreyfus, he did so because he felt the most fundamental principle of morality was violated by Dreyfus's conviction. Durkheim and some social scientists after him have felt that the sociologist cannot be ethically neutral. He does not come from Mars. He or she is part of the society and has the responsibility of enhancing its moral self-understanding. This is a conception of social science that I believe is worth fighting for.

In short, not only as a citizen and as a Christian, but also as a sociologist, I strongly support the radical middle position of which David O'Brien speaks. To dissolve all boundaries, to relativize all moral judgments, would not only threaten the survival of the traditional religious communities, it would also lead to a society in which no one would really want to live. But on the other hand, we do not need to create iron curtains between communities either. That too leads to pathology. To wish to maintain the life of one's own community, to see it as a community of memory and of hope, is not to deny that it overlaps with other communities, that individuals belong to more than one community, and that all communities are ultimately included in the human race. The dialectic of personal and group identity is close to the heart of a healthy personal and group life.

There is a fear in our loose-bounded culture that strong belief in anything, particularly in the area of right and wrong, means one wishes to coerce others into sharing one's view. But the proper practice in a democratic society, one consonant with our heritage as Americans, is that we do not try to force our views on others. Rather, on the basis of our conception of the right, we argue, we discuss, and we seek to persuade our fellow citizens of our view. We are also open to being persuaded by others engaged in the public conversation. And on the basis of the ongoing discussion we do change the moral consensus. Slavery was finally conceived to be an offense we could not tolerate. The majority of Americans were persuaded that slavery was not a matter of states' rights, of local option, but was absolutely wrong and could not be tolerated. A century later Martin Luther King, Jr., helped to change our consensus about race relations once again.

Most of my intellectual friends think the greatest danger to the continuation of the democratic conversation today comes from the radical religious right, from Jerry Fallwell and others who would coerce us into adhering to their norms. My own sense is that a far greater threat comes from the triumph of loosely bounded culture which, were it ever completely successful, would destroy both the moral norms that provide the terms for our democratic conversation and the communities that carry those moral norms and ethical concerns, including the religious communities.

In the face of serious dangers coming from both extremes, I believe that it is the middle course—maintaining group identities and group boundaries while remaining open to knowledge of and cooperation with others, including those of different faiths—that is authentically biblical and authentically American and that holds the greatest hope for our future.

Notes

1. Mary Midgley, *Beast and Men: The Roots of Human Nature* (New York: Meridian, 1980).

2. Richard M. Merelman, *Making Something of Ourselves: On Culture and Politics in the United States* (Berkeley: University of California Press, 1984) 30.

3. Ibid., pp. 30–31.

4. Ibid., p. 229.

5. Mary Gordon, *Final Payments* (New York: Random House, 1978) 3.

6. Robert N. Bellah, Richard Madsen, William M. Sullivan, Ann Swidler,

Conclusion

and Steven M. Tipton, *Habits of the Heart: Individualism and Commitment in American Life* (Berkeley: Universtity of California Press, 1985).

7. Ibid., pp. 221, 226, 235.

8. *The Unchurched American* (Princeton, NJ: Princeton Religion Research Center, 1978), especially pp. 9, 32, and 69.

Contributors

Robert N. Bellah is Ford Professor of Sociology and Comparative Studies at the University of California at Berkeley. His publications include *Tokugawa Religion, Beyond Belief, The Broken Covenant, The New Religious Consciousness, Varieties of Civil Religion,* and *Habits of the Heart: Individualism and Commitment in American Life.*

John Murray Cuddihy is Professor of Sociology at Hunter College of the City University of New York and author of *The Ordeal of Civility: Freud, Marx, Lévi-Straus and the Jewish Struggle with Modernity* and *No Offense: Civil Religion and Protestant Taste.*

Jay P. Dolan is Professor of History and Director of the Charles and Margaret Hall Cushwa Center for the Study of American Catholicism at the University of Notre Dame. He is the author of *The Immigrant Church: New York's Irish and German Catholics, 1851–1865, Catholic Revivalism: The American Experience, 1830–1900,* and *The American Catholic Experience: A History from Colonial Times to the Present.*

Lawrence Foster is Associate Professor in the School of Social Sciences at Georgia Institute of Technology and author of *Religion and Sexuality: The Shakers, the Mormons, and the Oneida Community.*

Frederick E. Greenspahn is Associate Professor of Judaic Studies at the University of Denver. He is the author of *Hapax Legomena in Biblical*

Hebrew. He has also edited several volumes comparing Jewish and Christian thought as well as *Nourished with Peace,* a collection of essays in memory of Samuel Sandmel.

Samuel C. Heilman is Professor of Sociology and Director of the Center for Jewish Studies at Queens College of the City University of New York. He is the author of *Synagogue Life: A Study in Symbolic Interaction, The People of the Book: Drama, Fellowship and Religion, The Gate behind the Wall,* and *A Walker in Jerusalem.*

George M. Marsden is Professor of the History of Christianity in America at Duke University Divinity School. He is the author of *The Evangelical Mind and the New School Presbyterian Experience* and *Fundamentalism and American Culture: The Shaping of Twentieth Century Evangelicalism , 1870–1925,* and co-editor of *A Christian View of History?* and *Eerdman's Handbook to Christianity in America.*

Mark A. Noll is Professor of History at Wheaton College. He is the author of *Christians in the American Revolution* and *Between Faith and Criticism: Evangelical Scholarship and the Bible in America.* He has also edited *The Princeton Theology 1812–1921: Scripture, Science and Theological Method from Alexander to Warfield, The Bible in America,* and *Eerdman's Handbook to Christianity in America.*

David J. O'Brien is Associate Professor of History at Holy Cross College. He co-edited *Renewing the Earth* and is the author of *American Catholics and Social Reform: The New Deal Years* and *The Renewal of American Catholicism.*

Jonathan D. Sarna is Associate Professor of American Jewish History and Director of the Center for the Study of the American Jewish Experience at the Hebrew Union College–Jewish Institute of Religion in Cincinnati. He is the author of *People Walk on Their Heads: Moses Weinberger's Jews and Judaism in New York* and *Jacksonian Jew: The Two Worlds of Mordecai Noah,* and has edited *Jews in New Haven, Jews and the Founding of the Republic,* and *The American Jewish Experience.*

Anson Shupe is Professor of Sociology at the University of Texas in Arlington and author of *Strange Gods: The Great American Cult Scare, Born Again Politics and the Moral Majority: What Social Surveys Really*

Show, A Documentary History of the Anti-Cult Movement, and *The Mormon Corporate Empire.*

Barbara Welter is Professor of History at Hunter College and the Graduate Center of the City University of New York. She is the author of *Dimity Convictions: The American Woman in the Nineteenth Century.*